The

GIFTS

of

READING

for the
next generation

The

GIFTS

of

READING

for the
next generation

ESSAYS *on*

NURTURING A PASSION

for READING

Inspired by Robert Macfarlane
Curated by Jennie Orchard

SCRIBE

Melbourne | London | Minneapolis

Scribe Publications
18–20 Edward St, Brunswick, Victoria 3056, Australia
2 John St, Clerkenwell, London, WC1N 2ES, United Kingdom
3754 Pleasant Ave, Suite 223w, Minneapolis, Minnesota 55409, USA

Published by Scribe 2025

Typeset in Minion by the publishers

Printed and bound in the UK by CPI Group (UK) Ltd, Croydon,
CR0 4YY

Scribe is committed to the sustainable use of natural resources and
the use of paper products made responsibly from those resources.

978 1 761380 97 6 (Australian edition)
978 1 915590 82 4 (UK edition)
978 1 964992 12 9 (US edition)
978 1 761386 28 2 (ebook)

Catalogue records for this book are available from the
National Library of Australia and the British Library.

scribepublications.com.au
scribepublications.co.uk
scribepublications.com

CONTENTS

For Alice

Ben Okri, 'Ten and a Half Inclinations'

1. There is a secret trail of books meant to inspire and enlighten you. Find that trail.

2. Read outside your own nation, colour, class, gender.

3. Read the books your parents hate.

4. Read the books your parents love.

5. Have one or two authors that are important, that speak to you; and make their works your secret passion.

6. Read widely, for fun, stimulation, escape.

7. Don't read what everyone else is reading. Check them out later, cautiously.

8. Read what you're not supposed to read.

9. Read for your own liberation and mental freedom.

10. Books are like mirrors. Don't just read the words. Go into the mirror. That is where the real secrets are. Inside. Behind. That's where the gods dream, where our realities are born.

10½. Read the world. It is the most mysterious book of all.

Foreword

ROBERT MACFARLANE

The poet Samuel Taylor Coleridge once memorably described himself as a 'library cormorant': he was so avid for books that he would pursue them greedily, almost indiscriminately — then gulp them down whole, one after the other.

As a child, I was a library cormorant, too: omnivorous and insatiable in my reading. Beano comics and Rupert the Bear annuals, volumes A and D of the *Encyclopedia Britannica*, Hugh Falkus' *Sea Trout Fishing: a guide to success* (though I was never successful), the operation manuals of certain items of household hardware I can no longer clearly recall (a tumble dryer, perhaps; but *why?*), poetry, natural history field guides whose painted pages I can still summon brightly to my mind's eye, forty years on, and of course novels, in many of which the landscape leaped forwards as a character in its own, complex right: *Forbidden Paths of Thual*, *The Box of Delights*, *The Weirdstone of Brisingamen*, *The Eagle of the Ninth*, Le Guin's Earthsea series, and later Robert Holdstock's deep-time dreamscape, *Mythago Wood*.

I gobbled all of these texts down — nonsense and candy floss and data and wonder alike. And the nights when my parents forbade me from keeping any lights on, in an attempt to force sleep upon me, I would uncomplainingly comply, wait for the footsteps to fade, then get out my small, black Mini Maglite torch, grip its handle between my teeth, lift my knees to make a tent under the sheets — and carry on reading in that tiny, glowing cavern. *That very night in Max's room a forest grew and grew ... and the walls became the world all around ...*

The book I remember 'becoming the world all around' more vividly than any other to me as a child was Susan Cooper's great fantasy novel, *The Dark Is Rising*, the second in a series of five books which together sank deep into my bones. Their characters — tall Merriman, capable of such warmth and such wrath; the Lady with her leitmotif of haunting, ethereal music; wise young Will; horned Herne — all stepped unhesitatingly into my imagination, and have never left. I was also profoundly influenced by Cooper's sense of landscape as a memory-shaping, time-slipping medium. Place, in *The Dark Is Rising*, is a potent agent. It carries auras and memories; it acts both archivally and prophetically. It *intervenes*. Such ideas were powerfully formative for me, and this sense of landscape as lively and memorious has, really, become the inexhaustible subject of my own work as a writer. I do not believe this would have been the case had I not read Cooper, and the tradition of wild-minded Anglo-American children's fiction to which she belongs, and which has since been marvellously extended by Philip Pullman, Katherine Rundell, and others.

When I met Susan Cooper herself in America in 2019, she told me how, when the air raid siren sounded during the Blitz, her mother would hurry her and her brother down into a nearby bomb shelter. There, by candlelight, Susan's mother would read and tell stories to the children to take their minds off the danger. Susan recalled — and it was a detail that lifted the hairs on the back of my neck as she told me — how, when the bombs fell, their detonations would cause the candle flame to quiver. The nearer the explosion, the more the flame shook. Boom ... shiver ... *Boom ... shiver ...* BOOM! SHIVER!

Cooper's mother read to her in the darkness of the bomb shelter — and helped make Susan into a writer. I read Susan in the darkness of my bedroom — and she helped make me into a writer. Now I in turn have read *The Dark is Rising* aloud to my children. *The gift gives on ...*

We must not, though, take the intergenerational, onwards-circulating gift of reading for granted. As the final essays for this volume were being gathered, the National Literacy Trust published a report on childhood reading for pleasure in the UK. Its headline finding was grim and hit hard: more than half (56 per cent) of children and young people aged eight to eighteen did not enjoy reading in their free time. This was an all-time low since recording began, and down over 15 per cent from 2016. Levels of reading enjoyment were weakest for children from disadvantaged backgrounds, of whom a third were leaving primary school without reaching the 'expected' level of reading literacy. One in five children taking part in the Trust's Young Readers Programme had never owned a single book. The Trust's research also found that children and young people were more likely to read if they had support from role models who read and loved reading, access to books, and a 'quiet space to read in'.

The formula is not a surprising or a complicated one. Children need to be able to read, to have something to read — and to have somewhere safe and warm to read it. If these three needs are met, miracles can happen. This is why public libraries are galaxies, wildwoods, time machines, and engines of social mobility — and why cutting the funding of libraries is both economic and emotional idiocy. This is why enabling children to fall in love with books at home and at school is not a luxury but a necessity. This is why reading is among the greatest gifts a child can be given.

The book you hold here in your hand is a celebration of those gifts and their giving. It gathers wonders and opens possibilities. It recognises the radical powers of reading: to transport, to propel, to inspire, to save, to hope.

Introduction

JENNIE ORCHARD

This book, like its predecessor, was born of two defining moments.

In the introduction to my anthology *The Gifts of Reading*, I wrote about the moment when I first read Robert Macfarlane's eponymous essay about gifting — and gifting books, in particular. 'It has almost always been the case that the gift which has spoken so "commandingly" to my soul has been a printed book,' he wrote. I couldn't agree more.

This inspired me to approach a number of authors and invite them to write on the same subject, including specific recommendations. Robert was immensely supportive and allowed me to include his essay as well as offering to write a preface. More than twenty others promised to contribute, and the responses to my brief proved to be rich and diverse. The resulting anthology was very well received, even though it was released in September 2020, the first of the Covid-dominated years.

Many people will remember 2020 as a year of changed plans, isolation, illness, loss, and even grief — but for some, the long periods spent sequestered at home provided opportunities, especially for the creatives who were able to spin gold from lives uninterrupted by social and professional obligations.

My own first year of Covid was marked by two memorable births — the arrival in the world of my first granddaughter, Alice, and the release of *The Gifts of Reading*. These two experiences were made different by the restrictions in place at the time — but each of them provided fulfilment and joy in abundance.

Robert Macfarlane wrote this in his preface to *The Gifts of Reading*: 'It is a beautiful, tangled skein of stories, filled with surprising echoes and unexpected interlockings. Here books take flight in flocks, migrating around the world, landing in people's hearts and changing them for a day or a year or a lifetime.' And Bron Sibree wrote a review for the *South China Morning Post*: 'Books, it is often said, are the gifts that never stop giving. And if ever there were a testament to that epithet, it is this inspired and inspiring anthology ... this collection, conceived and nurtured in a spirit of altruism, is freighted with such wonder and generosity it is also a testament to the best that resides in the human soul.'

Even as I was working on the first anthology, I had the idea of curating a second, originally to be called *The Gifts of Reading for Children*.

Now that I had a grandchild, I started to think about the books that I might want to share with her and to revisit memories of my own childhood reading experiences. Initially, I was thinking of the picture books — and all the other stories — that I had loved reading to my three sons (the most battered books on our shelves include *Goodnight Moon*, *Five Minutes' Peace*, and *The Elephant and the Bad Baby* — 'rumpeta, rumpeta, rumpeta'!), but soon I was also wondering about which books might help shape Alice, growing up in such a very different world.

But while books might help her navigate this world, they

would have to be books that she discovered for herself. I have far too many memories of books that I 'should' have read — books that my father had loved when he was a boy, classics that his best friend gave us every Christmas, books selected by tired teachers. Yet I have happy memories of our Saturday morning family visits to the local library when there were no restrictions in place.

There's a story in Markus Zusak's memoir, *Three Wild Dogs (and the truth)*, that resonates deeply. He is writing about his father, Helmut, who says that Markus is a much better father than he was because he reads to his children. Markus responds:

'And look what happened,' I said. 'I became a writer.

'What I neglected to remind him was that books were everywhere in our house when my siblings and I were growing up ... someone cared enough to have books in the bedrooms, the kitchen, the lounge, even if they were just lying around. Even my dad's *Reader's Digest*, which he read in the bathroom, was a signal that stories mattered.'

Like Markus, many writers have drawn attention to the crucial importance of books in the lives of children and young people:

'There are perhaps no days of our childhood that we lived as fully as the days we think we left behind without living at all: the days we spent with a favourite book.'
Marcel Proust

'When I look back, I am so impressed ... with the life-giving power of literature. If I were a young person today, trying to gain a sense of myself in the world, I would do

that again by reading, just as I did when I was young.'
Maya Angelou

'It is difficult to be young in this age … easy to feel lonely
… from an early age I needed to read in order to make
sense of the world around me. Books opened up other
worlds, other possibilities.'
Elif Shafak

And Kate DiCamillo, introduced to me via a *New York Times*
article written by Ann Patchett and published in March 2020,
'Why we need life-changing books right now', has written this
about books for children: 'We are working to make hearts that
know how to love this world.'

It soon became clear to me that rather than invite people to
write about the gifts of reading for children, it would make more
sense to broaden the concept and think about books to be shared
with the next generation, providing the contributors with greater
scope. And so *The Gifts of Reading for the Next Generation* started
to take shape.

I began to extend the Gifts of Reading community that had
emerged via the first anthology. Some of those who had been
involved previously accepted the invitation to contribute again,
but I had a long list of others I wanted to include. Not everyone
accepted my invitation, of course. And there were many more I'd
have liked to invite. As with the first anthology, it was important
to represent writers from many backgrounds — and this time,
even more so, writers from different age groups.

One of those who readily agreed to write an essay was Colum
McCann, author of not only many fine (and much awarded)
works of fiction but also *Letters to a Young Writer*. While
preparing to write his essay, Colum asked his son, JohnMichael,

what sort of books he thought young people should be reading. JohnMichael was quick to answer — 'whatever the hell they want' — and went on to write his own essay, a 'companion piece' for his father's (Colum's suggestion, very gratefully received).

Other younger contributors include Maisie Fieschi, daughter of Australian Children's Laureate Ursula Dubosarsky, who writes with considerable grace and courage about the book that helped her navigate a particularly challenging period in her life. Australian novelist Diana Reid has written about the importance of reading beyond the comfort of immediate 'relatability', of an infinitely varied literary diet; and Thelma Young Lutunatabua, co-author of *Not Too Late* (with Rebecca Solnit), has described the relief of retreating into the sanctuary of poetry when needing respite from the despair induced by the prospect of severe climate change.

Many have written about the solace provided by books at times of adversity: Nguyễn Phan Quế Mai and Wayne Karlin revisiting their experiences of the Việt Nam War, and Alice Pung reflecting on the hope provided by books in her childhood years after arriving in Australia with her family as refugees from the brutal Pol Pot regime in Cambodia.

The families of Shankari Chandran and Dina Nayeri were also refugees, from Sri Lanka and Iran, and their essays bear the imprint of these experiences. Shankari was the magnanimous first to commit to this new anthology and writes about the significance of the *Mahabharata*, 'the ultimate multigenerational family saga'. Dina is persuasive on the subject of re-reading a text at different times in order to discover different interpretations.

Horatio Clare writes about the profound gifts of reading aloud, especially for a son who is dyslexic, and Nardi Simpson offers an entirely different perspective on the experience of reading, in her case 'reading country', imbibing and interpreting landscape, far from the written page.

And then there are the vital contributions from the creators of books for children and young people: Papua New Guinea-born artist, author, and composer Matt Ottley; Welsh naturalist and author Nicola Davies; Australian actor and author Tristan Bancks; and former British Children's Laureate Michael Morpurgo, author, poet, playwright, and librettist, probably best known for *War Horse*.

William Boyd and Pico Iyer are among those who have generously written essays for both anthologies. This time, Will has chosen to revive memories of reading H. Rider Haggard, whose literary career was inspired by his experiences in South Africa. Pico has written about the enchantments of youth, many of them associated with his alma mater, Oxford, fondly recalling Alice and Lyra, Ratty and Mole.

Madeleine Thien wrote a memorable essay for *The Gifts of Reading* and has contributed again, this time writing with crystalline sensitivity about Walter Benjamin. She also offers a fascinating reading list, including a collection of Tang poetry translated by Wong May: 'True to the spirit of classics, these poems from 1,200 years ago read like they were still being written somewhere in the world — to be read today and tomorrow.'

Nikesh Shukla is the author of many books including *Brown Baby: a memoir of race, family and home,* named after a lullaby by Oscar Brown Jr: 'I sang it to you softly, Ganga … Here you were, a brown baby, born into a world that felt less welcoming to you than it should have done.' Like Nikesh, Nilanjana Roy, who writes a column called 'Reading the World' for the *Financial Times*, mentions the influence of James Baldwin, so apt at this time of the hundredth anniversary of Baldwin's birth. Nilanjana's own essay collection, *The Girl Who Ate Books*, is 'an essential collection for those who live to read and read to live'.

This list of authors represents a formidable array of talent and a cornucopia of contributions — but this isn't all. Queen's Gold Medal for Poetry winner Imtiaz Dharker has given us three poems from her latest collection, *Shadow Reader*. Nigerian-born Booker Prize–winning novelist and poet Ben Okri has allowed us to include his 'Ten and a half inclinations' as an epigraph. 'There is a secret trail of books meant to inspire and enlighten you,' he writes. 'Find that trail.'

In the reading list at the back of this book — 'The gifts of reading for the next generation' — there are suggestions from each of the contributors, some of them undoubtedly familiar but certainly many new possibilities, too.

Ann Morgan, author of *Reading the World (How I read a book from every country)*, is a new discovery (for me) but I am so grateful to Nguyễn Phan Quế Mai for connecting us. Ann's essay and her reading list — the longest — introduce books from many far-flung destinations, including Albania, Morocco, and Palestine: rich discoveries of authors, illustrators, translators, and publishers.

I would like to express a deep debt of gratitude to *all* those who have contributed to this anthology and the first. Writers are always stretched, with many demands upon their time, often struggling to make the living they deserve. It is therefore especially generous to write something knowing that there will be no financial reward. All of the writers who have contributed essays to *The Gifts of Reading* and *The Gifts of Reading for the Next Generation* have donated their royalties to Room to Read and U-GO, the two organisations that John Wood has founded. Instead of royalties, they receive rewards of a very different kind: the knowledge that millions of children and young people will benefit from the literacy and girls' education programs supported by their donations.

In 2025, it will be twenty years since I first heard about the work of Room to Read, soon after I had moved to live in Hong Kong for a few years. The Hong Kong chapter had held a fundraising event in the wake of the Boxing Day tsunami. So much money was raised on this occasion that a decision was made to launch Room to Read in Sri Lanka, one of the countries that had been devastated. Now, twenty years later, plans are on the drawing board for Sri Lanka to become the tenth country to join the U-GO family.

Room to Read's mission has remained the same since it launched in 2000: to create a world free from illiteracy and gender inequality through education.

U-GO, launched in 2022, focuses on funding tertiary education for young women, for 'the next generation', offering multi-year scholarships to ensure that the recipients complete their degrees.

The work of these two organisations is complementary, although in launching U-GO, John Wood broadened his partnership base. As with Room to Read, he will scale fast and plans to support 100,000 scholars by 2040.

John has long supported the idea that there can be no better ambassadors for organisations such as Room to Read and U-GO than the writers and artists creating books for young people around the world. Soon after launching Room to Read, though, he became aware that children in developing countries often didn't have any access to books, let alone books that reflected their lives. One of his early decisions was to create a local-language publishing program, developing books in languages such as Lao, Hindi, Tamil, Swahili, Sesotho, and Chinyanja, in places where mainstream children's publishers simply didn't operate. Since that decision was made two decades ago, Room to Read's book-publishing program has created more than 4,725 original and adapted children's books in over fifty-five languages and twenty-four countries, all of them written and illustrated by talented local creators. As journalist Kate Whitehead commented in the early days of Room to Read, it's 'the most influential children's publisher you've never heard of'. This work is ensuring that children don't just learn to read but become lifelong readers.

If you are holding this anthology in your hands, the chances are that you are a lifelong reader. It is my very great hope that these essays will revive literary memories but also illuminate the reading path ahead by offering an extraordinary range of reading choices for you, as well as for the children and young people in your lives. Please celebrate and share the gifts of reading.

I will conclude with a few final words from Robert Macfarlane, the ever-giving patron of this Gifts of Reading community, whose original inspiring essay has grown into two collections and created a group of literary benefactors with enormous hearts: 'Here, repeatedly, books and words are given and received as gifts, prompting in turn further generosity — including the giving of each of these essays. Truly, the gift gives on, and on, and on …'

TRISTAN BANCKS

I started reading to my boys when they were still in the womb. I'm sure it was a bit muffled in there, and they probably didn't fully grasp the plot of Diary of a Wombat *or* Edward the Emu, *but they were born hungry for stories ...*

Tristan Bancks tells stories for the page and screen. His books for kids and teens include *Two Wolves, The Fall, Detention, Cop & Robber,* the Tom Weekly series, and most recently, *Scar Town,* a suspense-thriller. Tristan's books have won and been shortlisted for many awards, including the Prime Minister's Literary Awards, ABIA, YABBA, KOALA, NSW Premier's Literary Awards, and Queensland Literary Awards. *Scar Town* was named the Children's Book Council of Australia's Book of the Year for Younger Readers.

Tristan is currently working with producers to develop a number of his books for the screen. He's excited by the future of storytelling and frequently addresses audiences of young people and adults at schools, festivals, and conferences.

Tristan is a committed Author Advocate for Room to Read and has led campaigns to raise money for literacy and girls' education programs.

Reading as a contact sport

In Children's Book Week 2024, a Sydney teacher took to the streets of Rozelle with a band of unruly students in tow, dressed as their favourite book characters. The teacher held a placard, 'My Nephew Just Won Book of the Year' on one side and 'Proud Uncle' on the other. Many stopped to take photos, including the local constabulary.

The man was my Uncle Mike. Many years ago, he had kick-started my reading journey, gifting books every birthday and Christmas of my childhood. Fiction and nonfiction, funny and serious. Mostly funny. I still have the copies of Roald Dahl's *The Witches* and *The BFG* that he gave me when I was eight years old.

When I speak in schools anywhere in the area, kids and teachers ask if I'm related and tell me how much they love him. He either taught them or their child, or he was a beloved colleague. He gave the gift of reading not just to me and my sister, but to countless others. Even now, in his mid-sixties, he's turning reading into a contact sport, an act of civil disobedience, just as it should be. Collaborative, fun, and a bit dangerous.

The public library

My mother worked hard to raise two kids on her own, so I would go to after-school care at the local neighbourhood centre. It smelt like toast and freshly peeled oranges, and the women who looked after us were funny and kind. The public library was next door, and we would go there on adventures. Partly to rub the soles of our shoes on the synthetic green carpet and build up enough charge to electrocute our friends. Partly to disappear into other worlds.

I disappeared into *Fungus the Bogeyman*, a cornucopia of grossness that satisfied my young mind on so many levels. I got lost in *Where the Wild Things Are*, too. Released the year I was born, Maurice Sendak's classic swept me away 'through night and day, and in and out of weeks, and almost over a year' to a place where Max and I were kings of all wild things. I spent hours searching for Lowly Worm in Richard Scarry's books. I discovered Mr Happy, Mr Sneeze, and Mr Tickle. I would settle into a beanbag with a pile of Golden Books: *Tawny Scrawny, Scuffy the Tugboat,* and my favourite, *Mister Dog: the dog who belonged to himself.* Decades later, my mother would gift all of these books to my sons.

But my life changed forever, at the age of six or seven, when friends and I stumbled across a picture book called *Where Did I Come From?* My memory is that it was shelved right there next to *Wild Things* and *The Very Hungry Caterpillar.* It quickly became a hot ticket. We didn't borrow it. No way. We just revisited it on a very regular basis, bringing other kids along to witness the funniest, weirdest, most mind-boggling book on the planet. Surely this wasn't how babies were made. Couldn't be. Reading it was a communal, educational, and subversive pursuit. It blew our little minds. An axe for the frozen sea inside. A gift, indeed.

Having read *Where Did I Come From?* dozens of times and committed every page to memory, I was puzzled when a copy appeared in our house when I was fifteen years old. I flicked through, remembering old times and wondering if Mum was going to give it to a small child. Then it dawned on me that *I* was the small child. This was 'the talk'. I still laugh about it with my mum. That book is the gift that keeps on giving.

Sick bay

I spent a lot of time in sick bay at school. Not because I was sick, you'll be pleased to know. But because they had the sickest (read: best) collection of pop-up books ever. I would feign illness, then skip down the hall to where Mrs Armitage was cranking out the stencils on the Gestetner machine (an ancient photocopier). The smell of that purpley blue ink smacking down on fresh sheets of A4 as they raced through the machine was music to my nose. I would lie back on the narrow sick bay bed, reach into the book box, and spend the morning spinning cardboard dials, pulling levers, and turning pages to see the world of the story pop up into three-dimensional life. This wasn't just words on a page or some nice pictures. These books were *alive,* and I loved them. Each book was a theme park ride, a physical adventure.

In Robert Macfarlane's essay 'The Gifts of Reading', which inspired this book, he quotes Lewis Hyde, writing, 'The gift moves.' Not just physically but emotionally, in the heart of the receiver. And, I would add, the giver.

When I first started writing books for young people, one of my guiding principles was to write 'books that move' — engaging, page-turning books, with characters you cared for and stories that were about something. I was told early on, 'Never be boring when writing for young people', and I took that on board — but I didn't want to write 'exciting' at the expense of meaning or emotion. So, perhaps kids' books should move in three ways — driving young readers through the plot, making them feel something, but also being given as a gift and inspiring the recipient to give, too.

The first book

Bookshop, library, cinema, and beach are my four favourite places. I remember a day in December 1985 when my grandmother ticked two of those boxes and gave me two indelible cinematic and literary memories. She took my cousins and me to see *Rocky IV* at Hoyts multiplex on George Street, Sydney, the biggest cinema in the world, as far as we knew. Outside in the street, after the movie, we straggled behind her, rehashing the plot, practising our boxing moves, and arguing over who was playing Balboa and who Drago, all the way down to the biggest bookshop in the world. The size of the Dymocks George Street store was difficult to comprehend when we were ten, eight, and six. It must have been fifty times the size of my local bookshop in the Blue Mountains.

We spent a couple of hours in the shop, reading in corners and under display tables. Then Nan bought us the first book I remember being purchased directly from a bookshop, that hadn't just somehow appeared at home. It was *Unreal* by a new Australian author, Paul Jennings. The short stories in this book were every bit as dark and funny and magical as Roald Dahl, but they were set in Australia and the kids were a bit like us.

The problem was that Nan only bought one copy. But there were two of us who desperately wanted the book. So, my eldest cousin and I took dual custody. At the end of the school holidays, we flipped for who got it first. Nick won. The next holidays, he reluctantly gave it back to me — and the following one, I to him. I seem to recall that one of us dropped it in the bath or had a sneaker wave wash up and drown it at the beach. The book was crispy and bloated, and there were bitter, hilarious arguments over who would buy a replacement. Nan's joint gift forced the reading process to be vital, alive, and communal, a point of deep connection between us. We would both go on to write our own books.

The body

By the end of 1986, on the cusp of high school, my friend Rachel introduced a few of us to Stephen King during reading time at the back of the classroom. *Thinner*, I think, was the first book. We quickly found our way to *Pet Sematary* and *Carrie* and *Cujo* and *The Shining*. Books nabbed from parents' shelves or passed on by my Uncle John, another influence on me becoming a reader, or bought from the cigarette-smoke-smelling second-hand bookshop at the back of the arcade. Books that some would say we shouldn't have been reading at age eleven, but that's exactly why we wanted to read them. As with *Where Did I Come From?*, this was reading as an act of defiance, a secret between friends, discovering things about the adult world that were heretofore unknown, and then discussing our discoveries.

The following year, we saw *Stand by Me*, about four kids who head out on a railway line, searching for a dead body. We were astounded to realise that this epic teen coming-of-age story was based on an adult novella, *The Body*, written by the very same Stephen King who had just written *Misery*. This guy was a genius. And the collection it was in, *Different Seasons*, also included *Rita Hayworth and Shawshank Redemption*, perhaps the second-best story we had ever read.

These are not the books that I would recommend to a twelve-year-old now. I don't have to. There are so many other options. I had no choice but to jump from *Danny, the Champion of the World* to *Cujo*. There were no such categories as Middle Grade or Young Adult back then, apart from books like *The Secret Diary of Adrian Mole* and *The Outsiders*. Now, I try to write the books that I would have loved when I was twelve, if they had existed — darker and more dangerous than Dahl, but more relevant to the eleven- or thirteen-year-old reader than King.

A line from the opening page of *The Body* and the opening

scene of *Stand by Me* has guided the writing of my middle-grade books: 'I was twelve going on thirteen when I first saw a dead human being.' For me, this captures the change that happens between primary and high school — that growing fascination with mortality and morality that books can explore in much greater depth and in more satisfying ways than a horror movie or a TikTok video.

Reading to my own kids

I started reading to my boys when they were still in the womb. I'm sure it was a bit muffled in there, and they probably didn't fully grasp the plot of *Diary of a Wombat* or *Edward the Emu*, but they were born hungry for stories, and I continued to read them to sleep until well after they could read independently. We discovered *Floss* and *The Last Train* by Kim Lewis (gifted by Uncle Mike), Kate DiCamillo's *The Miraculous Journey of Edward Tulane*. I read them Jean Craighead George's *My Side of the Mountain* and Michael Gerard Bauer's *Just a Dog*.

I have only one parenting tip that I gleaned from those years. The only thing that I know, for sure, worked with my kids and that I feel confident passing on. My sons were early wakers, so the rule was that if they were awake before 6.30 am, the only choice was to read. No Lego or games or TV, no beating one another up for entertainment. Just read. The choice of books was theirs, but if they didn't want to read, they had to stay in bed and sleep or rest. The plan was to have very well-read or very well-slept children. We were happy with either.

We had done our best to give the gift of reading, but once devices became a requirement for school, reading began to wane. My heart goes out to any parent fighting this battle now. The pressure to give kids time on devices for school, entertainment, and social interaction has never been greater. I might be wrong, but my feeling is that the longer you can hold out, the further you can stretch the attention span, the better chance of building a reader.

Room to Read

I have visited thousands of schools over the past seventeen years, invited by proactive teacher-librarians. I use images, video, music, maps, and anecdotes to take kids behind the scenes on the writing of my own books, but also to share the books I loved as a kid and as a teen, and the books that have had a profound effect on my stories.

In 2009, I read John Wood's *Leaving Microsoft to Change the World* and it changed my world. The book shared the story of the genesis of Room to Read, the non-profit started by Wood that has built school libraries, trained teachers, published local-language books, and funded girls' education in low-income countries. I had been surrounded by books as a child, but Wood showed me that many kids in the world have little or no access.

So, I dared a class of year 5/6 kids in a small primary school in northern New South Wales to raise $500 in a single day to buy 500 books for kids in Cambodia. The kids undertook challenges like 'Drop Everything and Read', a gold coin 'Book Swap', and a 'Sponsored Silence' where the noisiest kid in class was sponsored to be quiet for an entire day.

These challenges brought reading to life, made it fun, and also raised $572. We shot a video for YouTube, persuaded other schools to take on the challenge, and, with the help of a corporate sponsor matching donations, we raised over $20,000 — enough to build a school library in Siem Reap, Cambodia. We have continued this 'World Change Challenge' each year and have now raised over $270,000 for Room to Read programs in partnership with Australian authors, illustrators, teacher-librarians, and students. The gifts of reading in action.

The gifts of reading

There has never before been greater competition for human attention. Sometimes it is a battle to make time to read, and to find creative ways to share the gifts of reading with young people, to make it an adventure, a contact sport. Through books we give kids empathy, kindness, love, healing, and the space and time to be with their own thoughts, to reflect on their lives, to understand others. And these gifts are more precious now than ever.

Seven books for kids and teens that I most like to gift

This list is not just about the books I loved as a kid. It's also about the present-day receiver. Many of these have influenced my writing and I think they're some of the best in their field.

Herman and Rosie by Gus Gordon (picture book)
My Side of the Mountain by Jean Craighead George
Hatchet by Gary Paulsen
Holes by Louis Sachar
Once by Morris Gleitzman
We Are Wolves by Katrina Nannestad
The Sky So Heavy by Claire Zorn (young adult)

WILLIAM BOYD

*… there was another writer [that] I found even more
intriguing … This was H. Rider Haggard — a writer who
is pretty much forgotten today, I suspect — but whose
novels exercised a grip on my imagination
that I can still recall.*

William Boyd was born in 1952 in Accra, Ghana, and grew
up there and in Nigeria. He is the author of eighteen highly
acclaimed bestselling novels and five collections of stories. He is
married and divides his time between London and south-west
France.

Out of Africa:
H. Rider Haggard

I was an early and avid reader, so my mother always told me, and I can remember the first book that I 'owned' — a large-format, lavishly illustrated edition of Rudyard Kipling's *The Jungle Book*. This was not such a surprising choice, as I was born and raised in West Africa, in Ghana. Kipling's mythic jungle boy, Mowgli, and the wild animals he associated with, seemed not too far away from the world I myself inhabited as I roamed the countryside, the so-called 'orchard-bush' — also full of wildlife — around our house.

Another of the books I read and re-read was called *I Flew with Braddock* by the pseudonymous 'George Bourne', about an English bomber pilot in World War II. Then there were Enid Blyton's Famous Five and Secret Seven stories; Captain W.E. Johns' Biggles series; and, when I went off to boarding school in Scotland in 1961, at the age of nine, I remember devouring the Jennings school stories by Anthony Buckeridge.

So far, so typical, I suppose. But it was at that boarding school in Scotland, when I was eleven or twelve, that my reading took its first serious swerve and enjoyed a different character. My mentor was another boy at the school, a good friend called Philip Panton. Philip was plump and not very sporty, but he compensated for this by being a precocious reader. It was Philip who introduced me to J.R.R. Tolkien and the Lord of the Rings trilogy — and this was long before Tolkien had achieved any great renown. But there was another writer he steered me towards, whose work I found even more intriguing than the Hobbits and the Orcs of Middle-earth. This was H. Rider Haggard — a writer who is pretty much forgotten today, I suspect — but whose novels exercised a grip on my imagination that I can still recall.

H. Rider Haggard (the 'H' stands for Henry) was born in 1856, the eighth of ten children. He came from a wealthy squirearchical Norfolk background but, unusually for a boy of this class, did not go to a private school and did not attend university, either. Instead, at the age of nineteen, he travelled to what is now South Africa and started to earn his living as a junior colonial officer, acting first as a private secretary to provincial governors and steadily rising up the imperial administrative tree.

The time Haggard spent in Africa between 1875 and 1882, and the travels and experiences he had there, formed the basis of his literary inspiration. When he returned to England, he became a lawyer and a farmer — he wrote an excellent clear-eyed autobiographical account about the latter profession and its seasonal stringencies called A Farmer's Year (1899). He began to write novels, so he claimed, only as a way of making some extra money.

Haggard's literary career took off in spectacular fashion with the publication of his third novel, King Solomon's Mines, in 1885. This was the book that established his personal tone of voice and the highly individual literary atmosphere he created for the duration of his writing life. It was a long and productive one, also: Haggard wrote some fifty-eight novels, as well as copious works of nonfiction and journalism.

It's fair to say that Haggard more or less invented a literary genre — the so-called 'lost world' novel. These are novels of adventure and romance usually involving the search for a hidden civilisation, city, treasure, or tribe, full of witchcraft and magic, ritual and barbarity, and other supernatural trappings. *King Solomon's Mines* set the benchmark and was hugely influential. Jules Verne, Robert Louis Stevenson, Arthur Conan Doyle, Rudyard Kipling, John Buchan, and Edgar Rice Burroughs all acknowledged Haggard's influence.

The protagonist of *King Solomon's Mines* is a big-game hunter called Allan Quatermain. He embarks on a trek into the terra incognita of Central Africa in search of a missing friend and the legendary diamond mines that provided King Solomon's vast wealth. Quatermain was based on the famous hunter and scout Frederick Selous (whom Haggard met and came to know) and featured in some fourteen of Haggard's novels, also in four short stories. Allan Quatermain is also — reputedly — the inspiration behind the character of Indiana Jones.

Haggard's next extraordinary triumph was a novel entitled *She: a history of adventure* (1887) which proved to be even more enduringly successful. *She* has been filmed eleven times, the most famous version arriving in 1965 with Ursula Andress as the eponymous 'She'. Again, the novel featured a quest: two friends from Cambridge set off to search for a 'lost world' in Africa, a city called Kôr ruled over by an immortal white goddess known as Ayesha or She, as in She-Who-Must-Be-Obeyed. In fact, She is over two thousand years old and yet is still mesmerisingly beautiful. The novel's climax occurs when She strips naked and enters a column of eternal flame to prove her immortality. Disastrously, the reverse occurs, and her real age begins to manifest itself on her body:

Suddenly — more suddenly than I can tell — an
indescribable change came over her countenance. The

smile vanished and in its stead there crept a dry hard
look, the rounded face seemed to grow pinched …
Her face was growing old before my eyes! … Ayesha was
shrivelling up. Smaller and smaller she grew; her skin
changed colour and in place of the perfect whiteness of
its lustre it turned dirty brown and yellow, like an old
piece of withered parchment … Then she seemed to
understand what kind of a change was passing over her
and she shrieked … Smaller she grew, and smaller yet,
till she was no larger than a monkey. Now the skin had
puckered into a million wrinkles and on her shapeless
face was the stamp of unutterable age …

It's not hard to understand the grip of Haggard's fantastical
stories on the mind and imagination of a young reader. I was
utterly held by these novels and began to consume as many
Haggards as I could muster. Another of my favourites was *Eric
Brighteyes* — an epic Viking saga — written with the same verve
and excitement as his African novels.

It's fair to say that Haggard himself couldn't really fathom
how these astonishing stories emerged. He always wrote very
fast — *She* took him only six weeks — and sometimes he would
publish three novels in a year. Success bred success: his income in
1888 from sales of his books was over £10,000 — the equivalent
of £1,600,000 today.

I suspect it was the very speed of composition that unlocked
something in his unconscious mind; almost a kind of emotional
free association — rather like automatic writing — that
unwittingly created narratives, images, and startling scenes that
a more considered composition might have reshaped and dulled
or, given that these novels were written at the height of Victorian
propriety, suppressed. It's interesting to note that Carl Jung

himself used the example of She/Ayesha to illustrate his concept of the Anima, the feminine force in humankind. The potential psychological and psychoanalytical interpretations of Haggard's fictions are both tempting and manifold, as many modern critics have since explored and debated.

In the way that untaught, naïve painters can sometimes achieve remarkable artistic effects (one thinks of Henri 'Le Douanier' Rousseau, Alfred Wallis, L.S. Lowry, and Jean-Michel Basquiat, for example), so too, I believe, a similar creative naivety explains Haggard's particular potency as a novelist. Tellingly, he was not subjected to the English private school ethos, nor did he experience a university education, let alone Oxford or Cambridge. Instead, he went off to Africa to make a life for himself. These biographical details are, I believe, very significant — the key factors that shaped his imagination and made his creative mind work differently, aslant, idiosyncratically. In one sense, Haggard appeared a representative Victorian gent: with his neatly barbered grey beard, the wing collar, the tweed suit, he looked highly typical of his class. He was even knighted in 1912. But when he sat down to write his novels, he tapped into something else in his nature. Something strange and compelling poured out, not fully understood.

All novelists to a degree, either consciously or unconsciously, exhibit the value systems of their age. In Haggard's lifetime, the British Empire was at its apogee, circling the globe from Australia and New Zealand, through Burma, India, and great portions of Africa, and all the way to Canada. It is true that Haggard's novels reflect some of the prejudices of the era — racial, sexual, and societal — as indeed did the work of most of his novelist peers. And yet there is something remarkable about Haggard's African novels that makes them entirely untypical of their time. One of his recurring characters is a Zulu warrior called Umslopogaas

— a companion of Allan Quatermain and a completely nuanced and three-dimensional portrait of a remarkable individual.

Haggard's admiration for the Zulus and their attributes is very clear in his African novels. And what Victorian novelist would have written a novel featuring only African characters, as Haggard did when he wrote *Nada the Lily* (1892)? *Nada the Lily* is an origin story about Umslopogaas' early life and his love for Nada, the 'most beautiful of Zulu women'. It was widely acclaimed on publication, adding significantly to Haggard's reputation. This novel establishes, in a real sense, that Haggard was only interested in myth and story; that the judgements he made in his novels were determined by his chosen subject matter and the narratives that his unusual mind supplied. He was not using his fiction as a manifesto, keen to propound the typical assumptions and imperial bigotries of the time.

Rider Haggard is a curiosity in literature. In his lifetime he was as famous and successful as Arthur Conan Doyle, Rudyard Kipling, and Robert Louis Stevenson. Yet I sense he is something of an unknown writer today — even though, somewhat astonishingly, all of his dozens of novels are available in one form or another. Perhaps their unique appeal — with their bizarre lost worlds, their exotic quests, their violent battles, their evil demons and hallucinogenic drugs, their magic, their marvels and overwhelming passions — keeps the works alive and still attracts new readers, as I myself was drawn to them all those years ago.

Rider Haggard died in 1925 at the age of sixty-eight.

SHANKARI CHANDRAN

Books are the efforts of storytellers to honour human strengths and weaknesses. Our achievements and our failures are all recorded so that we can better understand ourselves, so we can better achieve our potential. Words are a gift. Books are a gift.

Shankari Chandran is an Australian Tamil lawyer and author of *Chai Time at Cinnamon Gardens, Song of the Sun God, The Barrier, Safe Haven,* and *Unfinished Business.* Her fiction explores dispossession and the creation of community, and she has received multiple awards and listings, including the prestigious Miles Franklin Literary Award in 2023 for *Chai Time at Cinnamon Gardens.* Shankari's short stories have appeared in two acclaimed anthologies, *Another Australia* and *Sweatshop Women* (Vol 2).

Shankari has spent two decades working as a lawyer in the social justice field, on national and international program design and delivery. She currently continues her work in social impact for an Australian national retailer. She is based in Sydney, Australia, where she lives with her husband and her four children. She first supported John Wood's work two decades ago when she was living and working in London.

A thousand stories

The earliest memory I have of my Appamma is her soothing me to sleep with stories from the *Mahabharata*, the ancient epic that is so deeply familiar to all Hindu children.

It is a thousand stories within a story. You could retell the *Mahabharata* in five minutes (two sides of the same family fight over their ancestral kingdom, almost everybody dies).

Or you could do what my grandmother did and regale your descendants, every night for many years, and still not get to the end because it's so long (as I said, almost everybody dies).

I remember the feel of her hands, strong and gnarled, like my father's are now, rubbing my back to help me sleep as she talked. I've always been a tense sleeper, and my husband thinks it's because I was raised on mythological sagas of fratricide and civil war.

Perhaps he's right.

My parents do not read fiction. Their extensive reading of spirituality, Hinduism, and our mythology is obviously *not* fiction. In recent years, my father has read my novels and found them to be a revelation. He swells with pride when he observes that my work is about the Tamil experience, and that it is infused with Hinduism. He says to me, 'You were listening.' (He also reproaches me for using the F-word in my books.)

I *was* listening.

From an early age, I can remember my parents drawing on the

stories from the *Mahabharata* to teach us life's lessons. Somehow, everything we needed to know was contained in this epic. My parents come from a long line of storytellers/exaggerators (aka Sri Lankan Tamils) and between family history, Sri Lankan political history, Hinduism, and human anatomy (they're both doctors), they were never short of material to share with us.

As a young adult, I often wondered what my approach to parenting would be. Of particular concern were the issues that consume me daily: justice, religion, literature, and laundry.

Would my children fight for justice, would they seek divinity, would they help with chores, and most importantly, would they be readers?

Would they feel as I do — that to spend time with words is the most beautiful gift? Would entering a library feel like entering a temple, as it does for me? If they listened, would they hear the voices of generations of people who have tried to understand and record the human condition?

Books are the efforts of storytellers to honour human strengths and weaknesses. Our achievements and our failures are all recorded so that we can better understand ourselves, better achieve our potential. Words are a gift. Books are a gift.

Perhaps like many parents, and like all Sri Lankan Tamil parents, I was expecting too much of my four children before they were even born.

When they were young, I read them *The Very Hungry Caterpillar*, *The Gruffalo*, *We're Going on a Bear Hunt*, and so on. However, as more children joined the family and chronic sleep deprivation set in, I was never that mother who lay down at night and read to them from Harry Potter or Lord of the Rings. I watched the movies with them repeatedly, and we have 'bookclubbed' the books extensively. But reading lengthy novels at night only ever happened in my fantasies of perfect parenting.

And of course, the first book I bought for my unsuspecting, (as yet) unconceived children was the *Mahabharata*.

It is believed that the story was narrated by Veda Vyasa, one of our most venerated sages. Realising that he was coming to the end of his earthly life, he decided to preserve the *Mahabharata* in writing, so that future generations would remember the Great War that shaped their destiny. He asked Ganesha, the Elephant God and Remover of Obstacles, to be his scribe, but he gave him two conditions. Ganesha must not stop writing once Vyasa began the story, and Ganesha must understand everything that he was writing. Ganesha agreed to the old sage's conditions but gave Vyasa one of his own. He declared that once Vyasa began his story, he must not stop telling it; he must narrate continuously until the very end. Narrator and scribe thus agreed on the terms, and Ganesha broke off one of his tusks, which he used as a divine pen. Vyasa sat down and began.

The *Mahabharata* was composed in the first millennium BCE, but in 1999 (four years before my first child was born), I bought the edition by academic Kamala Subramaniam, published in 1977. I was at Higginbotham's, the legendary bookstore in Chennai, India. The first time I had walked in, many years beforehand, my father had said to my brother and me those magical words that every book-loving child yearns to hear: 'Choose whatever you want.'

Most of the novels in my father's childhood home were school prizes won by him and his six siblings. While my parents were frugal and fiscally responsible in their uncertain immigrant youth (in retirement, the Carnival Cruise Line may have unspooled them), they understood the value of literature even if they had not felt its power. Public libraries, bookstores, second-hand bookstores, and book stalls at school fetes were places of endless possibility.

I particularly loved Higginbotham's in Chennai because it was in this cavernous place that I first discovered a universe of brown writers who interrogated and celebrated the lives of brown people. Rushdie, Mistry, Seth, R.K. Narayan, Ghosh, Desai — and later Roy, Lahiri, Divakaruni, Desai (junior), Selvadurai, and others. All of them helped me find myself in literature. I felt seen, understood, and valued through their work. Reading their books gave me the confidence to write; a sense that my own stories were valid.

These are not books for young children. They came later in my life, but their impact was considerable. Children should start with the age-appropriate readers recommended by their wonderful teachers and school librarians. 'What are you reading?' was a question I asked much more frequently than 'How much screen time have you had?'

That said (and before I spiral into an anxiety-fuelled rant about the dangers of screens and the impact they have had on children who once reached for a book before they reached for their toothbrushes), my children still love books.

I have one child who is challenged by reading but tries very hard with it, as she does with all things. She is a gifted visual artist and storyteller whose childhood game called 'Let's Pretend' transported her siblings to boundless worlds. I have another child who once asked me if he could take his Kindle onto the cricket pitch when fielding. He now only reads nonfiction, and occasionally has the patience to explain the world to me as he learns it. Another of my children reads slowly, deeply, and quietly. He keeps a list of stories that are loved by the people he loves, and is reading them in his own time. And my last child reads quickly, deeply, and furiously. He cannot start or end his day without 'just five more minutes'.

They are all young adults now, mature enough to read the

South Asian greats as well as a broad range of others, from the global classical to the global contemporary. They are also fortunate enough to have grown up at a time when they can see themselves and their lived experiences reflected through diverse stories in Australian literature, something I longed for but didn't have as a young person. My South Asian favourites now proudly sit alongside the work of Mohammed Ahmad, Christos Tsiolkas, Peter Polites, Yumna Kassab, and Maxine Beneba Clark. First Nations literature also enriches their lives and teaches them about our chosen home through the work of Nardi Simpson, Larissa Behrendt, Melissa Lucashenko, and others.

And of course, there is still the *Mahabharata*. My children never really took to the graphic novels (Amar Chitra Katha comics) that my cousins and I were obsessed with. They were collectible, as all comics are, and focused on stories of Hindu gods, goddesses, warriors, sages, and other notable Hindu figures. As the range matured, its subject matter also diversified, and we learned about other South Asian religions and their notable figures. These short comics were where we began our religious reading, before we were old enough to move on to the massive translated texts, and they were highly prized in my childhood. After the civil war started in Sri Lanka, my parents could no longer return home. They took comfort in pilgrimages to India and, to our utter delight, would return with new comics.

As I mentioned, my children never loved these comics the way we did, and to this day it mystifies (and if I'm being completely honest, disappoints) me. And so I have had to rely on the same oral storytelling tradition of my grandmother and my parents. I am somewhat embarrassed to admit in this safe space that I don't think I've done as well as they did (or as well as the comics), but I have tried. As we exited our front gate en route to their primary school, I would ask them what they'd like to talk about, offering a curated selection of topics: what they were reading, what I was reading, what I was writing, and the *Mahabharata*. I confess there were times when I only gave them one option. We would walk and talk all the way to school. It is my favourite memory from their primary school years.

At the risk of sounding like my parents, the themes and characters of the *Mahabharata* really do teach you everything you need to know about life.

At the centre of the epic is a bromance between the brave warrior prince, Arjuna, and Krishna, the god-in-human-form (aka avatar, before *Avatar*), who had befriended him. Krishna serves as Arjuna's confidant, diplomat, wise counsel, and skilled charioteer; what every hero needs.

The story goes that just before the war was about to begin, Arjuna threw down his weapons and refused to fight. The armies of his brothers, the Pandavas, were lined up on one side of the magnificent Kurukshetra battlefield. The armies of his cousins, the Kauravas, were lined up on the other side. Arjuna declared that he could not — he *would* not — kill his own family over the ancestral kingdom they were unable to share.

It is at that moment that Krishna reveals he is not actually Arjuna's friend, but that He, Krishna, is indeed Divine. He takes this opportunity to have a dialogue with Arjuna, who has dropped to his knees, hands folded in prayer. Still reeling from finding out that his best friend is actually God, and having a completely understandable pre-war panic attack, Arjuna represents a lost and confused humanity.

Krishna the God gives humanity 700 verses of Sanskrit poetry about human nature, the purpose of life, how to live life, and how to realise one's own Divinity. This sacred song of God (the *Bhagavad Gita*) apparently took Krishna forty-five minutes to deliver (a remarkable achievement given that I've never known a middle-aged Hindu male to wrap up a discussion about religion in less than three hours).

In summary, Krishna says there is formless Divinity inside all of us and around us. This is our true and shared nature, and our true purpose is to realise this. Trapped in a cycle of birth and death, we can free ourselves through right conduct, devotion, pursuit of knowledge, and control of the mind and body.

I have read many retellings of the *Mahabharata*, but the one I bought for my children in 1999 is my favourite. Subramaniam's explanation of the *Bhagavad Gita* is easy to understand. Like most sermons, it's dramatically lacking and tonally didactic, yet it evokes the complex and contradictory humanity of her characters, who are to be our moral guides in life. The heroes are flawed; they are human and therefore they fail. The villains are capable of goodness and greatness. The Pandavas and the Kauravas are cousins who should have loved each other like brothers. Instead, both sides of the family are destroyed, and all that's left are mothers and widows. There is nothing, no glorious kingdom to rule over for the Pandavas. They win the war, but every single one of their sons is killed. A whole generation of their young is lost to them. There is only grief and emptiness for the victors. For the losers, there is no earthly punishment. Of the hundred Kaurava brothers that were brought into the world, not one remains. All of them lie dead on the battlefield, in a pool of clan blood mixed with their mother's bitter tears.

The final chapter of the *Mahabharata* is not a Happily-Ever-After. It is a cautionary tale. In wars, civil or otherwise, the fight for freedom, for statehood, for justice and self-determination, is flawed. Each side of a conflict will have their moments, the days and years in which they will either redeem or repudiate their humanity. It is the nature of the species.

The *Mahabharata* speaks to the macro — the dynamics

of power, control, and war between all tribes. And it speaks to the micro — the dynamics of love, duty, loyalty, greed, fear, and sacrifice within all relationships. It is about nations, communities, and families.

Subramaniam's *Mahabharata* embodies what I love most about my favourite authors and books. It has the propulsive pace and game-playing protagonists of Highsmith's *The Talented Mr Ripley*. Like Greene's *The Quiet American* it offers subtle meditations on war and the hypocrisy of the lies we tell ourselves to enter conflicts. It is political and personal, like Le Carré's *The Constant Gardener*. The language is somewhere between the gut-wrenching simplicity of Mistry's *A Fine Balance*, and the devastating poetry of Roy's *The God of Small Things*. The women are strong, powerful, and vengeful, like the sorceress Polgara in the Eddings series I devoured as a child, although none of them wanted to be writers like me and Alcott's Jo March, my other go-to re-read. It makes radicalisation understandable and the reader empathetic, the way Shamsie's *Home Fire* does. The Pandava brothers are an unbreakable gang like those in S.E. Hinton's *The Outsiders*, who try to 'stay gold' but who are torn down and apart by the violence of the world they live in. The chilling despair and self-annihilation of the impending and post apocalypse is rendered as vividly here as it is in McCarthy's *The Road*, Bacigalupi's *The Water Knife*, and Golding's *The Lord of the Flies*. In this book, children see and speak the truth, as in Lee's *To Kill a Mockingbird*, and justice is equally unserved. It is mythology reborn and relived in the modern world, like in Gavriel Kay's The Fionavar Tapestry series.

Subramaniam's *Mahabharata* is the ultimate multi-generational family saga in the tradition of Allende's *House of the Spirits* and García Márquez's *One Hundred Years of Solitude*. She writes with the intellectualism of Baldwin, the activism of

Atwood and Morrison, and the integrity of Flanagan.

I have given my children many books since this one, including some of those listed above. I chose Subramaniam's *Mahabharata* as the first gift I would give them. Not the first book; the first *gift* — because it is the story of the human journey through the world, and the soul's journey within all of that. The world is chaos, brutality, beauty, and love. I know my children will need a guide, and my husband and I won't always be here for them. But we will leave them a library of books, a love of stories, and maybe some change in our pension.

HORATIO CLARE

When you read aloud to your partner or your child the room and the world beyond it seem to still, and the spirits gather to hear the story. Words uttered are more than words heard in the silence of the mind; they are things in the world, and the world responds.

Horatio Clare is a writer and broadcaster. His acclaimed memoirs, travel, and children's books include *Running for the Hills*, *A Single Swallow*, *Down to the Sea in Ships*, *Heavy Light*, and *Aubrey and the Terrible Yoot*. His latest book is *Your Journey, Your Way: the recovery guide to mental health*. He lives with his family in Yorkshire.

The gifts of being read to

'So,' my father would ask, after the bath and the doing of teeth, as if the answer was unknown, 'what's it going to be?'

'Shady Glade!'

'Right! *Shady Glade* ...'

And sitting on my bed in our basement flat in London, for the thirty-third time, he would recite (and pretend to read), in exactly the same warm, alerting, storytelling tone, as if he had never seen them before, the first lines. He would have just done the same thing for my brother, now in a deep doze on the other side of the room, with *The Gnats of Knotty Pine*, while in the kitchen in my pyjamas I gave my nightly reading of Peter and Jane and Pat the Dog to my mother.

His beautiful voice, which was soft and rich and clever, was the last thing I heard every day for years; being read to is the routine I remember best from my early childhood, before they split up, and we moved to Wales and our mother took up reading to us. The nights she gave us Astrid Lindgren's *The Brothers Lionheart* were spellbinding. Dad was a broadcaster. Mum had been an actress. They were super performers.

'That's a *nice* set of knives and forks and spoons! I'll 'ave that!' cried Burglar Bill, 'Boglar Boll' as my brother called him, every night for weeks, in the year before we switched to *Shady Glade*, in Dad's own voice, and with his characteristic grin. The word Tengil, the name of the murderous despot in *The Brothers Lionheart*, still shivers through me in my mother's hiss. I can still hear *Cannonball Simp* in both their voices.

Writing my first book, about the collapse of their marriage and our move to Wales, and partly imagining, partly reconstructing their relationship, I included a scene Mum had mentioned in which he read to her.

'John loved reading to me!'

'What did he read?'

'At the farm I remember *The Heart of the Matter* ...'

It seems a strange choice for a couple freshly embarked together, slightly stranger than watching a box set with your beloved with the same themes — grief, adultery, faith, death — if only because in reading aloud the reader is the narrator, performer, effectively the writer, imparting the tale to the other, aligned with the book and the sensibility of the work. But I can hear the exact quiet relish with which Dad must have read to her, in his beautiful voice.

When my turn to read to my child came, I discovered all the pleasures of the bedside performance. One is the chance of escape through absorption. When Aubrey was small, I commuted between home in the Pennines and teaching in Liverpool, in more or less constant movement through the weeks, and only when I was working with students or reading to Aubrey was my anxious and tugging inner self stilled. And I can recognise that absorption and pleasure on my father's face when I think of him now.

It's a particular time, reading to and being read to, a quietly magical time for a child, especially snug in your covers, watching and listening to an adult giving themselves entirely to entertaining you. Being an audience of two to the story of the book is lovely, too, a companionship something like equality across generations, across the gulfs between childhood and the adult world.

Dad took us on boating holidays after the divorce; with the little cabin cruiser moored for the night, and the black Thames slithering under the keel, he set about E.B. White's *Charlotte's Web*, and Russell Hoban's *The Mouse and His Child*. The mice are two clockwork toys, made of tin. They have no teeth, no claws, and no territory. They agonise over their defencelessness. 'But that is what is saving them!' I remember exclaiming. 'They don't threaten anyone!' And my father smiling. 'Exactly right,' he said.

My first piece of close reading, proto-literary criticism. Whenever he found a funny passage, his delight and amusement were beautiful; the cabin chimed with our laughter and snorted with giggles. Unlike me, Dad timed reading so that we heard a chapter or section and were then bid goodnight, kissed, and the light was turned off. When I began bedtime reading, to my then partner's six-year-old, Robin, I soon realised that the aim was not necessarily to entrance and delight, but to render unconscious.

First in Rochdale, and then during our years abroad, we did whatever Robin wanted, including Jeff Kinney's *Diary of a Wimpy Kid*, and manuals on Bionicles (a race of plastic space robots with which he was in love), and Derek Landy's *Skulduggery Pleasant*. Michael Morpurgo's *War Horse* we met in our tiny studio flat in Verona, and also Robert Westall's *The Machine Gunners*, one of my favourites ever, which Dad had sent to me from London in the years when he was there, and we were up the mountain, with a note — *I thought this might be up your street.*

Although I knew *The Machine Gunners* well, reading aloud is different, more powerful. In moments of this and *War Horse* I struggled not to cry, fighting not to embarrass Robin and break the spell.

With even the most gripping books I found I could change

gear, after the appropriate while, from an entertaining rendition, designed to engage Robin, to a soporific monotone, to knock him out. One evening in Verona we began one of David Walliams' books. The flat was a one-bedroom, and Robin slept on a sofa bed in the kitchen-diner. His mother, Rebecca, often curled up with him to listen, and often they both fell asleep.

There is a time then that readers aloud know, when you raise your eyes from the page and look at some one or two you love most in the world, your now dreaming audience, and though you do not think it consciously, perhaps, the truth is that their gentle sleep is a gift you have helped, that night, to give them, and it feels an almost holy moment. Not that night, though. I managed the first couple of pages, and gave them my best, but after a little while I stopped and put it down.

'I'm sorry. It's just *so* bad! It's *terrible*. Wait a sec. Even *I* can do better than this *crap* ...'

I wrote Robin a short story, and when he liked it, and his brother came along, I set about a longer one, a novel for children that became *Aubrey and the Terrible Yoot*. Something magical happened with that book. It came to talk to us, it seemed, to be read aloud at bedtime; it was a gift from those two boys to their reader, and a gift from me to them, and also more than that. When you read aloud to your partner or your child the room and the world beyond it seem to still, and the spirits gather to hear the story. Words uttered are more than words heard in the silence of the mind; they are things in the world, and the world responds. Sometimes, depending on where you live, in the hoot of an owl ...

Robin was six when I met him and about twelve the last time I read to him, so I knew something of what to expect and to try when Aubrey reached that stage. But I knew nothing about those first half-dozen years. The first thing I read to him, when he was

weeks old, was Coleridge's 'The Rime of the Ancient Mariner'.
We had left the flat in Verona now and moved to the top floor of
a villa in the Valpolicella. A long low woody room with sofas at
one end and our bed at the other, and a separate kitchen, and a
room for Robin — bliss.

It was a snowy winter, Aubrey's first; the mountains seemed
to come down to the valleys at dusk, great white wolves with
purple woods for fur, and the church bells ringing, tiny and
crystalline in the frost. He would wail last thing at night — we
know why now: like me, he is a night owl, often unready to go to
bed — and so I paced with him strapped to my chest slowly up
and down the long room, saying softly:

> He holds him with his skinny hand,
> 'There was a ship,' quoth he.
> 'Hold off! unhand me, grey-beard loon!'
> Eftsoons his hand dropt he.
>
> He holds him with his glittering eye —
> The Wedding-Guest stood still,
> And listens like a three years' child:
> The Mariner hath his will.

It is the show-off, the actor in me, who loves reading to him
so much, I know. But it is also a love of parenting in the root
meaning of the word, a *bringing forth*, of the listener's attention,
marvel, laughter, and thought. Reading aloud is also a self-
parenting, in the bringing forth of the voices, feeling, and tones
from the reader. And it is a team sport, as it were, while reading
to yourself is all about individual skill.

Not all children love to read. They absorb narrative through
talk and games and films and their friends and their YouTubers

and that is fine, I learned, despite my initial panic when neither Robin nor Aubrey showed any great love of print. They still loved stories, and they loved being read to.

Being read to is also to read, as millions of us have discovered through audiobooks. (And Andy Stanton's Mr Gum deserves a medal for making even the most word-averse children laugh and read on.) Every night in our little valley in Yorkshire, where we moved from Verona, with the owls owling outside, we read something. Robin was a fan of Hubert Reeves' *The Universe Explained to My Grandchildren* — you don't have to explore the whole cosmos; just starting with the age of the light from the stars as it reaches us is enough to whirl you both into a constellation of dreams. Aubrey loved Randall Jarrell's *The Animal Family*, an exquisite masterpiece about a hunter, a mermaid, a bear cub, a lynx kitten, and a boy rescued from a lifeboat. On those nights we both forgot we were reading — we were far away, in the place of somewhere and the time of always, where the greatest stories live. It is a busy place, that somewhere. *As I Walked Out* is there, and *Cider with Rosie*. *My Family and Other Animals* and Durrell's whole Corfu trilogy. We read Kipling's *Just So Stories* with much characterisation, and Rebecca read Aubrey Terry Pratchett and Harry Potter. These years were joyous, especially when the figures in his books demanded performance. For some reason the dragon in Julia Donaldson's *Room on the Broom* was a Brummie — *Oi' think oi'll 'ave witch an' chips for moy tea …*

If he was tired, Aubrey would ask me to read Mum's current Greek myth (Rebecca was teaching herself to be a Classics A-Level teacher at the time) or switch to something 'not exciting'. This was the cue to put down *The Hobbit* or whatever for whatever I was reading, and, I noticed, writing. The knock-out drop of his childhood proved to be my own *Down to the Sea in Ships* — I don't think he has ever made it past the second page, and we have read it often — which was gratifying if not flattering. As he and his days grew longer, the knock-out was often all we had time for, though he excels at the well-timed question or thought, only partly designed to keep you talking and put off going to sleep. (Do you remember those years when you kept and treasured a record of the latest you and your friends had stayed up — or claimed to have done?)

So now I had my will again! Three pages only of *King Solomon's Mines* and two pages of A.A. Gill down a gold mine in South Africa for the *Sunday Times*. The next night, his peerless essay on a visit to Kaliningrad. One winter, my sort of stepfather's memoir *Breaking Free*, by Gerard Morgan-Grenville, a now departed part of his family I wanted Aubrey to know. Aubrey could not take much of that, bless him, though there are scenes when Gerard is working for General Sir Francis Festing, who is Assistant Chief of Staff at the Supreme Headquarters Allied Powers Europe, and confronting, as far as they know, imminent war with the Soviet Union, and they are both hiding in a French chicken coop in the dark in the rain because Gerard has lost a key ... worthy of Jerome K. Jerome. (We read *Three Men in a Boat*, too.)

I have not yet finished reading to him and his mates, at sleepovers. I have always read, after Dad's example — bits to friends, to my family, to my mother often, in her kitchen at home, something amusing or wonderful that catches my eye. Our family stories are in many books I do not expect Aubrey to read himself, but I do plan to read to him from his grandfather's anthology, *Captured in Time: five centuries of South African writing*. We could pick up Rider Haggard's trail there ...

As is the way of memory, I expect Aubrey will recall more of these times, these nights, these books, as he grows older, if not perhaps as I remember them now, in great range and detail: he was only very young and going to sleep for most of them, after all. When we talked about this essay, I ran a few by him, to yeses, no's, and ums, until I said, 'Philip Hoare's whale! *The Sea Inside!*'

'I remember *that!*' he cried, immediately.

No wonder. The writer is hanging in fathomlessly deep water off the Azores and a sperm whale approaches. The whale sonar-scans the man with his clicks, and the two creatures hang there, the great beast and the little being, as Philip describes the way a whale can make a cannonball of sound, a weapon to stun a squid, and the two look at each other in a kind of whale's peace. It is the most beautiful passage, and we read it night after night, hanging beside Philip and the whale in exactly the same place at last, in that wonder between life and sleep.

NICOLA DAVIES

... the books I most often give to both children and adults are picture books. They cut to the chase. They deal with big things in a way that delivers clear understanding at an emotional level.

Nicola Davies is the author of more than eighty books for children: fiction, nonfiction, and poetry. Her work has been published in more than ten different languages and has won major awards in the UK, US, France, Italy, and Germany. Her books include *The Promise* and *King of the Sky* (both illustrated by Laura Carlin), *Tiny: the invisible world of microbes* (Emily Sutton), and *A First Book of Nature* (Mark Hearld).

Nicola trained as a zoologist, taking a degree in Natural Sciences from King's College, Cambridge. She spent some years as a field biologist and studied humpback and sperm whales, and bats, before joining the BBC Natural History Unit as a researcher and then presenter. Underlying Nicola's work is the belief that a relationship with nature is essential to every human being. She regularly runs workshops for children and adults to help them find their voices as writers and advocates for nature.

Nicola lives in West Wales.

Picture reading

The first book that I can remember reading was a volume of the *Encyclopaedia Britannica*. My father, the son of a South Wales miner and the first of his family to get a degree, was enthusiastic about learning. He was an evangelical atheist with an unshakeable belief in the power of science and knowledge to transform the world. So when the door-to-door encyclopaedia salesman called, Daddy was a pushover. We got the lot in one go, including the *Children's Britannica*. These revered volumes stood on special shelves, next to the radiogram (which would break if my sister played pop music on it) in what my mother called 'the drawing room'. 'You can look up anything!' my father said, gleefully, 'Anything. *Everything!*'

The children's encyclopaedias held no interest for me at all. Why go for something small and relatively skinny when bigger, fatter books were on offer? The grown-ups' ones were what fascinated me. Their funny, thin paper made a distinctive 'shushing' sound when you turned the pages. They had columns of text like Grandpa's old Welsh Bible. They were *so* big and *so* fat. Just manoeuvring a single volume off the shelf was a major undertaking for a small human. None of Mummy's 'nest of occasional tables' could take the weight. They had to be laid out on the carpet, like a body, and read whilst kneeling before the open pages.

I'd like to tell you that I read every word of every volume, cover to cover, by the time I was six. That's what truly clever, special, precocious children do, those who go on to Achieve Great Things; they learn to read early and acquire degree-level knowledge before they've lost their milk teeth. But I didn't. Like many children, I struggled to learn to read. Decoding letters didn't interest me at all. The spindly patterns that the teacher scratched on the board in white chalk meant nothing to me. They weren't even pictures. School was just a trial: other kids could go off like a firework; teachers were terrifying; food was horrible; lavatories freezing and full of pipes that groaned like demons. I longed for home-time.

And yet in spite of all that, I read, passionately. I read the same pages of my favourite volume of my father's encyclopaedias, again and again and again. I soaked up what they told me, remembered it, and still wanted to come back for more. Those favourite re-read pages were at the back of the last volume on the lowest shelf. They were at the time, I think, the state of the art in publishing: acetate pages printed with high-definition illustrations of the human body. There were two sequences of illustrations — one male and one female. Each began with a picture of a naked human, whose bland, open eyes stared out at me. It was not the nakedness that was interesting. I was still little enough, and hot water precious enough, to be taking baths with every other family member on a regular basis. I'd seen it all before. It was the succeeding pages that I adored, as they peeled off skin, muscle, connective tissue, and organs, layer by layer by layer, down to the bone. The last picture in each sequence was a skeleton, whose skull looked out where a face had been, just a few pages back. I deconstructed each body, page by slow-turned page, then reconstructed them the same way. Time after time.

What was going on in my head as I scrutinised these images?

Over sixty years later, it's hard to recapture it precisely, but I do remember how it *felt*. Although 'felt', with its adult meaning, of an emotional or tactile experience, is not quite the right word. I mean 'felt' in the five-year-old sense, where experience is not compartmentalised. Instead, physical sensation, intellectual stimulation, and emotion are mixed and swirled together, so that learning is a whole body, whole soul, whole mind thing. So I still remember how I 'felt', turning those pages of bloodless organs arranged so neatly within their human outlines. My whole self was absorbed in reading those images. I soaked up the information in those illustrations and transposed the anatomy onto my own small body. I experienced a sense of physical validation, as if the awareness embedded in my autonomic nervous system had been touched by a reaching finger of consciousness. And in this layer on layer of learning about my body and the bodies of other humans, I grew an understanding of my own finiteness; one day, I too would be a lifeless skeleton staring out with empty sockets.

Every time I revisited those images, lingering on different occasions on different pages, some part of those 'feelings' was reverberating inside me, teaching me things. Everything from factual information about what a heart really looked like, to the universal ultimatum of human mortality. These were the first gifts that reading gave me, through pictures: a sense of personal geography inside my own space, and geography inside the timeline of my own life.

My memories of those first gifts of reading have informed my writing for children throughout my career. They remind me that young children may not have much command of language, but their inner lives are complex and epic, with big ideas and emotions shifting like waltzing tectonic plates. I am motivated by wanting to write to that complexity, to honour and acknowledge it. That's why I love the challenge of writing picture books, writing important big stuff but doing it with little words, carefully placed, accessible to small vocabularies. This doesn't mean the meanings these texts embody are superficial; the right small words can suggest a deep, rich hinterland that opens under the gaze of a child and is expanded, deepened, and set alight by the pairing of words with illustration.

Writing picture books is incredibly difficult. It requires all the skills of language wrangling that I've acquired throughout my life, plus the ability to squirm my way back into my five- or six-year-old skin and to think, to be, without boundaries between head and heart, body and soul. I don't get it right often — sometimes for a page or two, rarely for a whole book. But I know when I do, because those pages, those books, are the ones that speak most clearly not just to their young target audience, but to all ages. The responses I get mean more than prizes or royalties because they make me feel I'm putting the first gifts I received to good use.

There are lots of examples — not least my agent telling me that she now understood how climate change worked thanks to a page in my book *Green* (illustrated by Emily Sutton). I carry these in my heart, like treasure.

I think most of the biggest jewels in my treasure chest have come from one story, *The Promise*, illustrated by Laura Carlin. The story is about a child who steals a bag of acorns and whose life is transformed as she, in turn, transforms her city by planting them. It's about a lot of things: tree planting, obviously, climate change, too. But at its heart is a child in a very bad situation, who changes her life through a deep connection with nature. Somehow, when I was writing it, I was right in that five-year-old zone. Laura's art does so much more than merely 'illustrate'. It carries layers of meaning that speak to the unspoken complexity of our inner lives. The resulting marriage of words and pictures proved very happy indeed. It is a story from which readers have taken multiple meanings, about transforming their own lives and their communities, about the environmental crisis and the importance of individual responsibility.

Most of all, though, it is uncanny how this book speaks to children and adults who are in very bad situations. Shortly after it was published, I had an email from an aid worker in Afghanistan who was helping set up community gardens to help with local food production and to heal the shattered mental health of war-ravaged people. She told me how much the story meant to the people she worked with, how they were moved by its message of transformation through planting.

'Your book is being passed from hand to hand across the country,' she wrote. That's my Koh-i-Noor diamond, but it isn't really mine, it's Laura's; or rather, it belongs to the power of picture books, their amazing ability to go right to the heart, to carry a message across boundaries of age and culture.

A few years ago, I was helping a friend try to sort out the many tangled strands of a documentary he was making about the women fishers on the coast of Senegal. There was the sisterhood of the women themselves, their oppression by the colonial powers of French capitalism, the way a brand of toxic masculinity was limiting their ability to thrive, the ecology of the coastal habitat, the role that the women's catch played in local nutrition and health, and so on and so on. We spent two whole days talking, with no real narrative result. I had to go out and I left my friend with a pile of picture books and advised him to read them. He looked at me as if I were mad. But when I came back at the end of the afternoon, he was full of admiration for their clear but sophisticated storytelling. And he had a plan for his film.

This is the reason the books I most often give to both children and adults are picture books. They cut to the chase. They deal with big things in a way that delivers clear understanding at an emotional level. So I almost always have a copy of Shaun Tan's *The Red Tree* on hand to give to a child struggling in adolescent gloom, or an adult swamped in midlife crisis. For those wondering where they, or their child, fit on our society's hideously rigid scale of male/female, there is the liberation of Jessica Love's glorious *Julián is a Mermaid*. And for anyone in an abusive relationship, from a year two bully to a controlling spouse, there's Maria Gulemetova's *Beyond the Fence*.

The ability of picture books to boil things down to a silver bullet of understanding is especially important when it comes to communicating about the environmental crisis: we do all need the factual information to have the tools to make changes, but the motivation for change is emotional. Picture books deliver the core emotional hit that can be a catalyst to changed thinking. So, if I want someone — child or adult — to understand why the fragmentation of tracts of tropical forest matters, I'll give them a copy of Barroux's *Where's the Elephant?* in which an elephant, a parrot, and a snake are driven into a smaller and smaller piece of forest as buildings replace trees.

Where's the Elephant? is a straightforward representation of the consequences of habitat destruction, but picture books don't have to address an issue head on. Their simplicity can be subtle, circumventing preconceptions and prejudices. In *Flooded* by Mariajo Illustrajo (the pen name of Mariajose Gajate Molina), animals inhabit a city where water levels are mysteriously rising. Everyone carries on as normal — although the small animals are already in over their heads. But when the biggest animals, too, are up to their necks, everyone finally listens to the Emperor Tamarin, who has been trying to warn citizens all along. Just in time, they pull together to dislodge the plug and drain the water from their city. The analogies with problems of the climate crisis are clear, but presented in this visually beguiling and humorous way they seem less dark, more surmountable. For children, *Flooded* gently defuses the ticking bomb of environmental anxiety and replaces it with the possibility of community action. For climate-change deniers, the story neatly depoliticises the issue and makes the necessity for change a no-brainer. This is a picture book I would like to give every MP and CEO in the country!

The first literacy we acquire as children is visual. It's not something of a lower order, or something to abandon when we learn that second kind of word-based literacy. I feel very fortunate that my vivid memories of reading the images in my father's encyclopaedia remind me of that. They remind me, too, that children can read and respond to sophisticated imagery that adults think is beyond their grasp. I was given another reminder of this by an eight-year-old, part of a group I was working with at the Tate Modern a few years ago. She and her class were looking at Lee Krasner's work *Gothic Landscape*, giving their opinions of what the picture showed. They had lots of great ideas. One little girl, whose name I didn't record but whose thoughts I did, said, 'It's about how a bird feels when it lands in a tree. What it sees when it goes fast and then slow again.'

So this child could grasp that a two-dimensional, abstract image could depict time, speed, and visual and emotional experience. It demonstrates insightful, sophisticated thinking in response to what most people would consider an image that was inaccessible to a child. I think it also indicates that our desire to 'dumb down' illustration for children is often a mistake, especially when it comes to representations of the natural world.

One of the problems we face in trying to initiate action to

restore nature and natural ecosystems, is basic ignorance. When I was little, in the sixties, I would guess that most people in the UK would have had some direct experience of nature, in gardens, parks, countryside. Many people could probably have named 'bluetit', 'robin', 'dandelion', 'daisy' at the very least, maybe even 'thrush', 'buttercup', 'bumble bee'. That was the kind of knowing and naming knowledge that was passed from adult to infant. Now, many people have no access to nature at all, and we have at least two generations who couldn't identify a dandelion even if their children's lives depended on it.

The trend for extreme stylisation of illustration in books for young children isn't helping. Neither is the publisher's need to maximise financial returns by making books that are not location specific, that can be republished in many languages across the globe, using the cartoon-style illustrations that show 'flower', 'bee', 'butterfly'. How any young child is supposed to recognise in pictures like these the *real* species that she might actually *see* poking from a crack in the pavement or buzzing over the grass in the park, I don't know. This is a problem created, at least in part, by the preconceptions of editors and fashion in book design. Illustration that is precise, scientifically accurate, is deemed 'old-fashioned'. But kids don't know about fashion, and the incredible popularity of Jackie Morris' illustrations in her book with Rob Macfarlane, *The Lost Words* (and its successor *The Lost Spells*), shows that there is an appetite for images that show wild species as they are. *The Lost Words* is another book that I have passed on to new parents and grandparents to share with children from the start, encouraging them to discover, and rediscover, the wildlife around them.

Children really enjoy visual detail, especially before they can read words. So one of the things I would encourage parents to do is to 'read' field guides together, pore over pages illustrating ten different species and talk about what distinguishes one from the other. This is the formula that made the Where's Wally books a publishing phenomenon. If children can spot the right 'Wally', then they can tell the difference between two kinds of bumble bee, or a kestrel and a sparrow hawk. They'll probably be better than the adults, so the adults can learn from their children's excellent visual literacy skills — and nothing is better for a child's empowerment than being able to explain something to its grown-ups.

Gazing at pages crowded with living things is good therapy for stressed-out grown-ups, too. Had a really bad day at work? Eyes sore from screens and words? Sit down with a cup of tea and a copy of the Reverend Keble Martin's *The Concise British Flora in Colour* and spool through the pages. I can pretty much guarantee your cortisol levels will drop, and you may even learn the difference between different kinds of speedwell.

I remember as a kid the I SPY series of books. There was one for every category of common wildlife and object. I admit that when I came to write this essay, I thought they were out of print. But no. A google search reveals they are alive and very well. There's *I Spy Birds, I Spy Creepy Crawlies, I Spy Nature, I Spy Butterflies and Moths*. The principle is just the same as it was when I was little — you spot and you score, five points for a Red Admiral and forty points for a Purple Emperor, fifteen points for a Greater Spotted Woodpecker and fifty for a Dotterel. These books are still a great idea, perfect for that phase when kids like collecting things. But only if their parents know that 'hills, mountains, and moorland' isn't quite enough guidance for you to be able to find a ptarmigan.

The books I'd really love to give children and their parents are books that feed and develop a visual literacy of nature. These books would build the habits of close observation and accurate naming that are the pegs on which more complex, nuanced understandings of the natural world hang. They would be guides, encouraging families to explore, discover, and learn together. Each volume would be limited in scope: like the I SPY guides they would approach the acquisition of new knowledge in bite-sized chunks. They would have beautiful, detailed illustrations that would excite wonder and curiosity, they would guide readers about how to look and where to find different species, and they would offer a few basic bits of information. They would also be graded, maybe even colour-coded, so readers could chart their progress from bronze level to gold, from identifying things that you could see on an urban stroll to things you'd need a tent and crampons to find. They would be books that sparked not just observation but, eventually, adventure and immersion in the wild. They would be books whose pages would be turned and turned, images read and re-read — as I turned and re-turned those acetate pages six decades ago.

I don't think these books exist.

At least … not yet! Maybe my real gift of reading is to help create them.

IMTIAZ DHARKER

*When we stop and listen to each other's voices, we make
a still space in the world, and that is a space for poetry.
It is needed now more than ever. Poetry travels without
a passport. It is able to eavesdrop on the world. It says
things the heart knows before the world catches up.*

Imtiaz Dharker is a poet, artist, and video filmmaker, awarded
the Queen's Gold Medal for Poetry in 2014. Her seven
collections, all published by Bloodaxe Books, include *Over the
Moon* and the latest, *Shadow Reader*. Her poems have featured
widely on BBC radio, television, the London Underground, and
Mumbai buses. She has had eleven solo exhibitions of drawings,
and also scripts and directs video films, many of them for
non-government organisations working in the area of shelter,
education, and health for women and children in India.

Three poems from
Shadow Reader

The welcome

You were running on broken glass,
a child chased by nightmares
down shuttered streets, until at last
you came to this door. Here

are rooms made of hope, shelves full
of voices that call you in. They say
you can stop running now, pull
out a chair and sit. For you, they lay

a table with a feast that tastes of places
in your dreams, honey from the hive,
warm bread, words like spices.
This is where people come alive

to speak their stories in ink and blood
on wild nights, dappled afternoons,
telling of fallen tyrants, drought and flood
under desert stars and arctic moons.
They spin legends and conjure myths
in mother tongues and other tongues

that give your accent to their dance with death,
their love of life, the songs they sing.

You have been welcomed in
to books that smell like ancient trees,
standing here with broken spines,
opening like thoughts set free

and as the pages turn, your breath
quickens with something you always knew
in your blood like remembered faith.
When you open the book, it opens you.

The key

The room is holding itself close
like the hush when you know
it will snow or the sky goes yellow
before a monsoon rain starts falling.

You sit in a corner on the floor
where bookshelves meet
and find that the span of your arms
can hold a continent or more.

Even if you have no country
that would claim you,
no handful of mud to call your own
or home you want to go to,

this could be yours.
Language starts to crack
the way an egg hatches
and a beak appears.

You feel the heat
of the earth waiting for rain,
trees in the forest, bending
to the wind, see the life

of the woman on the train. You hear
what the books are saying.
You are the key.
You turn. The world opens.

Reader

You come to the books
to take you away, but they
open to welcome you home
and you stay.

URSULA DUBOSARSKY

As I read and re-read the stories, I knew more than anything that I wanted to enter this world, this realm of ideas, of beauty, of the imagination of the impossible. This is what reading is for. This is what books are for. This is where I wanted to be, always, all the time.

Ursula Dubosarsky was born and lives in Sydney, and wanted to be a writer from the age of six. She is now the author of over sixty books for children and young adults, and has won many national and international prizes for children's literature. She has been nominated for the Hans Andersen and Astrid Lindgren awards and was appointed the Australian Children's Laureate in 2020. In her spare time, she can be found playing the ukulele and reading cake recipes. Her latest book is *Ethel the Penguin*, illustrated by Christopher Nielsen.

(i) Some children never stop reading

Years ago, I was asked to write something about why I love reading, why I think books are important, and in particular was there a special book in my childhood that had hooked me, or even changed me in some profound way.

I found it terribly difficult to write about. Everything I could think of seemed like a truism, hardly worth putting down on paper. To me it was like saying food is a good thing. As for choosing that one special life-changing book — there were so many books I read and loved as a child, and they formed and still form a huge dense forest in my head. How could I pick one out? I could have chosen one of the several that I still know by heart, that I read over and over again as a small child, each time with a supernatural freshness. My favourites were *Biquette the White Goat* by Françoise, Wanda Gag's *Gone Is Gone*, and Dr Seuss' *I Had Trouble in Getting to Solla Sollew*. I loved them then and I love them still, but why I love them, I can hardly explain. I love them the way you love a person, because you just can't help it.

As I grew older and the books grew longer, and I could no longer memorise them, it was the same kind of love. Lying on my bed at eleven, I read the opening sentence of Rumer Godden's

An Episode of Sparrows, a story of children in post-Blitz London engaged in what might now be called guerilla gardening:

> The Garden Committee had met to discuss the earth; not the whole earth, the terrestrial globe, but the bit of it that had been stolen from the Gardens in the Square.

I understood nothing. I didn't know what a Committee was, what a terrestrial globe was, or what the Gardens in the Square could possibly mean. But such a vortex of tantalising mysterious language, doors and windows, swinging open and closing and swinging open again — it was impossible not to keep reading. And re-reading, as I did with all the books I loved, and still do, recreating them over and over again in my private imagination.

Despite being such a fervent reader, I was actually a little later than average learning to read. I didn't manage to grasp the knack until about halfway through my second year of school. Now the great thing about being the last in the class to be able to do something is that the moment when you finally can do it blazes into your life as a kind of miracle. There was a poster on the wall of our classroom, with a giraffe reaching up to the sky with its long spotted neck, and the word 'giraffe' in round black letters underneath it. One day, gazing idly over at it as I often did, I realised abruptly that rather than guessing the word (not a hard guess!) I could actually *read* it. Giraffe! The letters clicked together like a jigsaw. After all those months of dogged teaching and repetition resulting in apparently no progress at all, I could read! It was like a silent explosion in my head — the great wall fell, as Emily Dickinson might say. Even now, for me the word giraffe exudes a mystique, the key to all the mysteries … Having mastered giraffe, almost at once I became a fanatical reader, reading everything I could find, all the time, in every place, greedily and rapidly, to the point that the girl who sat next to me at school bit my finger to make me stop turning the pages so quickly. She bit me quite hard. I remember the little row of teeth marks.

Nonetheless, there I found myself years later, struggling to write something about the wonders of books and reading. By chance I happened to be browsing a second-hand stall at the local school fete and I picked up an old creased red booklet. I recognised it at once. It was a reader produced by the Infants' Reading Committee of the New South Wales Department of Education, used in classrooms in the 1960s to teach young children to read. The title of the little book was *Gay Days*. Written and illustrated by Katherine Morris and Eveline Laird, it's a simple booklet, made up of stories and poems with lists at the back — 'Words We Know'.

I opened *Gay Days* and felt a wave of wonder. Every word, every illustration, every story, every character was intensely familiar and potent. Trance-like, I turned the pages of this, my humble version of 'Chapman's Homer'. There they all were, my old friends, celestially clean and unnaturally joyous — Mother, Father, Jill, Ken, and Pamela the baby. Mother smiles while cutting the divine bread or arranging the flowers. Father packs the picnic basket in the boot of the smooth, bright car. Baby sleeps while Jill and Ken throw a huge buoyant blue ball into the air, jumping, leaping in the waves. Everything dances in a dream — cake, rocking horse, garden, beach, house, long pyjamas — and giraffes! A day at the Zoo! Of course there are giraffes ...

Now, we little, learning, solemn, reading, biting children, we knew perfectly well that nobody lives like this. The smallest child can recognise hyperreality, especially of this most intoxicating kind. This was not anybody's real life. Utopia glittered through the turning pages, piercing the heart painfully with longing and addictive awe. As I read and re-read the stories, I knew more than anything that I wanted to enter this world, this realm of ideas, of beauty, of the imagination of the impossible. This is what reading is for. This is what books are for. This is where I wanted to be, always, all the time.

And so then, with *Gay Days* open on the desk in front of me, instead of writing an article, I wrote a poem:

Some children never stop reading.
I remember when I learned to read. I was six.
Slowly, strangely, the letters gathered meaning —
That procession of long-spotted necks,
'Giraffes' reaching upwards across the page
Of my very first reader. A Day at the Zoo
With Jill and Ken. 'Here is the cage
Of laughing monkeys — look!' says Father. Blue
Is Mother's dress, blue the sea, the sky.
Home in the yellow car, sunlight fading …
Shhh, Baby is asleep, Goodbye! Goodbye!
The elephant's trunk is waving.
Words and pictures, the dream revealing
That's why some children never stop reading.

(ii) Children and writing: in the service of the dream

I wanted to be a writer when I was six, when I found out what writing and reading was. I would have wanted to be a writer before that, though, if I'd known. Before I could write on paper I wrote in my head, making up stories, like most children, with toys or sticks or lolly wrappers. When I saw my own children in the bath with their toys, or in a corner with shreds of paper, deeply concentrating, talking to themselves in some secret elaborate narrative, I recognised that's exactly what I do when I'm writing.

The first story I remember writing down at school, as opposed to simply imagining in my mind, was in first class, about a family of penguins drifting through the water on an iceberg, waving at other families who drifted by on theirs. Now the penguins were represented not by little bits of plastic or paper, but words. I recall so strongly that feeling of pleasure in writing it, like enjoying a bowl of ice cream and chocolate sauce. I wanted to swirl it around in the bowl and make it last forever. There was no sense of deliberate effort at all, as later, alas, particularly in school, writing often seems to become. It was as natural as playing a game.

I was reminded of this recently while reading a 1971

collection of essays, *Playing and Reality,* by the British child
psychoanalyst D.W. Winnicott, which includes a discussion
on what is known as the transitional love object — the teddy
bear, for example — in the psychological development of
children. It struck me reading Winnicott that everything he
says about children playing with a peculiar precision describes
my experience of the writing process — how 'the playing child
inhabits an area that cannot be easily left, nor can it easily admit
intrusions', a state I think all writers are familiar with, and that it
is a precarious and exciting activity in which:

> the child manipulates external phenomena in the service
> of the dream, and invests chosen external phenomena
> with dream meaning and feeling.

Writing down a story, and then indeed publishing it, is I
suppose simply an attempt to make that precarious and exciting
state of play slightly more permanent, like freezing a dream, and
hoping it won't melt too soon. And, of course, one can't help
but think of the Brontë children in that dreary claustrophobic
parsonage, playing with their twelve wooden soldiers, the twelve
Young Men, an extraordinary and fascinating extended elaborate
narrative game that lasted over four or five years, written down
but just for them.

In the first three or four years of my infant and primary
schooling in the 1960s, writing revolved around what was called
composition, once a week. The teacher would provide a topic for
a story, and we would write about it in a lined book. It was a
simple and unstrained regular activity that I enjoyed and didn't
think about much.

When I was nine, I changed schools and my new teacher,
Miss Pattison, had a different approach. By this stage, the early

1970s, I think it was probably known as creative writing rather than composition. Miss Pattison, too, set aside a particular time each week but it was for something she called, rather alarmingly, the first time we heard the word, 'brainstorming'. Looking back, I now see that brainstorming consisted of attempts to reach into the unconscious mind to see what sort of ideas might be hiding there, by playing us odd sounds on a tape, or snatches of music, or holding up parts of a painting or photograph, or reading out slices of sentences, which we would then write about. Again, it was really like playing a game, not work, and we loved it.

Like a game, but Miss Pattison took writing seriously, certainly as seriously as maths. Further than that, she was serious about what you might call originality. Not everyone is, as we know. Quite often people are made anxious by originality in writing, and it can sometimes seem in children's writing that acquiescence and normalisation are valued more than originality. But Miss Pattison loved the playful and the ridiculous. I remember once when she asked us to write a story with the title 'Caught with an exclamation mark'. How delighted she was with one boy, who wrote a story about a man running down an alley, pursued by the police, who finally caught him clasping a giant exclamation mark to his chest. Caught, red-handed, with an exclamation mark!

The incident I'm going to tell you about today seems to me to illuminate something about children and writing. It's about a visit made to our class by the school inspector. The inspector called. In those days, the school inspector was a familiar member of the cast of characters in the great enterprise of the New South Wales state primary school system. The inspector would appear at the back of the classroom like a dark angel, watch in silence, take notes, and just as ominously depart.

On this occasion, we were warned some days beforehand

that this particular school inspector, Mr Berthouse, would be coming to inspect the class. Miss Pattison gave us a good talking to — highest standards of behaviour, etc. etc., were expected. We understood that the inspection was of Miss Pattison, not of us, but that the burden was on us to show that she was a good teacher. We were very attached to Miss Pattison. She was not at all a woman who sought to be loved or even liked, but she was energetic, highly conscientious, and, in many ways, passionate and admirable, and we wanted to please her.

The day arrived, and in walked the unappealing Mr Berthouse. He had an unfortunate resemblance to our feared deputy headmaster, Mr Norton, to whom our more soft-hearted principal delegated all the daily canings of naughty children. At least Mr Berthouse wasn't carrying a cane, although he did produce a long fold-out wooden ruler from his pocket that he waved about in the air like a fencing rapier. He roamed up and down the aisles between our desks — there were forty-one children in the class — snapping questions here and there, throwing a bit of maths on the board, then a bit of spelling or general knowledge.

Finally, he announced that he had heard we were good writers. Mr Berthouse looked unconvinced. He wanted to see for himself, he said, so we were now to write a composition.

Mr Berthouse was clearly an extemporaneous sort of fellow who didn't muck about with a lot of preparation. I suppose, in fairness, he spent his life slipping in and out of classrooms generally spreading terror and getting children to do a bit of writing. He gazed about the room looking for something we could write about — classrooms in those days were not what you could call graciously decorated. There was a half-dead pot plant on the windowsill that I wouldn't have minded writing about, but he didn't like the look of it. At last, he settled on a kind of hessian wall hanging, not very big, not very attractive, a geometric representation of an egg in an egg cup in semi-psychedelic seventies colours, hanging lopsidedly next to the blackboard.

'Write a story about that!' commanded Mr Berthouse, pointing at the egg cup with his very, very long ruler. 'Get on with it.'

I admit these might not have been his exact words, but they are the words that matched his personality.

So we all bent our heads down and tried to write. I have not the slightest memory of what I wrote, but I do remember the feeling of blankness, tension, and failure. What on earth could I say about this egg cup? I could think of nothing. How different to our brainstorming sessions, when ideas tumbled out of us like hundreds and thousands on top of a cake. We wrote with nib pens in those days, which we dipped in inkwells. Our teacher was proud of this, although she couldn't have been very proud of me, leaving as I did great Rorschach blots all over the page. But we wrote, or tried to, and at the end of an allotted time, Mr Berthouse took our books away to inspect them.

Well, word soon got around. Catastrophe! Mr Berthouse thought our writing was hopeless! Lamentable! He couldn't believe how bad it was. Miss Pattison was in tears in the library, being comforted by our glamorous librarian! Miss Pattison was getting the sack! These were the rumours that spread, and there was a lot of head-shaking from other disappointed teachers. How could we let Miss Pattison down like that? How could we have been so bad?

Miss Pattison, having presumably dried her eyes, if indeed they were ever wet, came fiercely into the classroom the next day, on fire. She had a dramatic manner that was quite compelling, even when reading out a spelling list, so when she was angry and alight, you felt you were in the presence of something significant.

Miss Pattison was ashamed of us. When she thought of what some of us could write, and the rubbish we provided for Mr Berthouse! She couldn't believe it, what was wrong with us? She was deeply disappointed. But she was there to tell us, we were very, very lucky. Mr Berthouse was a busy man, but he had agreed, after much pressing from the headmaster himself, to give us another chance. Mr Berthouse, in fact, was waiting outside the door. He was coming right in. You know what I expect, said Miss Pattison, icily. ONLY the best possible writing, with NO exceptions. She swept out of the room.

We sat in gloom. No, gloom is too mild a word. Guilt, and dreadful anticipation, perhaps not the best psychological conditions for producing good writing.

In marched Mr Berthouse.

He gazed at us, miserable lot that we were. This time, he'd done a little preparation. He turned to the blackboard and wrote up in beautiful chalky writing (and it's not easy to write beautifully on a blackboard) the following words in one long prose sentence:

I wandered lonely as a cloud, that floats on high o'er vales and hills, when all at once I saw a —

With a lovely long dash after the word 'a'. The chalk screeched.

'Continue the story from this point!' commanded Mr Berthouse. 'You have twenty minutes.'

He then settled down in Miss Pattison's chair, in our teacher's chair, and waited, folding and unfolding his long wooden ruler.

Now my great misfortune here was that I knew the poem. We hadn't read it at school, but I had a book at home that I'd bought at a fete, an old school anthology from the 1940s, printed on nasty yellow-smelling paper that tore as you turned each page. I was very fond of it, and liked learning the poems, which I would then recite to an audience of soft toys in my room with the door closed. I'd line the toys up on my bed — I had a blue dog and a koala, a couple of dolls and a sad orange clown. My favourite poem for performance was by the Scottish poet Robbie Burns:

> My heart's in the Highlands, my heart is not here,
> My heart's in the Highlands a-chasing the deer;
> A-chasing the wild deer, and following the roe,
> My heart's in the Highlands, wherever I go.
>
> Farewell to the Highlands, farewell to the North,
> The birthplace of Valour, the country of Worth;
> Wherever I wander, wherever I rove,
> The hills of the Highlands for ever I love.

I used to get pretty worked up over this poem — the depth of nostalgia I felt for those never-seen highlands was amazing. But I was also reasonably fond of Wordsworth's daffodil poem and knew it off by heart as well. And knowing it, alas, made it impossible to get what were the perfect words out of my head. Yet I knew I had to think of something of my own, something original, as Miss Pattison would put it, had to crawl miserably out from under the awesome weight of the genius of Wordsworth or my poor teacher would get the sack. This turned out, in fact, to be the most clearly demonstrated and self-conscious encounter I've ever had of what is the inescapable experience of all children, all writers, all artists, of the paradox that is at the heart of creativity, described again by Winnicott in terms of a game:

> In any cultural field, it is not possible to be original
> except on a basis of tradition … the interplay between
> originality and the acceptance of tradition as the basis for
> inventiveness seems to me to be just one more example,
> and a very exciting one, of the interplay between
> separateness and union.

I wasn't myself exactly excited that day as I struggled between my separateness and union with Wordsworth, but I did somehow manage to write a poem of my own. I don't remember any of it, and it was most certainly a poor effort, but whatever the case, we all performed much more to Mr Berthouse's apparent satisfaction, and there was no more talk of sacking or tears in the library.

I wonder why these events with the school inspector have stayed so clearly in my mind? I suppose it must be something to do with the stark contrast between writing as a performance to please authority and writing as a kind of game, both private and shared, both secret and public. I've now published over sixty books for children of all ages, and my newest one is called *Ethel the Penguin* — a story about a family of penguins that I seem to have been writing since I was six years old. Sometimes I wonder if everything I've written is an iteration of that very first penguin story, which appeared, miraculously to me, out of the end of my pencil in a windy classroom nearly sixty years ago …

It's a strange experience, looking at a book you've written — by the time it has turned into a physical object like that, it almost feels as if someone else has written it, or even more that it somehow wrote itself. Actually, it makes me quite uneasy — what have I said in this book? The writer is often the last to know.

What do I know? Like many children's writers, I go into schools fairly frequently on request to take writing workshops with children, so I'm often confronted by worried faces, children wanting to do 'good' writing, desperate to please 'the writer' who must somehow know. That tends to make me anxious in turn — I don't want to be their version of the fearful Inspector Berthouse. Of course, I don't have a long wooden ruler or wear an undertaker's suit, but there are so many ways of exerting authority that can demoralise the young, and I suppose we're not always conscious of them. So I try to keep on the top of my mind Winnicott's beautiful phrase, 'in the service of the dream'. That's what we're there for, playing a game together — with pictures, with music, with toys, and always with words, wonderful words — much as Miss Pattison did with us all those years ago in those brainstorming sessions, in the service of the dream.

MAISIE FIESCHI

Atrum post bellum, ex libris lux.

Maisie Fieschi, daughter of Ursula Dubosarsky, studied Australian Literature at the University of Sydney before starting her career as a fiction editor at Random House Australia. In 2012, she moved to Paris and worked as a freelance editor. She now writes English-language books for French children and is working on a novel. In 2022, she attended the Breadloaf Writers' Conference. That same year, she began working at the American Library in Paris, near the Eiffel Tower. Maisie warmly invites everyone reading this to stop by and visit if you're ever in Paris!

Sanctuary

My first great fortune was to be born to a mother who not only wrote children's books but loved them. Growing up, our shelves always overflowed, creating a personal library that became the landscape of my childhood. From an early age, I discovered the unique pleasure of being tucked up in bed, alone with a book. A book that I chose. No one insisting I must read it. No one telling me how to read it. A book I chose myself, because something made me pull it from the shelf.

Perhaps my favourite in my mother's collection of children's literature was her set of C.S. Lewis' The Chronicles of Narnia — 1960s paperbacks from her childhood. They had bright covers, drawings inside, and, on the back, the price was listed in Canadian dollars. These were exotic treasures for a nine-year-old living on the far-off island of Australia.

Of all the books in the series, *The Horse and His Boy* became my obsession. It tells the tale of Bree, a talking horse, and Shasta, a young boy, who flee slavery in search of Narnia. Along the way they join forces with another horse and a young princess, and endure a journey fraught with peril.

I devoured *The Horse and His Boy*, listened to the audio cassette on a loop, and found myself returning again and again to a particular scene: the horses and children have undergone countless trials, and the princess has been clawed by a lion and needs medical care. The group stumble upon a hermitage. A peaceful, protected oasis, with a 'pool of perfectly still water', 'the hugest and most beautiful tree', and a 'high wall of green turf'. A gentle hermit welcomes the weary warriors.

Yes, I thought as I read, *the heroes deserve this. They've done enough. They will stay in the hermitage, forever protected, and they will rest and play and be safe*. But no, the hermit tells Shasta. Shasta cannot stay. Shasta must leave 'without a moment's rest' to warn King Lune of an impending attack. 'Run, run: always run,' says the hermit.

And then C.S. Lewis writes this passage, which seeped into every part of my body, and is now a part of me:

> Shasta's heart fainted at these words for he felt he had
> no strength left. And he writhed inside at what seemed
> the cruelty and unfairness of the demand. He had not
> yet learned that if you do one good deed your reward is
> usually to be set to do another and harder and better one.

It seemed so unfair! So unfair!

How could Shasta be asked to do more? And yet, Shasta did as he was instructed. He ran, he warned King Lune, and he saved Archenland. The hermit had been right.

I held on to that scene, those words I had discovered and claimed as mine at the age of nine. They became my private talisman, a secret source of strength, known only to me. I carried them with me, and I have needed them.

In 2012, when I was twenty-four, I moved to Paris on my own, driven by a desire to see the exotic worlds I'd read so much about. I scraped by as a freelance editor, and a year later I met the love of my life, Simon, a French social media manager. We got engaged.

Our Parisian life unfolded like every clichéd Audrey Hepburn film — until 7 January 2015. Simon was the second person shot during the attack on the *Charlie Hebdo* offices. The satirical cartoon magazine was targeted by Al-Qaeda militants who wanted to silence its writers and deny readers their freedom of choice.

Unlike twelve other people that day, Simon survived. But his survival came at a steep cost to him, and to us all. Shot at close range with an AK-47, the bullet tore through his body, shattering as it pierced his lung and permanently damaged his spinal cord. He spent a week in a coma, a month in the ICU, and then seven gruelling months in a military hospital, undergoing intensive rehabilitation. I was by his side every step of the way.

I gave up editing — it had little meaning to me anymore. Not much did, other than Simon's recuperation, and our families. Meanwhile, from the moment the news broke of the terrorist attack, many around the world responded with a chorus of blame. The victims deserved it! Drawing provocative images was an invitation to violence! From the hospital, from the gravesides, we were bombarded with polemics, from the left, right, and centre.

Was it not enough that Simon's colleagues were murdered, that Simon was permanently disabled at the age of thirty-two?

We now had to continuously defend ourselves to the world? It seemed so unfair!

I remembered *The Horse and His Boy*. I found the ebook and read aloud to Simon as he lay in his hospital bed. 'If you do one good deed your reward is usually to be set to do another and harder and better one.' The words reminded us we were not alone. And they galvanised me. What did I believe in?

I believe in literature, in the access to information, in the use of the law and debate to determine what society sees as the ever-changing 'limits' to freedom of speech.

I believe in books.

After nine months of unimaginable suffering, Simon and I married in September 2015 at our local town hall, officiated by a great hero of ours, the formidable Paris mayor, Anne Hidalgo. Surely this should have been the end of our ordeal? The movie should fade to black. But this was only the beginning.

By some miracle, Simon can walk, though with great difficulty and only for short stretches, relying on a crutch. The neurological pain, however, is relentless — severe, unpredictable, and a daily reminder of the damage inflicted. Some days, Simon feels as though his entire arm is on fire. I witness him suffer, and I have suffering of my own. A spinal injury does not heal. There is no cure. The psychological wounds of a terrorist attack also linger — they can be managed, but never erased.

Then there has been the labyrinthine struggle for insurance, a near-nine-year battle to secure compensation for Simon's injuries and inability to work. At the same time, our lives have been consumed by three major terrorism trials of the various criminals who aided and abetted the attack. Each trial stretched over three months, with Simon having to testify.

And in 2019, I also ended up in hospital. I had a 4.5-kilogram borderline tumour. All this while, it had been silently wreaking havoc, destroying one of my ovaries, necessitating major surgery. I was literally cut in half.

There is no end, and it seems there is no eternal sanctuary, earned through our suffering. What is asked of us can seem cruel, it can feel unjust. But that is what it means to fight for something you believe in, be it love or freedom of expression. It's never just 'one good deed'. The reward isn't a sanctuary — or at least, not for long. The reward is to be set to another, harder, and better task.

In 2022, I found my way to the American Library in Paris. It was a choice: I wanted and needed to be among books. Joining the Library, the world opened up to me again, just as it had in my childhood, wandering through my mother's book collection. Once a week, I would retreat to its shelves, indulging in solitary afternoons among the stacks, surrounded by books curated by generations of librarians I would never meet. In those moments, I was simply myself — free of political labels, free of the burdens of victimhood, free of *Charlie Hebdo*.

The American Library was my personal refuge, and it revitalised me. This was worth fighting for. I began volunteering at the Library, and before long I joined the team. I learned the Library was founded in 1920, building on a book collection created for American soldiers during World War I. The American Library's motto is 'atrum post bellum, ex libris lux': 'after the darkness of war, the light of books'.

My work at the Library became about more than just my own solace — I wanted to ensure that others could find their haven and their compass in books, as well. My role is to find new ways to engage readers, young and old, and to show them that the Library is a sanctuary of stories, a place where books are not just preserved but celebrated. It is the most fulfilling job I've ever had, and certainly the most meaningful.

Yet, it is far from easy. We are an independent library, accepting no government funding — a decision that protects us from censorship but leaves us financially vulnerable. We fight on, because to believe in something is to continue the work, moving from challenge to challenge, 'another and harder and better one'.

The work is hard — that is what it means to fight for something meaningful. No single book, no political movement, no institution holds all the answers. But the collective wisdom housed within literature can guide us through our darkest times.

PICO IYER

… the books that I'd wish for young friends can only be, deep down, the ones that truly changed my life.

Pico Iyer has spent the past fifty years essentially just reading and writing, resulting in seventeen published books, on topics ranging from globalism to the 14th Dalai Lama, and from the Cuban Revolution to Islamic mysticism. His books have been translated into twenty-three languages, and, for more than a quarter of a century, he has also been a constant contributor to *The New York Review of Books*, *Harper's*, *The New York Times*, and more than 250 periodicals worldwide, while writing introductions to more than ninety other works. His latest book is titled *Aflame* and records his first 100 retreats with a group of Benedictine monks high above the sea in California. His five talks for TED have received more than 10 million views so far.

The enchantments of youth

The first fan letter I ever wrote was to Michael Bond, the author of stories about the adventures of Paddington Bear. Paddington came into the world just one year after I did, appearing on Paddington Station in London, alone with his battered suitcase, much as I would do in the years to come, on my way to boarding school. He was friendly, polite, and well-meaning — eager to get on with his new neighbours in the middle-class England of the early 1960s. But he was also more or less guaranteed always to do the wrong thing, as a small foreigner given to clumsiness and the grubbiness that comes from keeping marmalade sandwiches under your hat. I realised, almost as soon as I met him, that I'd found my secret brother and, in truth, my twin.

Mr Bond was kind enough to write back to me, inundated though he must have been with correspondence, assuring me that more books were on the way and including a bear's pawprint at the bottom. Writers thus came to seem to me almost as lovable as bears. And when finally I arrived at university, my first (and most important) task was snagging an interview with Mr Bond when he passed through town.

In the years to come, as I began to scribble for a living, I found myself writing on Paddington for *The New York Times*, for the *Times Literary Supplement* in London, for anyone who'd ask (and many who didn't); the subject seemed inexhaustible. But I could never have guessed then that Paddington would prove to be such a universal hero, incapable of growing old or losing his bright-eyed optimism. Only a few months before the death of Queen Elizabeth II, there he was, taking tea with her, watching wide-eyed as she removed a marmalade sandwich from her trademark handbag — 'for later'. In Japan, when I look around, he's everywhere, the mascot of one of the largest banks, the focus of major exhibitions.

Even now I can't begin one of the tales of his adventures without descending into helpless laughter; nothing this side of P.G. Wodehouse can so reliably brighten my day and lighten my heart. And I've come to see that Paddington keeps many unexpected skills under his hat, speaking as easily in Chinese as in English, or in the 21st century as in the era of elevenses and cocoa. When asked to recommend books for the young, I can mention only the books that bring me instruction and joy even now that I'm in my sixties, and Paddington (who has found new life through several delightful films) is one friend who never disappoints. The political officer at the British Embassy in Amman took a large diplomatic contingent to watch *Paddington 2* in Jordan, perhaps because the little bear with his suitcase, though born in Peru, has become one of Britain's most beloved ambassadors.

*

My second literary fan letter was sent to Ursula Le Guin, after I had been transported to unseen and unguessed-at places by her Earthsea trilogy. Few writers of my lifetime combine wisdom and grace as Le Guin did, and none that I encountered was more fearless in imagining other worlds: my father used to teach her visions of alternative societies in his classes on Anarchist

Thought, while my mother shared her novels in the classes she offered on Religion and Literature. Yet none of her books speaks so well to every age — in the life of the world, or our own — as her trilogy, later expanded, on how to become a wizard.

When Harry Potter took his place within the collective unconscious, a part of me was grateful — he, too, had been standing on one of those British railway platforms, along with Paddington and me — but I couldn't help thinking that the true guidebook to magic would always be Le Guin's. Daughter of two celebrated anthropologists, steeped in Taoism and Indigenous cultures, sometimes forced to veil her first name because distinguished magazines didn't want to publish women, she knew everything about a hero's journey, the talismanic power that lies in words, the necessity of dragons, and the shadows inside even the brightest heart. Underneath the clarity of a story that I had no trouble following at eleven, she was really mapping a journey every adult knows as we do battle against our inner demons, trying to jump across abysses in our understanding, and working to become masters of a destiny that will always be at the mercy of forces far greater than we could ever be.

To this day, the Earthsea series is one I gladly foist on any friend who's interested in contemplation and imagination — and by a happy coincidence, it is the rare series that my Japanese wife cherished in adulthood much as I had done decades before I met her. If Paddington showed me how to navigate the whirlpools and frowns of the world, Le Guin began to tell me how to survive those places deep within me.

*

To be born and grow up in Oxford is of course never to be far from enchanted ground.

The world of Narnia had been created just five minutes
from our house, and so, too, had Middle-earth; Alice had
passed through her looking-glass just up the road. That musty
town of gargoyles, eccentric scholars, and quaint curiosities has
never been short of fantastical imaginings. A bookshop in the
centre of town sold only Puffin books — the Penguins meant
for children — and when I descended into the basement of
one of my honorary godmothers (a scholarly and upstanding
Englishwoman who became a Buddhist nun), I could follow
Tintin to Tibet and South America and the Arab world — even
to the moon — and dream of becoming a wandering journalist
with equally few concerns about expense reports or troublesome
editors.

There was a dodo at the quirky museum near the University
Parks, and the men who prevented undergraduates from
returning late were, for some reason, called 'bulldogs'. Oxford
was like a vast library in which the bookshops seemed to merge
with the green lawns of quadrangles so that one was moving
constantly through a world of reality spiced with magic. Lyra and
her daemon would come to live nearby, in Philip Pullman's more
subversive fantasies, and *The Wind in the Willows* seemed to gust
around the nearest country pub.

So I would send anyone who loves both language and magic
towards Alan Garner or T.H. White as well as Jane Yolen or Peter
Beagle; the British seem always to have favoured childhood much
as Americans have become great celebrants of adolescence. But
the books that I'd wish for young friends can only be, deep down,
the ones that truly changed my life.

Paddington's stories are very simple ones, set in an England
that now looks a bit antiquated, and perhaps most ideal for those
who wish to enter a more formal and innocent world in which no
good deed finally goes unrewarded. But they found me at a time

when I was ready to take instruction, and they made me believe the world could never be so bad as the newspapers suggest.

'How wonderful Darkest Peru must be to produce bears as cheerful and unfallen as this one!' I thought when very young. And — well on the way to becoming something of a determined bear myself — 'As soon as I get the chance, I'll go there to see if I can meet any bears on their home terrain!'

More or less the day I graduated from school, I took a job for three months to save up some money and then boarded a bus in the Mexican border town of Tijuana, bumping all the way down, along the Pan-American Highway, to Peru.

Upon arrival, no bears were in sight — but what came into view was an equally exciting prospect, of writing and travelling amidst the improbable wonders of the world without ever (I hope) losing too much of the resilience and courtesy in which the small bear had trained me. In time, I'd lose my heart to D.H. Lawrence and Keats and even Hermann Hesse, but by then Paddington had taught me to doff my hat before every stranger and the wizards of Earthsea had reminded me that the deepest — and most powerful — strangers are always the ones to be found within.

WAYNE KARLIN

… I may have been reading to illuminate the terrain around me and within me, to help me keep intact the person I wanted to be in a situation that wanted me to be someone else.

Wayne Karlin is the author of nine novels, a collection of short fiction, and three books of nonfiction. His stories, poems, and articles have been published in many literary journals and newspapers. He has received two Fellowships from the National Endowment for the Arts (1994 and 2004), the Paterson Prize in Fiction for 1999, the Vietnam Veterans of American Excellence in the Arts Award in 2005, and the 2019 Juniper Prize for Fiction. His most recent novel, *The Genizah*, was published by Publerati in September 2024.

Stories save lives

I have a photograph someone took of me when I was in the Việt Nam War.

It is daytime and I am lying in front of some stacked sandbags on the slope of a hill. You can see a machine gun barrel sticking over some of the sandbags, and leaning next to me is a rifle, its magazine — the rectangular container holding bullets — inserted. Above my head, from a pole supporting a piece of canvas, hangs a cartridge belt, sagging with other magazines, a canteen, and a large knife. The deadly accoutrements of war are all around me. But I have shed them: I'm shirtless and in my hands is a book and my eyes are focused on its pages.

The war is all around me, but I am elsewhere. *There is no Frigate like a Book/to take us Lands away,* wrote Emily Dickinson. I don't know what land I am in, but it is not Vietnam-the-war.

I don't remember what I was reading. It might have been something read purely for escape, a book that let me go into a magic wardrobe and get lost in C.S. Lewis' Narnia rather than being on that muddy, barbed-wire-rung hill, or on a quest with the Hobbits through Tolkien's Middle-earth, a world — so unlike the one around me — where everything evil was contained in one ring and all you had to do was get rid of it, *my precious,* and good would win and everyone would live and everything would end happily. Or it may have been some of the Jack London tales

I loved, allowing me to run off that hill into a snowy landscape in the mind of Buck, the dog in London's stories after whom I'd named my own first dog. Or maybe it was Steinbeck's Tom Joad moving out of the dust to search for a more just world, or Hemingway's Frederic Henry, ready to lay down his arms, to say farewell to a war which no longer made sense to him.

So yes, I may have been reading to escape into different lives and different worlds. Or I may have been reading to illuminate the terrain around me and within me, to help me keep intact the person I wanted to be in a situation that wanted me to be someone else, someone hard and brutal and diminished. To save the life of the man I wanted to be.

'Stories save lives,' the great storyteller Tim O'Brien wrote in his novel *The Things They Carry*.

At the moment that photo was taken, some fifty or so kilometres away, deep in the jungle near one of the pathways we called the Ho Chi Minh Trail, a sixteen-year-old girl named Lê Minh Khuê may also have been reading *The Call of the Wild* or *A Farewell to Arms* or *The Grapes of Wrath*.

She carried those American novels on her back, in her rucksack, and sometimes she would imagine the words in them pushing through the canvas and into her skin. She was a member of the Volunteer Youth Brigade of the People's Army of Việt Nam, my enemies. Her living conditions and her duties, and those of the other girls in her company, were dirty and dangerous. The hidden trails in the thick snake- and insect- and sometimes tiger-infested jungle where they lived were used to bring soldiers and weapons and ammunition south to the war. The Americans — those who were not in her books — shelled and bombed the trails when they could discover or estimate where they were. The girls' job was to keep open whatever section of the trail they were assigned, which they did, often while under attack by our aircraft, by filling in bomb craters or by exploding or defusing the bombs that didn't explode. They also helped guide the soldiers along their section of the trail, sometimes lining the way while wearing white shirts to form human curbs for the trucks driving with their headlights off, to avoid being spotted. Many of her friends and many of the soldiers died — and one of the other duties Lê Minh Khuê and the other girls performed was to build coffins and bury the dead. She did this work from the time she was fifteen for four long years.

And she read stories. The Vietnamese literature she loved helped her find courage and strength in herself, connected her to a long history of resistance, and a culture and a nation worth defending with her life. The American literature she loved also helped her find courage and strength, but it tore something in herself, as well. She loved the Americans in her books. She hated the Americans killing her friends and trying to kill her. If she saw one of their aircraft — say one of the helicopters in which I flew, looking for her — go down in flames, she would cheer inside. Yet in the books she read — the stories of the hated Enemy, the Other — she saw her own humanity reflected.

'Imagining what it is like to be someone other than yourself,' wrote the storyteller Ian McEwan, 'is at the core of our humanity. It is the essence of compassion, and it is the beginning of morality.'

But imagining what it is like to be another person is discouraged when one is in a war and has to sustain a hatred of the enemy, to kill the part of oneself that might imagine what it is like to be 'someone other than oneself'. Look again at those objects — other than the book — in that photograph of me in the war. The machine gun, the rifle, the instruments engineered to hurl projectiles made of soft cores of lead encased in harder metal into the body of another human being, where they will penetrate flesh and tumble on through whatever is in their path: brains, lungs, kidneys, hearts, and bones, puncturing, slashing, splintering, shredding those organs, which are the same as those contained within the delicate ecosystem of your own body; destroying not only their necessary physical functions but also memories, hopes, apprehensions, sudden joys and the lingering melancholy of sunsets, and all else that is encased lovingly or fearfully in the fragile brain, or the fragile heart and soul, the same fragile framework of flesh and bones, thoughts and emotions of the one firing that projectile.

To find some excuse of difference to help you feel that the Other is not you is the process of dehumanisation. To dehumanise others, you must kill your own humanity. You must kill something necessary and sacred in yourself.

To be torn about that, as Lê Minh Khuê sometimes felt while reading her American books, was to save her own humanity. To save herself. It kept alive something precious in her: a realisation that continued to clarify for her over the years after the war, as she began to write her own stories, stories that always revealed the quiet complexities and capacities and capabilities of the human heart under the white noise of politics or prejudice or preconception.

Sometimes the life that stories save can be your own.

*

I first met Lê Minh Khuê in 1993 at a program held by the Joiner Center at the University of Massachusetts, Boston, which brought together American and Vietnamese writers who had been combatants on opposite sides of the war. After the war, she had become a writer; today she is one of Việt Nam's best-known novelists and short story writers. We gave presentations and readings and ran writing workshops. But mainly, for a month, we former enemies lived together, and during that time there would come a point when we would ask each other, 'Where were you?' and 'When were you … ?' trying, as it were, to ascertain if we had ever been in a place at a time when we would have tried to kill each other. Lê Minh Khuê had avoided asking or answering that question — we had started our first conversation by showing each other pictures of our children, my son and her daughter — but by the second week I felt we were comfortable enough with each other so that at breakfast one morning, with just the two of us there, I asked her about her war.

When she named some of the areas where she had been, and the times she had been in them, I realised that I may have flown over those places when I was a helicopter gunner, that she could have been there, on the trails under the jungle canopy, and if I'd seen her then, I would have killed her. The realisation of that naked truth stabbed me and filled me with grief. There was nothing abstract or distanced by time or conditional about it; it was as if I actually *had* killed this human being who was sitting across the breakfast table from me, her face emerging from under the canopy of leaves that had hidden her from me in the war, when if I had spotted her all I would have seen was enemy, and if she had seen me, I would have been something inhuman, shelled in helmet and flak jacket in the centre of a terrible noise and wind pressing down around her. For a few seconds we just stared at each other, then she reached over, touched my arm and nodded gently, acknowledging what had passed between us, reassuring us both that it was over. At that moment, we became each other's stories.

As I got to know Lê Minh Khuê more, and she recounted her time in the war and told me how she had carried and read books by American authors, it struck me that I had never read stories from the people who had once been my enemies — none of them had ever been available to me. I remembered the photograph I had kept, when I lay near my machine gun on a muddy hill and found solace in the pages of a book that allowed me to leave that place and live inside the lives of other human beings. How would it have changed me if I had read the stories of those beyond the barbed wire perimeter at the slope of that hill or below the jungle canopy over which I sometimes flew? The stories of the people against whom I was defending myself and my fellow Marines, the Vietnamese I was supposedly defending against other Vietnamese: the people about whom I actually knew nothing?

The author and educator Rudine Sims Bishop compares literature to a window and a mirror. 'All children, and I think all adults, as well, need mirrors and windows — mirrors in which they can see themselves; windows through which they can see the world. And everybody's children are disadvantaged by not having that.'

After our time in Boston, when Lê Minh Khuê returned to Việt Nam, we continued to correspond. We decided, with the help of another writer, the great postwar novelist Hồ Anh Thái, to create a collection of stories by Vietnamese and American writers in the hope that they would offer windows into the lives of those separated by distance and language and culture, by hatred and damage and pain and war; that in those lives readers would find mirrored their own loss and pain and in that necessary revelation, healing and hope. We wanted to give others, from both sides of the war, the same transformative experience we had experienced at that breakfast table.

The book, we decided, would not contain war stories, stories about combat, but rather stories that would centre on the ways the damage of the war — the physical and psychological and spiritual woundings that endured even after the last shot had been fired — had continued to affect not only the lives of those who fought, but also their families and descendants.

We also felt that for the book to truly weave together stories of the war's lingering pain, it also had to include stories from the Vietnamese who had been allied with the United States, many of whom had fled the country after the fall of South Vietnam, and so we invited a third editor to help find and include those stories. Trương Hồng Sơn (*Trương* Vũ), is a former South Vietnamese Army officer who left Việt Nam as a refugee; he became a NASA scientist as well as an artist and literary scholar. When he was a kid in school, he told me, he had hated being forced to read Vietnamese poetry and stories, but after the war, when he fled his country, adrift in a small boat somewhere off the Philippines, he found that 'remembering those stories and poems saved me'. They saved his mind and spirit and gave him the will to survive, and later, in America, they saved the country he had lost, allowed him to keep it alive in his soul. Sơn knew and introduced me to the emerging literature from Vietnamese American writers, some in Vietnamese, some translated, and some, from the next generation, grown up in America and writing in English.

The dream of creating the collection, which we decided to call *The Other Side of Heaven*, brought me back for the first time, since the war, to Việt Nam. I returned to a country at peace.

But the process of bringing that dream to reality also revealed the many ways the war was not over. The mainstream American publishers I first approached seemed interested only in narratives in which the Vietnamese were the backdrop for the actions, conflicts, and trauma of Americans, an attitude that reflected the way the Vietnamese had been viewed by America in the war itself. For some American veterans, the parallels between the American and the Vietnamese stories, the echoes of suffering in the minds and souls of the former enemy, were too disturbing. In Việt Nam, there was resistance to including stories from Vietnamese who had been on the other side. They were anathema: 'puppet-soldiers' and traitors — a stance in turn held by many among the older generation of the overseas Vietnamese community; a symmetry of resentment and loss that generated threats and abuse, directed from all sides at the editors and writers when, eventually, the anthology was published. People had lost so much, so many.

Yet for the editors and writers, that psychological resistance to letting the war go underscored the need for the book and clarified its purpose.

The Other Side of Heaven: postwar fiction by Vietnamese and American writers was published in 1995 by Curbstone Press, a visionary independent publisher that believed strongly in the way stories could connect people. The profits from its sales were all donated, with the contributors' agreement, to a new obstetrics/gynaecology wing in a hospital in Huế, and later to Project RENEW, a Vietnamese NGO dedicated to finding and clearing the vast and deadly number of unexploded bombs, shells, and mines still maiming and killing people in Việt Nam.

The stories, literally, saved lives.

Through Curbstone, with the help of Lê Minh Khuê and Hồ Anh Thái and many others in Việt Nam, over the next two decades we were able to create a series called 'Voices from Việt Nam' and publish another anthology, novels, and short story collections, and bring them to American readers (these books are listed at the end of this essay). In the years since, meeting those writers and reading their stories, and those of the many other Vietnamese and Vietnamese American writers who I am glad to say are now being widely published in the United States and elsewhere, has transformed my life.

Gentle transformation is the great gift of reading. A story or a book lets us live not just our own lives but many, many more, and in those lives we find reflections of ourselves, of who we are and who we may strive to be. 'Somehow I was sure that if people were willing to read each other, and see the light of other cultures, there would be no war on earth,' says the teenage girl Hương in *The Mountains Sing,* the great novel by Nguyễn Phan Quế Mai. Perhaps this isn't quite true. But perhaps it would make it much more difficult to decide to kill each other. Perhaps stories can save lives. And perhaps they may allow those who feel they have lost something of themselves, some diminishment of the heart — as if it were pressed inside a circle of sandbags on a muddy hill — to regain the beat of their own humanity, thrumming into and with the beat of so many other human hearts.

The Other Side of Heaven: postwar fiction by Vietnamese and American writers (1995), co-edited with Lê Minh Khuê and Trương Vũ; *The Stars, The Earth, The River: Short Fiction* by Lê Minh Khuê (1997);*Behind the Red Mist: fiction* by Hồ Anh Thái (1998); *Against the Flood*, a novel by Ma Văn Kháng (2000); *Past Continuous*, a novel by Nguyễn Khải (2001); *The Cemetery of Chua Village and Other Stories* by Đoàn Lê (2005); *Love After War: contemporary fiction from Viet Nam*, co-edited with Hồ Anh Thái (2005); *An Insignificant Family* by Dạ Ngân (2009); *Apocalypse Bell* by Hồ Anh Thái (2012); *In Whose Eyes: Trần Văn Thủy, the memoir of a Vietnamese filmmaker in war and peace* (2016).

COLUM McCANN

When I think of young readers, I envy them the early book that will cleave open the world. That first rush of recognition. The tingle along the spine. The crackle of the pages. The immediate widening of the world. The mystery. The powerful alignment of knowledge with the imagination. The thought that the world, now, will probably never be the same again.

Colum McCann is the National Book Award–winning author of *Let the Great World Spin* and several other novels including the international bestseller *Apeirogon* and, most recently, *Twist*. His work has been published in over forty languages. He is the co-founder of Narrative 4, a global organisation that uses the art of storytelling to foster compassion and change in communities around the world.

The words made flesh

Almost two decades ago, Robert Nuranen, a fifty-seven-year-old teacher from Hancock, Michigan, was searching through the attic of his family home, when he opened a box and a dusty copy of a book called *Prince of Egypt* fell out. He flicked to the back cover and discovered that it was a library book forty-seven years (!) overdue. Over the years, the book had been misplaced and boxed and re-boxed and misplaced again.

Nuranen went to his local library and laid it down on the counter in front of the startled librarian. She totalled the fees, which came out to $171.32. He left the library with a receipt from a transaction that was due on June 2, 1960, when he was ten years old.

I'm not sure where I read the story, or why I remember it so well, but there are times we come upon parts of our old lives that bring us around to where we once were. John Berger has said: 'If I had known as a child what the life of an adult would have been, I never would have believed it, I never could have believed it would be so unfinished.' *Unfinished* it always is — until it can't be any longer. Many of us would give as much as $171.32 — if not a whole lot more — to be able to return to the past in such a tiny, intimate manner.

One of the curious things about time, and its passing, is how, on occasion, it can actually return to us almost fully formed. We may not remember what happened yesterday, but the texture of decades ago can hit us with the force of an axe.

I was seven years old when I first read Mary Lavin's *The Second-Best Children in the World*. It was a book that my father, a journalist with the *Evening Press*, brought home to me. He and my mother read it at my bedside. It was not my first book, but I can still remember it as if the bread is just now coming out of the oven.

I knew nothing about Mary Lavin at that stage, in 1972, but the story that she conjured up (about Ben who's ten, and Kate who's eight, and the other, Matt, who is 'so small that I can hardly see him at all') was rhythmically and psychologically powerful to me. The kids decide that — in order to give their parents a rest — they will go on a long trip around the world. As they don't want to wear out the soles of their shoes, they walk always on their heels, but soon their shoes grow too small. They return home, having grown up and experienced all sorts of adventures, but Lavin doesn't treat it as a moment of terror or loss. Instead, the parents come running from the house with open arms and call them the 'best children in the world'. The kids disagree, and their answer is a pour of cool water along the spine. Ben, Kate, and Matt say that if they were actually the best children in the world, they never would have left in the first place. So they're *second* best. And happy to be so. They have gone and they have come back changed. They would have experienced nothing if they had not left. To be best is to be static. To be second best is to slide a little knife blade of difficulty into the journey.

It strikes me now, years later, that the book is a song for the emigrant. There is something in the emigrant's spirit where he or she realises that they will always, only, be second best. Leaving is a form of memory-making. It is also a way to inflict a form of damage upon oneself. Emigrants seem to want to wound themselves in order to remember where they came from. This is neither a pillar of light nor, I hope, a whine. We leave, we go away, we walk on our heels for a while, we outgrow our shoes, and occasionally we are given the grace of being able to go home.

This is what books do. Like countries, we leave them for a while, but having been there we are always going to come back, in one form or another. Occasionally, they will sit in the attic. But they will be found eventually, one way or another, even forty-seven years later.

*

When I think of young readers, I envy them the early book that will cleave open the world. That first rush of recognition. The tingle along the spine. The crackle of the pages. The immediate widening of the world. The mystery. The powerful alignment of knowledge with the imagination. The thought that the world, now, will probably never be the same again.

Jorge Luis Borges once said that he always imagined that paradise would be a kind of library. Through literature, we enter an infinite place. All the corners meeting other corners. The shelves extending themselves unto other shelves. Spine upon spine. A room full of voices. A cacophony of possibility. One corridor leading into the next. The journey becomes what Dylan Thomas might have called 'an adventure in the skin trade', where new skin is developed, and other skin is sloughed off in the process of the long picaresque journey of reading and, indeed, mattering.

There are many times I recall now my own adventures in the skin trade. There was the time when my father wrote a kids' soccer book and asked me to read it for him: my whole consciousness of literature was shaped from this moment. I

was astounded that things that seemed very real to me (Georgie
Goode scored a goal! The rain came down in the second half!
Georgie's caravan was burned!) could actually emanate not only
from our coal shed at the side of our house, where my father
wrote, but also from inside his head. The sound of his typewriter
tapping away became the music of my childhood.

When I think back, my mind is decorated with a series
of mirrors created by books, flashing lights and sounds and
language, echoing them down through the years, meeting other
years, layering my life.

There was the moment, at the age of fifteen, when I cracked
open Jack Kerouac's *On the Road* and a whole new sense of
possibility came over me. It was a book that eventually led me
towards travel, and I embarked on my own Kerouacian journey
across the United States on a bicycle. I didn't need Neal Cassady
when there were so many that I would meet on the road.

And then there was Benedict Kiely's short story, 'A Ball of
Malt and Madame Butterfly', which seemed, at the age of sixteen,
a whole new way of writing to me. Madame Butterfly, a half-
Japanese Dubliner, was a woman of 'questionable virginity'.
When a suitor starts regaling her with an obscure Yeatsian love
poem, she turns around and says that he would 'puke you with
poethry'. I began to read all of Kiely's work. It was amazing to me
that he lived just five miles from me in Donnybrook. I eventually
knocked on his door and he became, for many years, a mentor.
Still one of my favourite books of all time is his pitch-perfect
novella, *Proxopera*.

And still they go on, these books. They continue to spin in
my head. They meet one another and reignite their own history.

Some of them are obscure. Some are not. There's *Fup* by Jim
Dodge. And there's *The Dixie Association* by Donald Hays. There's
Whitman. And there's Toni Morrison. And there's Hopkins.

There's Desmond Hogan. And Ciaran Carson. And there's Louise Erdrich (Oh! how I felt when I read those first sentences in *Tracks* — 'We started dying before the snow and like the snow we continued to fall. It was surprising there were so many of us left to die.'). And then there was Jim Harrison, guiding me down the road with the extraordinary *Letters to Yesenin*. It did, in fact, come to me like a burning bush and a pillar of light. I had decided to stay in the country of literature.

Michael Ondaatje literally took my breath away with *Coming Through Slaughter*. I sat there, stunned by beauty. And then there was E.L Doctorow. And Don DeLillo. And Edna O'Brien. And Isabelle Allende. And James Galvin. And Salman Rushdie. And Joan Didion. And then friends of mine: Marlon James, Michael Cunningham, Dan Barry, Téa Obreht, Ishmael Beah, Joe O'Connor, Terry Tempest Williams, Darrell Bourque, Chimamanda Ngozi Adichie, Christine Dwyer Hickey, Roddy Doyle. It is embarrassing, in fact, to even begin this list, because I know there are so many names that I could write, and I paralyse myself with the notion that I will leave someone out. I have a whole phone book, an encyclopaedia of them. They are friends who have met other friends who have all become words.

The word made flesh. And dwelt amongst us.

*

While preparing to write this essay, I asked my son, JohnMichael, what sort of books he thought young people should be reading. (Please see his own essay on p.129 of this anthology.) He was quick to answer that a young person should read 'whatever the hell they want'.

Nothing wrong with a comic book. Nothing wrong with a mystery. Nothing wrong with a philosophical tome. In fact, any book is a good book. I find it difficult to think of a book that is inherently evil, although *Mein Kampf* might take that mantle, but not so much for the content of the book as for the content of the author's heart.

Books become doorways. They propel us into new rooms and sometimes into a whole wide landscape of new thoughts.

There is, on occasion, a mystical element to the books that shape our lives. Have you ever walked into a bookshop or library and experienced that strange sensation of being led to a particular shelf? And then, not knowing why, you reach up to a place that is almost out of reach, to a name you don't know, or a title you have never heard of, and you take the book down, and you crack it open, and it seems, there and then, designed specifically for you? I have no explanation for this feeling, even though it has happened to me many times. I have been led to an unfamiliar part of a bookshop. Why, I ask myself, have I been drifting towards the nonfiction section, or the ancient history section, or to the architectural section, only to find something that ploughs open my ribcage and reaches in for my tired heart and squeezes it into life?

I am not a big believer in the supernatural, or the fated, but there is certainly something spiritual that occurs when we find the right book. It becomes a companion and leads us back into ourselves.

Which leads me, in turn, to the most important book of my life. Often, when you mention *Ulysses* by James Joyce, you can actually hear the eyeballs roll. People think that it's either an obvious choice, or it's a pretentious one, or that it's somehow too difficult or too obscure. But it is none of those things, at least not for me. It is, in my opinion, the greatest novel ever written, almost nuclear in its spin: profound, profane, prodigious, provocative, prophetic, propulsive, progressive, protonic.

So much so that it has led me to a moment that I need to confess: there is a beautiful copy of *Ulysses* in the New York Public Library on 42nd Street. It has been there for many years. A first edition. Signed by Joyce to his friend, James Stephens. The collision of book and place is, for me, a sort of Borgesian paradise. So when I had a chance to see the copy, about ten years ago now, I was delighted.

Along Fifth Avenue. Into the library. Up the stairs. Into the rare book room. The book was opened carefully and methodically by library staff who wore special gloves so oil from their fingers didn't mark the pages. I was supervised every moment of the way. I leaned over the pages, breathed them in. As Joyce says: *The ineluctable modality of the visible.*

Part of the charm of books is that they disintegrate. No book can be protected forever. There are simple laws of nature. Even if we sealed our books in hermetic tombs, some distant day entropy will gnaw at the pages. It's called age — it's the most democratic thing in the world, and it happens to the best of us, even James Joyce. So when the book was put away, a tiny flake of page fell from inside onto the blue cloth beneath. This happens. Books will flake. A crumb, really. Just a crumb. The library staff didn't notice it. The book was put away. Wrapped, protected, humified. But the miniscule flake still lay there on the cloth. I stared at it. It would soon become dust.

And then I did what any heartsick lovesick booksick wordsick worldsick joycesick fool would do … I ate it.

There have been other times in my life when *Ulysses* has entered my body. This is the beauty of books. They arrive inside us in the most peculiar ways. The messy layers of human experience get ordered and reordered by what we take into our minds. Books can carry us to the furthest side of our desires. We can travel, we can remain, we can hide in plain sight. We can hoist our history on to a page. We, too, will die and disintegrate, but the amazing thing is that the stories don't die with us.

Death takes away everything, except what we need to tell others. This, too, then, is the beauty of literature. It allows us this manner of living. Literature is, in a very pure sense, a place where we can learn to remain alive.

Perhaps I should apologise to all at the library for touching my finger against that tiny flake of *Ulysses*, then putting it on my tongue in the manner of a man who has known other churches. But the fact is the blue cloth would have been collected, and then someone would have shaken it out, and the tiny flake would have been swept away, and it would have been gone. Ashes don't return to wood. Words, on the other hand, stay with us.

So, young reader, read whatever the hell you want, yes, but also read *Ulysses*.

JOHNMICHAEL McCANN

In order to catch a fish, you must dive in. I dove into literature for reasons that cannot be mistaken for an interest in books. A decade later, I've yet to come up.

JohnMichael McCann is a 2021 graduate of Colorado College, where he self-designed a major in Peace and Conflict Studies. After graduation, he embarked on a series of adventures. In a journey that mirrored his father Colum's earlier travels, JohnMichael lived in his car, exploring the American South to gain a more fulsome understanding of his country. Since jettisoning the car mattress, he has taught English in Việt Nam and driven a rickshaw through the streets of New York. Through these varied experiences, he has gained a deep appreciation for all that is human, messy, and imperfect, while developing an unabashed reverence for pluralism. He holds fast to Lawrence Ferlinghetti's belief that: 'Printer's ink is the greater explosive.'

Reading to impress

I started reading in high school to impress a girl. We met one January in circumstances that I've long since ceased to remember. She revered spoken word poetry. I didn't know what it was. I had decided that books and literature belonged to rooms of stale air. She told me of the Nuyorican Poets Café and other places where music mingled with poetry. I was enthralled, at first by her. I started hanging around The Bowery, looking for traces of Allen Ginsberg and Frank O'Hara. Just before spring break I told her I had feelings for her. She said she loved chatting and my friendship.

In May of that year, I got a job at the door at Bowery Poetry and worked two nights a week until I left for college a year later. The words of Walt Whitman lined the hallway in giant letters. I loved the atmosphere. There was a strict three-minute time limit at the open mic, and I cackled at the polite and less polite ways it was enforced. A drummer, saxophonist, and pianist would play into the poetry, a concert that I relished. After I left The Bowery, poetry stuck around.

At first, my interest in poetry was strictly a way to appear interesting. To be seen reading *Howl* in the dining hall. I memorised a few poems to show off at parties, trying to give the impression that I knew vastly more than I did. I started to re-read Whitman and found that The Bowery had snuck into the pages.

There was something in his words that felt like the jazz of the place. Whitman bequeathed himself and cheerfully shared his curiosity about celestial matters. This gave me permission to explore my ignorances, and I came to understand that reading could be enjoyed under any lights — it was not a strictly public matter.

I began to explore. Gabriel García Márquez. Toni Morrison. Nabokov. Herman Melville. Italo Calvino. They all gave me things that today still feel impossible. Their best works catch lightning in a bottle. Márquez's *One Hundred Years of Solitude* made me feel like I was on saxophone trying to keep up with a crescendo that began eighty years ago. Morrison's *Jazz* brought me to my city a hundred years ago and spun me in circles. Nabokov's *Pale Fire* stunned me with its audacity as the narrator encouraged me to skip the long-form poem that was the novel's centrepiece. Melville's *Moby Dick* made me feel as if I was on a years-long sea journey. I remember careening through the seas towards the ending. My gratitude was immense, because no matter what happened, I wouldn't be stuck on this goddamned boat. Calvino's *Invisible Cities* took me through countless cities, looking for the places that he describes and cannot possibly exist.

Between all of these books there have been countless other works that impressed me, that I enjoyed, but I no longer remember. Most books will prove to be a somewhat ordinary experience, enjoyable and good, but often not excellent. These books, though, as all books, are still worthy of celebration.

The only way we get excellent books is if there are books and people willing to risk themselves. Also, just because a book didn't change my world doesn't mean it didn't or won't change someone else's, or mine in the future. The chance of happening upon the previously unsayable is why I read today. I travel, also, in search of the elusive impossible — but a book is far cheaper than a flight to Greece.

I read with the hope that a few years from now I'll still be able to describe how a book is currently making me feel. Feeling the pressure mount as a strong start turns into an excellent middle, I hope against hope that everything will stay together, that whatever they've done for the past two hundred pages, they can somehow sustain for another fifty. Another twenty-five. Another twelve. At some point it doesn't matter if the train comes off the rails, because what they have done already is so rare. A broken hallelujah. The best books split your life into the time before and after you read them.

Like any relationship, books change with time. Maybe on the second reading a few faults appear. Other times you re-read a book and find that it's aged like a fine wine and only continues to get better. In the rarest of instances, a book becomes a prized possession that only truly becomes yours when you share it with someone who, you hope, will understand why so much coffee and wine have been spilt over the re-readings. *Howl* and *Leaves of Grass* are two such books for me.

In order to catch a fish, you must dive in. I dove into literature for reasons that cannot be mistaken for an interest in books. A decade later, I've yet to come up.

ANN MORGAN

… young book-lovers around the world have helped redefine my relationship to reading. They have turned it into an ongoing process of adjustment and self-questioning, of growth and change.

Ann Morgan is an author and speaker based in Folkestone, UK. In 2012, she challenged herself to read a book from every country, recording her quest at ayearofreadingtheworld.com and in the nonfiction book *Reading the World*. She is also the author of two novels: international bestseller *Beside Myself* and *Crossing Over*. A fellow of the Royal Literary Fund and Literary Explorer in Residence at the Cheltenham Literature Festival, she continues to blog about international literature. In 2021, Ann launched her Incomprehension Workshop, an interactive session that invites readers to play with not-knowing and embrace discomfort and questioning. She has since run versions of the workshop online and in person with book-lovers around the globe. Her next nonfiction book, *Relearning to Read: adventures in not-knowing*, released in 2025 by Renard Press, draws on the ideas explored in the workshop and her ongoing adventures with international literature.

Presents from strangers

In the town where I live, there's a bookshop with a difference. Selling books is only part of what it does. There's a reading room at the back where you can make yourself a free cup of tea or coffee. There are craft activities and tables where people sit with their laptops, or linger for a chat, particularly in the winter, when the shop advertises itself as a warm space. There's also a board pinned with handwritten tokens showing sums of money donated by customers. Anyone who visits can put these towards a book, no questions asked. Sometimes, the people who lift tokens off the board are young people and children — more than a quarter of Folkestone's under-sixteens live in low-income families, and the ward in which the bookshop sits is particularly deprived. Now that the local library has closed, the tokens board makes that special feeling of acquiring a book — of hugging it to yourself on the way home, buzzing with anticipation — possible for many who wouldn't otherwise get the chance.

I know how transformative such bookish generosity can be. Back in 2012, a stranger's gift changed my life. Four days after I set up ayearofreadingtheworld.com, the blog where I recorded my literary quest to read a book from every country in the world in a year, I got a message from someone called Rafidah in Kuala Lumpur, volunteering to choose and post me my Malaysian book. This offer astonished and electrified me:

135

here was someone saying that my reading was valuable, that it was worth supporting, that it had meaning. Indeed, far from simply saying this, Rafidah was going out of her way to affirm it — taking the time to visit a bookshop, select a book, package it up, and post it internationally. Surely this was an awful lot of bother to go through for a random blogger on the other side of the world?

I was inspired and bewildered in equal measure; part of me doubted the book would arrive. I suppose, up to that point, I'd been in the habit of thinking of reading as a private, personal thing. More than a little self-indulgent. Even a little selfish. I knew it could have great benefit to the reader — books had unlatched my thinking many times over the preceding thirty years — but I found it hard to see why my choice of reading matter should be of more than passing interest to anyone else. Certainly, you wouldn't catch me parcelling up titles to post to strangers in other countries (or so I thought back then).

But Rafidah's book did arrive. In fact, there were two of them: Shih-Li Kow's *Ripples and Other Stories* for Malaysia and *Fistful of Colours* by Suchen Christine Lim as a possible choice for Singapore. Over the months that followed, many other people made significant efforts to support my project. They visited bookshops and libraries on my behalf, shared manuscripts with me, and, in the case of two of the UN-recognised nations that had no commercially available literature in English at the time, even wrote and translated stories for me. Slowly, my disbelief turned to wonder. There was something powerful here: sharing stories was a universal human impulse that, in the face of all our difference and difficulty, had the potential to bring us together across all kinds of barriers.

Even now, more than twelve years later, I regularly hear from readers and writers around the planet wanting to share ideas, information, and books. Many of the people who contact me are young. Sometimes, like the boy who sent me a video from Beijing recommending a textbook that explains why 'tomatoes can be really quite dangerous', they do so for school assignments. At other times, young people contact me to let me know about initiatives inspired by 'A Year of Reading the World'. One of my favourites involved high-school students in a small town in Mexico, who started giving away second-hand books at bus stops, making reading matter freely available to those who couldn't access it by other means. There was also the formidable Aisha Arif Esbhani — 'Pakistan's Ann Morgan', as I was amused to see one news website call her — who, at the age of twelve, set herself the challenge of reading her way around the world.

From time to time, however, the messages come entirely independently, unconnected to any institution or larger project. Instead, they seem to stem simply from enthusiasm. A young person somewhere has found my blog and been sufficiently inspired by it to take the trouble of writing to me, often in their second or third language. As with Rafidah all those years ago, some of these messages contain offers to send me books. I heard recently from a youngster in Georgia, for example, who wanted to see if I knew about one of her nation's classics, the epic poem *The Knight in the Panther's Skin*. If not, she would be happy to send it to me, 'with a telegram from London', the next time her family visited the UK.

The warmth and optimism in such messages is powerful, as is the unalloyed conviction that sharing literature is valuable and that people all over the world have worthwhile, intriguing tales to tell. I see this faith in readers of all ages, but most particularly in the young, and I am glad to have created a space online where people feel confident that their stories will be welcomed and valued. This is one of the reasons I maintain a 'Book of the month' slot on the blog — to honour and channel some of the many recommendations and book gifts I continue to receive.

Sometimes, the messages I get from young readers enlarge my understanding of what stories can do. One of my most memorable exchanges involves a young man, Esmat, who first contacted me some years ago when he was at school. He'd found my blog and loved the idea of reading books from different countries. He could read English because his father had taught him using the Dr Seuss stories when he was little, but there was a problem: he lived in Afghanistan. There were no English-language bookshops near his village, and Amazon didn't deliver there. How was he to get books?

Taking a leaf out of Rafidah's book, I offered to send Esmat some stories. This proved to be easier said than done. Not only was there the challenge of finding a courier company that would take a package to eastern Afghanistan, but there was also the problem of selecting suitable titles. From the tone of Esmat's emails, he was around fifteen or sixteen. I wanted to choose books that would grip and interest him, but I didn't want to cause him problems by sending stories that contained inappropriate material or themes that were too mature. Although this was the pre-Taliban era, I was aware that there were growing sensitivities around freedom of expression in Afghanistan and knew that there were probably local taboos that did not align with mine. Might certain cover images cause Esmat problems? Would plots that seemed innocuous to me draw outrage down on him or his family by virtue of some detail that I had barely registered?

In the end, in the face of so much I couldn't comprehend, I felt I had no option but to stick with what I knew best and what had always lain at the heart of the connections I've been privileged to share with readers around the world: great stories. I selected a range of what struck me as some of the most compelling and brilliant books from countries likely to be new to Esmat's literary landscape, packaged them up, and sent them off.

Several weeks went by. I got a crackly phone call from a depot in Kabul. Then, an email dropped into my inbox: my package had arrived. A few days later, Esmat sent another message. He had started reading New Amsterdam Books and Saqi Books' translation of *Broken April* by Ismail Kadare, a novel built around the intergenerational blood feuds in northern Albania. Although it was fiction set in another part of the world, it seemed to him that he was reading about his own village: he recognised the menace and trauma in its pages all too well. In fact, it had inspired him to write about his own community one day.

Esmat and I exchanged a few more messages after that. Then the correspondence tailed off. My emails went unanswered. At first, I was unconcerned. But when the TV news started showing footage of the desperate scenes at Kabul airport in the wake of the Taliban's takeover, I began to fear the worst. I sent more messages that received no response. Finally, in November 2022, an email arrived. Esmat was in the US. He had just finished a master's in literature. During the course of his studies, Dostoevsky had made him fall in love with his life, 'including all the insanities in it', and he was hoping to forge a career as an artist. We've swapped a number of emails since then and also spoken over Zoom. Recently, Esmat sent me a link to his website, plzbkind.com, where he shares his artwork and writing. 'I am forever grateful for what you did for me [all] those years ago,' he told me. 'I was moved, and changed forever, and I am indebted to you for that.'

What Esmat doesn't realise is that our exchange and the others like it I'm lucky to have with enthusiastic readers around the planet enrich me in exactly the same way. Wearied and saddened as I often am by the cynicism and insularity of the book industry, these conversations keep me connected to what matters about storytelling. They give me the faith that keeps me coming back to the desk. They remind me of the power that narrative has to unite us, creating common ground for people who might appear to share nothing. When we read the same story with openness, respect, and curiosity — Esmat and others like him have taught me — our minds move along the same track. That shared journey through imaginary terrain creates a bond: it makes us teammates on an expedition. Even when our responses and conclusions differ, we have been experiencing similar things. We can compare notes, swap tactics, and reminisce. And we can use this to open up our own storytelling: by reflecting on and contrasting the ways that our minds meld with a text, we can identify and reveal truths about ourselves.

This process is not always easy. A while ago, I was contacted by another young adult keen to share stories. Like Esmat, this correspondent loved the idea of international storytelling. Seeing that all the works I had read in connection with their nation were by people in the diaspora, they wanted to share some writing from inside their home country. We had a warm exchange and even arranged a video call. But when I started to ask questions about conditions in their country — one of the world's most censored societies, according to Index on Censorship — and whether it was safe for the young person to talk to me, the wheels came off. I received a waspish reply: my correspondent was happy to discuss storytelling and cultural exchange, but they didn't want to touch politics. They were disappointed that I seemed to have fallen into the same trap as every other Westerner they encountered online: fixating on this one aspect and ignoring the richness, humanity, and fullness of life in their country.

This response forced me to reflect. Was I falling prey to stereotypes? Was my questioning driven by an ugly, colonial hangover that made it impossible for me to see people in certain parts of the world as fully human? Did my questions serve a Western agenda? I knew from work I'd done with refugees on the UK's Kent coast, as well as reports on a variety of news platforms, that there was at least some truth to my perception that freedom of expression was under threat in this place. But wasn't it possible that my sense of this had been distorted, overblown perhaps because this view made my country look good? Because it helped perpetuate the creaky notion of the West as the saviour of the developing world?

It took me a while to craft my response. In the end, I wrote back thanking my correspondent for their generosity in sharing time and books with me. I was grateful and inspired by much of what they'd told me. But I wanted to challenge them gently on one thing. I understood their desire to avoid politics: when I started ayearofreadingtheworld.com I was determined that it would be apolitical — a space where all people could share and celebrate stories. I hoped it was still a site that welcomed everyone, and I strove to keep it open and respectful. But over time I had come to realise that championing storytelling was political. It stood against polarisation, silence, oppression, and hate. In that respect, I believed my correspondent was political, too, and I thanked them for it.

I didn't expect to hear anything further. If I'd received a message of that kind twenty years ago challenging some of my most fundamental assumptions, I don't think I would have responded. But — as so often seems to be the case — my young correspondent turned out to have much more grace, capacity for self-reflection, and humility than I did at their age. They wrote back saying that after thinking carefully they'd also realised storytelling was political. It was impossible to keep the two things separate. They've since gone on to share several excellent articles they've written about different aspects of their society with me.

Conversations like these with young book-lovers around the world have helped redefine my relationship to reading. They have turned it into an ongoing process of adjustment and self-questioning, of growth and change. It is a practice that spills into other areas of my life, infusing interactions of all kinds and teaching me to read the world in the fullest sense.

These exchanges have even led me to develop a new approach to reading — one that privileges not-knowing and questioning over reading to understand. To explore this, I created the Incomprehension Workshop, which I launched in 2021 and have since run with numerous groups of readers around the world. Turning the comprehension exercise — that staple of classroom English teaching — on its head, the workshop presents texts likely to be outside the comfort zone of most anglophone readers. Instead of requiring answers, I invite participants to focus on what they don't understand, what surprises, shocks, angers, amuses, or upsets them, and what they would like to know more about. By exploring these responses and asking questions openly and respectfully, we discover more about our assumptions and biases, the things we expect from stories, our habits of thought and the explanations we reach for to plug gaps in meaning when facing the unfamiliar. We learn to question knee-jerk reactions — discovering that resistance or irritation can often be the X-marks-the-spot that signals treasure buried beneath. And by playing in an environment where there are no right answers (indeed, often no answers at all), we learn to reconnect to our instincts and resist the urge to filter our responses for fear of looking foolish.

As ever, young people are often the most enthusiastic and impressive participants. Whether it's the schoolboy who piped up during one of my sessions at the Cheltenham Literature Festival to talk in eloquent terms about how disconcerting it was to read something that presented communism in a positive light, or the publishing student at Exeter University who mapped fantasy onto ancient Pacific Island myth, I am continually inspired by the readiness of young readers to connect with and expand the possibilities of not-knowing.

Perhaps the most successful iteration of the workshop took place in March 2024 with students at Dibrugarh University in Assam, north-east India. I was nervous beforehand: although I'd run sessions with readers of many backgrounds, I'd never before worked with a group made up entirely of people raised in a very different education system to my own. I was concerned that the concept might not come over well, or that the students would be too reserved and shy to engage sufficiently, leading to excruciating misreading on all sides. But the reality made nonsense of my fears: the participants were among the most energetic and creative I have ever encountered. They seized the invitation to play and ran with it. Extraordinary possibilities flowered in that room.

At one stage, encountering a patchy record of the griot Nouhou Malio's performance of *The Epic of Askia Mohammed*, which was translated from Songhay into French and then into English by a team of academics, leaving all sorts of gaps and non sequiturs, half the room were convinced that they were reading a spy's transcript of two people plotting an assassination. This was an explanation I would never have arrived at in a million years, and it revealed fascinating differences in the ideas and assumptions closest to the surface in our relative world views. The excitement in the room was palpable and the responses kept coming — so much so that I had to bring the session to an end with the threat that if we didn't stop we would end up locked in the venue all night! Afterwards, a university professor shared a video message from a literature student saying how much the workshop had meant to her and, in particular, how one reading from a science student had blown her thinking open.

Much like the messages in my inbox, young people's responses to the Incomprehension Workshop can sometimes be challenging. Shortly before I went to Assam, I ran a session at a local sixth-form college. I was there at the suggestion of the team at the Folkestone Bookshop, who had recommended me to one of the staff looking for a local writer to come and speak to the students. It being World Book Day, I decided to start the workshop by getting everyone in the room to write down and complete the statements: Stories are …; the world is …; reading is …

At the end of the session, after we'd worked our way through a series of extracts and played with the idea of reading by not-knowing, I invited some of the students to share what they'd written. Grudgingly, one girl at the back read out her version: 'Stories are exciting; the world is crazy; reading is boring.' She looked at me, a mixture of wariness and defiance in her eyes as her classmates tittered. I felt a flash of irritation. In the depths of my being, a Victorian schoolmistress stirred, determined not to entertain such impudence. Then I remembered the journey I had been on and how, so many times over the years since I set out to read the world, limitations have proved the key to new strengths. Knee-jerk irritation could often point to something worth excavating — wasn't that one of the ideas that I'd been exploring with these young people only moments before? This wasn't about me, I realised, any more than the readings we concoct in the Incomprehension Workshop are really about the text: it was about this girl expressing something, sharing something, recognising something. There was honesty in what she'd written. And that disconnection between the enthusiasm for stories and the notion of reading being boring — that was intriguing. There was something worth exploring here.

Once again, a young reader had given me a gift, the latest in a long line of gifts both tangible and intangible that continue to ricochet between myself and others, started by that package of books sent by Rafidah to my much younger self all those years ago. It was my job to work out how to read it.

MICHAEL MORPURGO

'I have travelled the world for my stories, discovering places and peoples, their histories and their tales. I collect story-thread from all over, weave it on my loom, and pass it on to young readers.'

Sir Michael Morpurgo OBE is one of Britain's best-loved children's authors. He has written over 150 books, served as Children's Laureate, and won many prizes, including the Smarties Book Prize, the Writers' Guild Award, the Whitbread Book Award, the Blue Peter Book Award, and the Eleanor Farjeon Lifetime Achievement Award. His best-known book is *War Horse*, which was adapted for stage, receiving standing ovations at the National Theatre in London and later on Broadway, and then became a film directed by Stephen Spielberg.

With his wife, Clare, Michael is the co-founder of Farms for City Children. He was knighted in 2018 for services to literature and charity.

Perchance to dream

As a species, we have always looked up at the stars and wondered. And when we wonder, we ask questions, investigate. When we don't find the answers, we often make up our own.

This wondering about ourselves and our existence, about all we see and witness around us, the wind, the tide, the sun and moon, and the seasons, about who or what began all this, about good and evil, life and death, about love, and war and peace, about why we are as we are, why we are here at all. These profound and difficult questions have fascinated and troubled and inspired humankind since the beginning.

Of course, it is this wondering that should lead us, and sometimes has led us, to new knowledge and understanding. On our journey to an understanding of the environment around us and of the human condition, we have invented and shared stories. These stories have been told down the generations, defining the people who have told them and loved them and believed them. Yes, often they confirm what we hope for, what we want to hear about ourselves and others. They can be comforting and reassuring, but also monstrous and terrifying. Collectively, they reveal the human experience of life through the ages, all over the world. These are the stories our ancestors have known, that gave them and now us understanding and empathy, belief and hope, made them and us wonder.

To gather these seed-corn stories from places and cultures from all over the world is so important now, more important than ever, as our world shrinks around us, as we people grow exponentially in our numbers, and travel and intermingle and migrate, as we become more and more inter-reliant. We bring with us our myths and legends from all corners of the earth. And as always, these stories necessarily evolve through the generations. Indeed, they have to be constantly retold and adapted for each generation so that they remain fresh and relevant, full of new life.

These myths, legends, and stories should not be read just as tales of the olden days or faraway places. I think of them more as I think of early medicine. Modern medicine as we know it grew out of an ancient understanding of the importance of the plants and herbs that grew all around us, of a deep knowledge and understanding of nature and of ourselves, both body and spirit. We know now that there was often wisdom in the ancient ways of healing, and these ways inform medical science today. So it is with ancient myths and legends.

Our stories and poems and dramas of today have grown out of their predecessors, made us who we are. Most importantly, they can help us to empathise. For me, developing empathy through knowledge and understanding of others is the single greatest benefit of literature and education. Literature is a pathway to a deeper understanding of ourselves and others, of the human condition, from Homer to Shakespeare to Dahl to Pullman to Ben Okri to Lemn Sissay and to our new Children's Laureate, Frank Cottrell-Boyce.

Of course, I am most familiar with the stories of my own childhood. I grew up with King Arthur and his knights, Robin Hood and his band of merry men. As a story-maker, I have adapted many ancient myths and legends. For me, it is wonderful to return to these ancient tales I know so well and retell them for the young of today. In the same way that an artist can learn from copying the works of the Old Masters, so I learn from these stories that have endured for thousands of years.

And more than once, like so many writers and others, I have been inspired to visit the places where these ancient stories were born. I have travelled the world for my stories, discovering places and peoples, their histories and their tales. I collect story-thread from all over, weave it on my loom, and pass it on to young readers.

I have two true stories to tell you. The first is about my search for King Arthur. Like the great poet Alfred Lord Tennyson before me, I was writing about King Arthur. It wasn't on a whim. I never write on a whim!

Here goes. I go to Bryher on the Scilly Isles for my holidays, every year if I can. One summer I arrived and went as usual to buy our vegetables at the farmer's stall just down the lane from where we were staying. I was just choosing some new potatoes when the farmer came out and invited me in. He had something to show me, he said. And he seemed quite excited. He took me into his greenhouse. On his work table, there lay something covered, under a sack.

He didn't immediately show me what it was. Instead, he told me about it: 'I was driving along in my tractor the other day, ploughing, when I suddenly felt my back wheel get stuck in a hole. I got out, looked down, and there was this lying there at the bottom.' He pulled back the sack.

It was an ancient sword, rusty but complete, and with it what looked like a mirror and the remains of a cloak. He told me archaeologists had been to look and thought he must have driven into a grave over a thousand years old, that these might be the goods from the grave, the remains of some ancient chieftain.

Maybe, I thought, this might date back to around King Arthur's time.

So I'd come to buy potatoes and discovered quite by chance a possible link to one of my childhood heroes. I knew at once I was going to write about this sword and how it came to be there. To me, this was at once Excalibur, King Arthur's sword that he had pulled out of the stone, the very sword that his faithful knight Sir Bedivere had refused time and again to throw into the lake after the wounded old king's last battle. Although he told the dying king that he had, he never did. In my book, in my story, he kept it. In my mind, this sword had to be Excalibur, and the farmer had driven his tractor over Sir Bedivere's tomb. No question about it. I was remaking the legend.

Then I remembered something. On the wall of a hotel on St Mary's (the largest of the Scilly Isles), there is a plaque stating that Alfred Lord Tennyson had come to Scilly and stayed there when he was researching the whereabouts of King Arthur's grave. This was at the time when he was writing his Arthurian poems, way back in the 19th century, and he was seeking inspiration.

He knew, as I know many of you might know, that after the last battle, in which King Arthur had killed his own son, Mordred — who had betrayed him — the old king, dying from his wounds, was borne away from a beach in south Cornwall, near the battlefield, and placed on a burial barge by several queens dressed all in black. No one had ever discovered where that barge went, where he was laid to rest. Tennyson thought it had to be on the Scilly Isles, which were only twenty-five miles across the Atlantic from the Cornish beach. He was there to find out where that barge had taken the king. He never found out. I did. I got lucky. I got scientific.

I had a map of the islands. I spread it out on the bed in our room, and tried to work out, or guess, to which of the hundred

and more little islands King Arthur had been taken. I ended up
— promise — closing my eyes and letting lady luck and my blind
finger circle around and dictate where it should land. I opened
my eyes. The tip of my finger was right on a tiny island called
Little Arthur on the Eastern Isles. True.

I went out there the next day in a boat. There I found a small
beach where a boat or a barge could beach easily, and beyond it
we could see a deep dark cave. That was enough for me. Arthur
was there, I was sure of it. In the legend, as you know, he never did
die. He is waiting there to this day on Little Arthur, ready to come
back as our king when we need him. And do we need him now!

Legends live on, if you retell them. I sat down and wrote my
book. I called it *The Sleeping Sword*. Read it if you can, and read
Tennyson's Arthurian poems, too. They're not bad! But don't
forget, I was the one who found where Arthur is resting.

I told you there was a second true story, and it's even better.
So good you won't believe it.

I had grown up, as many of us have, with that most well-
known tale of Ancient Greece, the tale of the Trojan Wars, of
the great heroes who fought in the years-long siege of the city of
Troy, of Odysseus and Achilles, of King Menelaus, of Hector and
King Priam, of Helen and Paris who had been the cause of the
whole terrible tragedy.

And most memorable of all, of course, is that great wooden
horse, which the Greeks left behind as a gift on the beach, as
they apparently gave up, abandoned the siege, and sailed away
home. We know all too well how the Trojans, rejoicing in their
supposed victory, were deluded and deceived, how they brought
this wooden horse in through gates of the city, and how the
Greek soldiers hidden inside crept out in the dead of night and
opened the gates to let the Greek army in to massacre the Trojans
in their sleep.

It was that supreme chronicler of Greek legend, Homer, who told the whole epic story in *The Odyssey*. Homer lived on the island of Ithaca. This was also the home of one of the great heroes of the Trojan Wars, Odysseus. He had left his wife, Penelope, to go to the wars. He was gone twenty years, ten years of war and ten years of heroic and fantastical adventures before he reached home at last after the war was over.

Meanwhile, Penelope, longing all the while for his return, had been fending off pestering suitors by telling them that she would make up her mind which one of them she would choose only when she had finished her weaving. She never did finish because every night she unpicked the work she had done that day.

Then one day Odysseus arrived home. Let's just say, it didn't end well for those persistent and pestering suitors.

But here's the magic for me of story-making — a magic I've tried to pass on to children all my teaching life. Here's the thing, this story was to have a new life, something that might make the hair stand up on the back of your neck.

My wife, Clare, and I went to Ithaca three years ago, simply on holiday, not for research. For me, research is so often happenchance, not intentional. We were staying in a small house on a pebbly beach called Dexa, near Vathy, the main town on the island. And what did we discover? We found out we were staying on the very beach that Odysseus walked up when he returned from the Trojan Wars, disguised as a beggar, to reclaim his wife, Penelope, and his kingdom.

We went see his supposed palace. We walked among the olive trees, climbed the huge stones that were still there, took our photos, the bleating sheep all about us, their bells tinkling, the smell of thyme in the air. And we visited Homer's house, too, where no doubt he had written his great stories, where he had walked and talked and lived out his life. All that was left of his house were great tumbled stones, and among these legendary stones were growing some ancient olive trees. I picked some legendary olives, almost the same olives Homer must have eaten. I've planted one of them back at home in Devon — but that's by the by. One day, when I'm very old, I'll be able to eat one of Homer's olives and write my own *Odyssey*!

That same evening, there was a magical happening, a true happening. We were back on our beach. We were reading. Hardly anyone was about. I was reading *The Odyssey*, of course, in a wonderful new translation by Emily Wilson, when we noticed an old lady dressed in black walking slowly along the seashore. We'd seen her often in the cool of the evenings, coming down with her family. She was doing what she always did, keeping the beach clean of any plastic washed up in the shallows.

She stopped suddenly and waved us over. She was bending down, picking something up as we came closer. She was holding it out to show us in her cupped hands. It was a flying fish. It lay limp, but it was silver and glowing in the evening sun. Neither of us had ever seen one before. Then she spoke, in halting English.

'It is dying,' she told us. 'They are washed up here on my beach quite often.' She held it a little closer to us. 'They talk, you know,' she went on. We must have looked doubtful.

'It is true,' she said. 'Listen.' And she stroked the head of the flying fish very gently with the back of her forefinger.

The fish opened its mouth and uttered plaintive little sounds, again and again. The fish was speaking to us, trying to tell us something, something important. Maybe it was about dying, I thought. And then I thought of something else, prompted, I am sure, by having just visited the home of Homer, by the story I had been reading. I wondered and I thought: this beautiful silver flying fish must be, has to be, Proteus, the Greek god, who can turn himself into any creature he likes. And he is trying to tell me something. He wants me to tell a story about him, this island and its people, its tortured history, from ancient times to modern times.

That very same evening, after supper in a taverna, we were walking home round the bay in Vathy, talking about little else except Proteus, our talking fish, when we passed by a modern-looking house with a verandah. Sitting there was an old man, a drink in his hand. I greeted him in my best Greek. He replied in broad Australian: 'Hello.' We stopped to talk. I asked him what an Australian was doing on Ithaca. He told me his life story. Here it is.

This man had grown up on Ithaca. In 1954, when he was a boy, there was a terrible earthquake on the island. Many died, and much of the island was reduced to rubble. The boy, now alone in the world, became a refugee. He was sent to Australia, where he had an uncle living in Melbourne, his only living relative. There he grew up and became a Greek Australian. All his life he'd had this idea, a determination, to make his fortune and go back to Ithaca, rebuild his family home, then spend as much time as he could in his retirement on the island.

In one day I had been gifted two wonderful stories, one rooted in an ancient legend, the other a legend of our time. I fused the two and made it my own. I called it *When Fishes Flew*. I think it might be just about the only story ever told by a fish, a fish who is a god, with an Australian heroine who is not!

It is out of such myths and legends ancient and modern that we make our stories. I know that for sure. Every one of these tales has, of course, a specific origin, a place, a people, a language, that created it. But every one of them is also universal, and once we have read it, it belongs to us because we have lived it, and imagined it.

We will, because of these stories, go on learning, wondering, dreaming, and searching for wisdom and truth. And if the search for wisdom and truth and creativity is not at the heart of the education of our children, then surely we are wasting their time and ours, and we are most certainly not enriching their lives.

That is why stories and storytelling of all kinds should be centre stage in education, why a library and art room must be at the heart and soul of every school. Let writers and storytellers and dramatists come into every school, often. Let there be dance and music and song, let there be storytelling from three to half past in every primary school, and with no comprehension testing afterwards. It is what cannot be tested that is important, not just in education but in life. Let the children simply leave with the wonder of the story lingering long in their minds, perchance to dream. That story might be the one, that author might be the one, to sow the seed of a life-changing love of books and ideas, might encourage them to create their own stories. This is so often how a child finds her or his own voice, how they become story-makers themselves.

And let every child have the opportunity to go to the theatre twice a year, to a concert, to a museum or art gallery, all of this free of charge. It is their right, their heritage. Heritage is stories, so open the windows and let the stories in like fresh air. Let them breathe in stories, breathe deeply.

And just as important, let every child spend time exploring the countryside, feeling close to nature, to hills and fields and woods and streams and seashores. To care for the world of nature, they need to feel they belong, to feel the harmony of it all, to understand that they are part of it. Let them wander and wonder, let them drink in the world about them, their world. We know we have first to care and empathise before we can live well and fully, and before we can create our own ideas and stories. I know that from being a child, a father, a grandfather, a great-grandfather, from being a teacher and a story-maker for nearly sixty years.

I think we all know it.

DINA NAYERI

'It's a gift, then, to revisit books, like revisiting a city every decade, allowing yourself to wander down new streets, to notice different landmarks. It's a rare pleasure, too, to be interested in a story enough to return to it again and again, to allow it to mingle with your joys and sorrows and to watch it change colour according to the atmosphere of your heart.'

Dina Nayeri is the author of two novels and two highly acclaimed books of creative nonfiction, *The Ungrateful Refugee* and *Who Gets Believed?* The latter was a National Book Critics Circle Award finalist and a finalist for the Dayton Literary Peace Prize, and *The Ungrateful Refugee* was a finalist for the *Los Angeles Times* Book Prize and the Kirkus Prize, and won Germany's prestigious Geschwister Scholl Prize. A 2019–2020 Fellow at the Columbia University Institute for Ideas and Imagination in Paris, and winner of the 2018 UNESCO City of Literature Paul Engle Prize, Dina has won a National Endowment for the Arts literature grant and the O. Henry Award, and was selected for *The Best American Short Stories*, among other accolades. Her work has been published in more than twenty countries and in *The New York Times*, *The Guardian*, *The New Yorker*, *Granta*, and many other publications. Her essays and stories on displacement and home are taught in schools across Europe and the US. Dina has degrees from Princeton, Harvard, and the

Iowa Writers' Workshop. She was born in Iran and currently lives in Scotland, where she is a Reader at the University of St Andrews.

You read it wrong

My students often ask me what they should read, and my answer is often disappointing: read whatever you want, I tell them, but be sure to re-read it later, when you're older, have made mistakes, are in love or grieving. My students are often quick to judge stories, their morality simple and iron hard (as mine once was). Sometimes, they spend all their energy on correcting offensive words in an old text or attacking a sinful protagonist, missing the context, the meaning, and every small beauty. Sometimes, they toss aside a book because, by page thirty, they don't feel the story represents them or those they care about. When I offer my own favourites, I worry they'll misunderstand and discard them, too. So, I say, 'Promise you'll read it again in ten years.'

I want to say to the next generation that it's okay to be uncomfortable in someone else's story. I want to tell them that it's not enough, after a long education, to amass a library of books that you've loved in precisely the way everyone else has loved those books. Better to delve into dark waters with a book that frightens you, one you can return to in crucial moments, when you crave to be ugly or errant or strange. That book will change with (and *for*) you, even (especially) if it enraged you the first time. The books I loved in my youth were often those I misread — again and again — to suit my latest fears and longings. Re-reading transformed those stories for me and inspired in me a firestorm of dangerous thoughts. I admit, it takes a big dose of courage now, to dredge them up from my memory.

*

The first time I read *Lolita*, I knew I was reading it wrong — and I didn't care.

I had a habit of plucking unripe opinions like green plums, making a sport of choosing the warped, sour ones. No doubt Nabokov's intention was lost on me like the meaning of so many other books. Nothing I could do about that. At eighteen, I had spoken English for only eight years and was dazzled by each new word, every crafty phrase and cleverly stacked sentence. When Iranian adults expelled their chewy, mangled English (rich and sensory as I now find it), I felt their choices as small assaults on art and beauty. I had been stateless, yet I thought rooting in Oklahoma would be a worse fate than returning to Iran to be hanged. Before I reached Lolita's age, I had lived in a refugee camp. I spent my teenage years in a too-poor, too-Christian family wishing I was rich and free. Then I got into Princeton. Then I read *Lolita*. My truest reaction, a traumatised, fatherless girl lying in the lower bunk of my dorm strung with Christmas lights, was that Lolita was lucky. She was rescued by the handsome Francophone who had read great books, who wielded the English language the way few others could. She was freed from that provincial mother, that silly jealous shrew. Why live with a woman who can't speak five sentences without humiliating herself, when you could be with a poet? Could it be so bad to allow him to marvel at your body now and then (he's an aesthete!)? Better that than to be forced under a scarf, or into jean shorts that hung below the knee in an Oklahoma summer.

'He put her in school, for God's sake!' I said to my roommate.

Humbert Humbert would've let me shave my legs. He would've insisted on it.

Humbert Humbert would've let me read bawdy books.

Humbert Humbert would've taught me French and only the wittiest English.

And anyway, in Iran, girls younger than Lolita were married off to uneducated mullahs. My own grandmother was married at thirteen and pregnant before she knew what sex was — she thought she had snakes in her belly. At least this lucky American girl could leave Humbert and take his money, as soon as she was old enough to figure out blackmail. She could run to the police. She could write her story. She could raise money for her education, or start a company, or be on the news. She could become an actress in Hollywood. An Iranian girl, given so much freedom, wouldn't sit around and suffer.

'Americans are so fucking soft,' I said to my roommate, who was from Mexico. She nodded and told me my analysis of *Lolita* was super weird, but yeah, true about Americans.

So, when it came time to write an essay, I kept my weird thoughts to myself. I wrote about obsession, art, and how the right words can beautify ugly things. I wrote about escaping death after a revolution, as Nabokov had done, though his family had money and we didn't. I wrote about the struggle and joy of the English language, and a kind of exile story that offended me — the American road trip — because it was brooding and selfish and unnecessary. I underlined every gloriously sinister detail, and I wrote about the burden of Humbert's sick gaze ('lips as red as licked red candy', 'the seaside of her schoolgirl thighs'). I knew what a correct read looked like to an undergraduate teaching assistant.

My honest opinions would have damned me. How could I confess that the only character I found worthy of saving was the predator with the excellent brain? I felt nothing for the women, who exhausted me, but I didn't judge Nabokov for writing them that way. My imagination was a bud and I had no empathy, but I was cynical and had years of experience hiding behind veils. I was a self-loathing immigrant from the East, taught by the church to be equally disgusted by my urges as I was by my origins, and I thought I saw Nabokov in ways others couldn't: if you come from the old world with its ugly, deviant ways and messed-up people, then fiction is a comfortable place to hide; it is dangerous to trust the Western listener with true stories. In fiction, you can show your strangeness, your bad breeding, and your frightening instincts without claiming them as your own. I admit, a part of me thought that with *Lolita*, Nabokov was confessing something. If I had met the author, I would have said, immigrant to immigrant, both dirty and opportunistic in our pressed academic robes, with our good shoes and foreign secrets: 'Save it, agha. We both know exactly what you were doing there.'

I thought I was so clever. Every day, I thrived on shocking my classmates, my neighbours, my friends. They rewarded me with gasps and whispers — attention. It never crossed my mind that it takes some kind of damage to be jealous of Lolita.

*

Though *Lolita* had stirred the sleeping feminist in me, *The Handmaid's Tale* woke her with a gong. Maybe I couldn't rage at Humbert, but I could loathe the men who put women in Handmaid costumes (their hair covered like in Iran), and hanged them, and beat them, and took away their names, and plucked out their eyes.

A few years ago, I joined a WhatsApp group of progressive NGO women in London. One morning, I woke to find them blowing up my phone over Atwood.

The Handmaid's Tale is hugely problematic.

It was early morning, and I hadn't slept. The literary world was fighting again, this time about whether Bernardine Evaristo should have won the Booker alone (instead of sharing it with Margaret Atwood). I had had enough of this conversation: here were two great writers, both wildly influential, whose voices would be heard. Forever. They were fine. It felt like the least important battle of all the nonsense battles so far — over a second sticker. Why was this woman trashing *The Handmaid's Tale*, one of the great feminist novels of our century?

Because it had appropriated women's experiences in oppressive countries.

Because it had imagined white women in traumas that happen to women of colour.

Because it ignored LGBTQ women.

Because, in committing these sins, it had turned a profit for Atwood.

I lost it. On whose behalf were these privileged women wringing their hands? Atwood had modelled the hangings in her book on Iran, *my* home country. And yet, *The Handmaid's Tale* had helped me deal with those memories of the Islamic Republic: how the teachers had threatened my mother's life, how I was forced under a scarf, how I waited by the door for my mother to return from prison. The day the moral police spilled into her car, then her office. I had lived in Gilead. No one, I believed with my whole body and mind, could call the book problematic unless they had lived in a theocracy or had a PhD in Literature.

I was angry for weeks. I had a hair-trigger in those days and, even though my biggest academic insecurity had been that I would misread English books, I fired off my own accusation. *You don't have a clue what this book means for people,* I said (or something to that effect). *I can't believe anyone could read it that way.*

*

Because my reaction to *The Handmaid's Tale* was so rooted in my Islamic Republic trauma (and my nostalgia for home), I considered reading Azar Nafisi's *Reading Lolita in Tehran*. When it had hit the shelves in 2003, I'd been startled to see it. I knew Nafisi was a scholar and she would have a sophisticated, respectable, and 'right' interpretation of the story. I didn't want to be corrected, though, so I avoided it for years. When I finally read it, I loved it, but found that it didn't change my own readings — because I was me. And I'm not a scholar, I'm a deeply physical, creative weirdo who forces everything through the sieve of her own fickle emotions.

More than a decade passed before I read *Lolita* again. Now I was thirty-two and in my second debilitating exile: divorce and a move to graduate school. I was softer, more doubtful in some ways, surer of myself in others. I had imagination and empathy now, though mostly for myself and people who had lived my precise kind of life. My hard shell had been ripped off by this new kind of displacement.

I was raw — and again, I read it wrong.

Unlike the first time, I was enduring a humbling. If at university I fancied myself a winner, at thirty-two I was a cursed thing, doomed to repeat the same displacement drama again and again. Having failed at marriage and chosen the wrong career out of cowardice, I had moved to Iowa City to become one of the oldest MFA students at a writers' workshop I chose because my brother once admired it aloud. I imagined that if you love writing enough to go to Iowa for it, then you must be free of New York–style vanities.

The first thing I learned at Iowa was that our New York–style vanity was *all* we had in common. Because I had spent my twenties in corporate settings, I knew nothing of their language or values. Here, I wasn't the cleverest or the best. I had no identity at all.

One night at a party, I listened as they gushed about a book I had once read. They spoke in the lush, unapproachable way of literary scholars — philosophical, aesthetic, pulling from many directions, making the thinnest connections profound through abstraction. They talked about the grotesque and the delinquent, the intersection of beauty and morality ('the ugliness of purity and the beauty of the grotesque'). They talked about politics and truth and the transformation of the publishing world in the last half century. They talked about Lolita herself, objects of desire, and who gets to be a fully realised character.

I felt so stupid and unprepared.

Steeped in narcissism, errancy, and despair, I developed a habit of taking long night walks. I downloaded *Lolita* read by Jeremy Irons, whose voice soothed me. I walked and listened to this book I had forgotten, noting all that had escaped my attention the first time.

How could I have missed that it was *funny*? That Nabokov's humour was as sharp as the grandfathers back home who had been raised on the great Persian poets and village raunch? I laughed through the description of Humbert's first wife — her lover, the taxi driver, asking Humbert about her diet and her periods and what she should read. I relished Humbert's mind-fuckery with the stupid doctors, the last one with 'a knack of making patients believe they had witnessed their own conception'.

But this wasn't the stuff I was meant to be noticing. To pass as a writer, I needed to pick apart the prose, to smell the subtle thematic notes. I walked on, straining to hear.

Then I arrived at Mrs Haze, Lolita's mother. Where in my first reading Humbert had consumed me, now I noticed only her. I was humiliated for her. Because the true reason I was walking the streets and listening to novels wasn't to fit in with my new literary classmates, but to pass the time as I waited for a new man to text — a younger man. Though, at thirty-two, I was free, I could no longer be a young object of fantasies. I was now the older, admiring one. The one who chased, who was thwarted, humiliated. I was the one who had to wait. I was Mrs Haze.

'To make someone wait:' wrote Barthes, 'the constant prerogative of all power, age-old pastime of humanity.'

Of all the brutal passages in *Lolita*, the sentence that distressed me most in that second read came after Haze asks Humbert if he'd rather sit awhile on the piazza or go to bed alone and nurse his tooth. To the reader, Humbert responds simply, cruelly, in a new paragraph, at the end of a section: *Nurse that tooth.*

Screw Nabokov, I now thought. Screw his sexism and ageism and his pretentious language. Another rich boy, raised trilingual, now old and shaking with unspent desire.

I deleted Jeremy Irons' voice from my phone just as the long-awaited text arrived.

I started to reply:

I hate it here. Everyone is smarter, better read, faster thinking. I want to go home. I typed these words then deleted them, because I didn't know where home was anymore. In the following weeks, I absolved Nabokov, pouring my disgust into the villain, Humbert. Afraid of his voice, I finished my second wrong reading using the paperback.

*

Two years later, in New York, I had lunch with friends who had gone into the corporate world. I mentioned a devastating book I had found. It got no press and sold no copies but had nonetheless astonished me.

'If it didn't sell though …' one of them began— I knew what was coming and unsheathed my rage — '… seems the market disagreed with you about how awesome it was.'

'The market has no clue what's good,' I said. 'Great books get missed all the time.'

'Then what makes them great?' said the other. 'Who decides? *You?* That's the whole function of a market. People think it's good and it sells. Nobody likes it, it doesn't.'

'By that logic, *Fifty Shades* is the best book in decades.'

'Yeah, so maybe you missed something good about it.' I loved my friend, but right then, I could have slapped her.

We fought. They went on about the efficiency of markets and all the ways of making the subjective objective ('Sales are a fair and unbiased way to quantify it!'). I went on about the inadequacy of collective taste, about 'real' art, and about having enough sense to leave the judgement of crafted things to craftspeople, the teachers and writers whose books had withstood scrutiny ('Any garbage can go viral if a celebrity's involved.'). Everyone went home angry. I wondered later who had won. The world would continue to bestow success as it always does, and much would depend on the whims of those who don't know how to read — the ones who pay seven figures for *Fifty Shades* or *American Dirt*. Money would follow money. Attention would follow attention.

Then in 2017, a man wrote a novel about a girl who grows up raped by her father. Though the man wrote from the girl's perspective, he gave her no mind, no heart. He lingered too long on her rape — a cynical choice. Half the reviews mentioned *Lolita*, as if the subject was enough to earn that man a place beside Nabokov. I couldn't finish it. I was a new mother and couldn't get through the rape scenes. I posted a comment to that effect. *I'm sure it's brilliant*, I lied, *but I'm going to stop reading now.*

A poet wrote me that I had offended her. *Just because I'm not a mother doesn't mean it's easier for me.* She wrote a long message, about how I had read it wrong.

A few years later, I heard the literary world fighting about whether *Lolita* would be published today. One editor said he wouldn't dare publish it now, as it would never get past a committee of millennials at his publisher, let alone withstand public scrutiny. It was the first time I thought about how my favourite books come into the world, and how they end up in my hands — how many other people's readings impact that and how vital it is that *those* people see beauty in unlikely places. I don't believe in wrong readings, but what about the brilliant books that never made it out of a finance committee? There is such a thing as lazy readings, cursory readings, thoughtless readings. How to prevent those, except to convince my students to take their raw curiosities, their weird perspectives (not their shame, their risk-aversion, their material fears) into their private communion with a piece of literature?

*

Sam and I met in our late thirties. He was a writer, too. He told me he used to work in the kind of high-end kitchen store where manicured women with no intention of preparing food shopped for decorative cookware. He carried a copy of *Lolita* in his pocket because an ugly thing written with depth and beauty was the only antidote to the hours he spent in the company of such high-polish vapidity. Watching people buy items they planned to forget (they were all Mrs Haze), he craved deviance and darkness and well-crafted obsession.

We began sharing stories and books we loved, aberrant minutiae that thrilled us.

I told him about an Iranian man who had tried to give a testimony in a church outside Amsterdam. I was there to translate for a group of new arrivals from Iran.

The pastor had asked the congregation to share recent bouts of sudden gratitude: small gifts from God. The Iranian man was the fourth to stand. The woman before him had spoken of a phone call with her best friend. A Dutch man said a few words about his wife. In the familiar broken English of my teenage years, the Iranian man described a little girl who had greeted him that morning with a handshake. He spoke of her charming dress, her innocent smile, the softness of her hands, and how she made him briefly forget all the ugliness he had fled. He said he felt blessed that she allowed him to kiss her cheek. *He misses his children*, I thought. Then I noticed that others were whispering. The man sat, awkwardly, unsure of his error. He hung his head for the rest of the sermon. I wanted to reach out and squeeze his hand.

'That's so weird and interesting,' said Sam.

We started to save our ugly stories for each other. As I moved through the day, I looked for strange details, like snagged threads in the universe, that would fascinate him. He did the same. 'I saw a turd on a bollard,' he said. 'How did it get up there? What creature has legs that high? Or did someone scoop it up and put it there?'

One day, with our baby asleep in her stroller, we walked into a sex shop. Sam was telling me a revolting story he had heard from a doctor friend. The cashier, a student in her twenties, gaped at us with undisguised horror. 'Over eighteen only,' she snapped.

'She's not doing any shopping,' said Sam.

'She's a minor!' the cashier informed us, her disapproval like a hook pulling down the sides of her mouth.

'She's not sentient,' I shot back. This wasn't a pre-teen we were dragging in to watch us browse for lube, which, by the way, I needed because I had *given birth*. 'She's a pair of lungs and a gastrointestinal system.'

The cashier glared at us until we left. Outside, my heart pounded. I was ashamed and fascinated by that exchange. I wanted to pick it apart, like a good scab.

'Well, that felt awful,' Sam muttered on the way out.

I felt gross, like I had been both right (in my logic, she wasn't 'underaged', she was a sleeping infant) and deeply wrong, because there can't be a line for the workers there — our case was obvious, but how would they draw the line if the child was one or two?

I read *Lolita* for a third time as a mother and writer, and I felt implicated somehow. Children are so fragile, so easy to objectify and forget in the periphery. Humbert Humbert no longer strikes me as brilliant or intimidating. He's neither a saviour nor a prize worth pursuing. He horrifies me, though I am interested in his point of view, because it is ugly and specific and aberrant. And I know that I have been ugly and aberrant (in much less harmful ways, but still). I no longer know or care what a right reading looks like. I know that the book's merit comes from my many wrong readings, that it changes as I change, pummelling a raw bruise each time precisely because the characters are complex and true. Each enrage and move and baffle me in their own time. This time I mourn Lolita, as I would if she were my child. Would *Lolita* be published now? Many more loathsome books are published now. And beautiful ones aren't given the space to breathe. Others are drowned out by lesser voices. Artists and audiences grow ever more cynical. And those holding the money still believe their metrics infallible.

I'm not powerful or persuasive enough to change the minds of all the finance people who buy books using sales figures as a measure of quality. And I'm too old to convince the young that beauty can be hidden inside ugly, triggering things. A decade after my MFA, I still spend literary dinner parties hovering by the snack table.

It's fine. No one is equipped to decide what's good, though I'm thankful for those who honestly try, who invest in the tools of our craft.

I tell my students to read what sparks a dark curiosity, what wakes the ogre within, and I tell them to read it as if the book is their secret; no one will judge them for being entranced by the wrong things. I tell them not to judge other people's interpretation either (even if it feels like their friends missed the best thing about a story and that it's your duty to reach into their head and fix it). I tell them that the heart remakes itself. It's a gift, then, to revisit books, like revisiting a city every decade, allowing yourself to wander down new streets, to notice different landmarks. It's a rare pleasure, too, to be interested in a story enough to return to it again and again, to allow it to mingle with your joys and sorrows and to watch it change colour according to the atmosphere of your heart. Best of all, re-reading inoculates us from many of the dogmas and insecurities that plague young readers — like the notion that a book is about one thing, or that there is a right way to read a book. How can there be when you've read it five different ways in twenty years?

I hope my fourth wrong reading of Nabokov's masterpiece surprises me. I hope I find loathsome new threads that drive me to laughter or devastation or humiliation or anger, that it shrouds and breaks up my crystalline views. I hope Sam is there — and our daughter, too — and that we're still inclined to dig into the grotesque, to suspect flawless things. I hope my daughter sinks into unsettling stories with mischief and mutiny in her heart, that she lingers for many long hours in the dark water, and that she protects her strangeness. I hope we're undiminished in all our errancy, reading wrongly together and writing our best work for ourselves, unafraid of what we uncover.

NGUYỄN PHAN QUẾ MAI

*Later, I would come across these lines from the poet
Phùng Quán: 'Có những phút ngã lòng, tôi vịn câu thơ
mà đứng dậy' — 'During moments of difficulty, I hold
on to the verses of poetry to pull myself up.' I realised
that as long as I had books to read, I was not poor. That
realisation made me less afraid.*

Dr Nguyễn Phan Quế Mai is the author of thirteen books in
Vietnamese and English, most recently the internationally
bestselling novels *The Mountains Sing* and *Dust Child*, and a
book of poetry and essays, *The Color of Peace*, released in June
2025. Her writing in Vietnamese has received some of the top
literary awards in Vietnam including the Poetry of the Year
Award 2010 from the Hanoi Writers Association. Her writing in
English has received many international awards including the
PEN Oakland/Josephine Miles Literary Award, the International
Book Award, the BookBrowse Best Debut Award, and the
Lannan Literary Fellowship in Fiction. She was also Runner-
up for the Dayton Literary Peace Prize. Quế Mai's writing has
been translated into more than twenty-five languages and has
appeared in major publications including *The New York Times*.
She is an advocate for Vietnamese literature and is the translator
of eight books. She was named by Forbes Vietnam as one of 20
inspiring women of 2021. She has a Ph.D in Creative Writing
from the UK's Lancaster University.

How reading saved me

Dear Precious Reader,

If you are holding this book in your hands, you are someone who cares deeply not just about books but also about the creators of books. I want to thank you with this very personal essay, which includes many details so intimate and painful, I have never, until now, revealed them to anyone. Reading the essay, I hope you will experience how my love for reading has saved me, has changed my life, enriched me, and enabled me to become a better person.

Looking back at the last fifty years of my life, I see that some of the darkest times happened when I was a fifteen-year-old girl living in Bạc Liêu — a small town located at the southern tip of Việt Nam. This was in 1988 and Việt Nam was under the American trade embargo, isolated from most of the world. Things were difficult. My parents were teachers and farmers who laboured around the clock, so outside school hours my two brothers and I also worked in our family rice field and garden. I harvested our vegetables and sold them in the market and on the streets. I was keen to help my parents, so in addition we also made bamboo curtains and carpets on commission for a cooperative in order to earn money and help put food on the table. Along with those tasks, I woke up early in the morning — as early as 4.00 am — to catch tiny shrimps and mud crabs from the ponds and rice fields around our house.

But that wasn't the worst time. Even though things were tough and I was exhausted at the end of each day, I was filled with determination and hope for the future. I knew how lucky I was to have a family who loved me and would do anything for me. My parents always took good care of me, bought me many books to read, and infused in me a yearning for knowledge. I knew education and knowledge would be the key for me to open a better future for myself.

Our worst nightmare hit us when I was about to enter high school. I still remember so vividly that day thirty-six years ago, when I found my mother howling in our kitchen. She was banging her head against the large clay jar that stored our drinking water. My father and brothers weren't home, so I had to try my best to pull her away. It took my mother a long while to calm down, and when she did, she told me, between sobs, that the person whom my parents had trusted to invest a lot of their money had disappeared. This woman had taken all of my parents' savings, as well as a large amount of money they had borrowed from other people. Even today, I can't imagine how this woman could have earned my parents' trust, but apparently she managed to cheat many people, some of them government officials and managers of banks.

That night, my parents' creditors overwhelmed our house. I watched helplessly as these angry men and women shouted, demanding that my parents should return their money immediately. They had heard about our misfortune and feared we would run away, too, like their debtor. My parents tried to calm the situation and begged them to give us time. They assured them that they had every intention of returning every single cent that they owed.

At that time, Việt Nam was experiencing a terrible economic crisis: our centrally planned, socialist economy wasn't functioning as well as everyone had hoped. Inflation was as high as 400 per cent. Every one of my parents' creditors wanted to have his or her money back as soon as possible, especially when they saw that my parents had few chances to repay their debts: their teaching salaries and earnings from our field and garden were meagre, not even enough to feed their three growing children. So the creditors returned to our home every day with threats and demands.

One night, I heard shouting coming from our living room, then watched helplessly as a group of creditors charged into our dining area, bedrooms, and kitchen, taking away anything of value that they could get their hands on. Gone was my clay pig — my savings bank in which I had stored the lucky money my parents had given me during the previous Vietnamese New Year celebrations. Gone was my bicycle, which I needed to go to school and to our rice field. Gone was my cassette tape player, which I needed to learn English. Gone were our chickens and piglets, which I adored and considered as my pets.

The only objects they didn't seize were my books. Apparently, these didn't seem valuable enough to the creditors.

My world was shattered, along with my faith in human beings. I didn't know if I could trust the adults around me. Even though some of the debtors were our relatives, they had ignored my parents' pleas.

Our belongings were not worth nearly enough to cover the huge amount of debt we owed, so my parents started to ask their friends and relatives for help. But all they received were apologies or silence. My parents started to work even harder, desperately, to try and find their way out of debt. My brothers and I did our best to help. I was very frightened when the creditors threatened to sue my parents and take them to court. We had never had problems with the legal system before, and I feared the court would take away our house.

There was no one in whom I could confide my fears. Nine years earlier, my family had moved to Bạc Liêu from a small village in North Việt Nam, more than 1,800 kilometres away, so I didn't have many close friends. I felt isolated, too ashamed to talk about what we were going through. The 'For Sale' sign in front of our house was a declaration of my family's downfall. The loud, angry voices of the creditors, whenever they visited our home, encouraged our neighbours to gather, whisper, and gossip. Some of the creditors were the parents of my classmates, so of course everyone in my class knew what was happening.

During that darkest time, it was books that saved me. I had always loved to read, but until then I hadn't realised that books contained the magic power of allowing me to disappear into them, such that I could temporarily forget about my family's problems and my fears about the future. In the books that I read, I lived through the characters' struggles and understood their strengths. I saw how the challenges they faced transformed them and enabled them to grow. Some of the titles that I loved at that time were *Dế Mèn Phiêu Lưu Ký* (*Diary of the Adventures of a Cricket* by Tô Hoài), *The Boat and the Sea* (poetry by Xuân Quỳnh), *One Thousand and One Nights* (a collection of folktales from the Middle East), and *The Adventures of Pinocchio*. These were the titles that I would later bring into my debut novel, *The Mountains Sing*.

During that difficult time, I also devoured books of Vietnamese fairytales and poetry. Later, I would come across these lines from the poet Phùng Quán: 'Có những phút ngã lòng, tôi vịn câu thơ mà đứng dậy' — 'During moments of difficulty, I hold on to the verses of poetry to pull myself up.' I realised that as long as I had books to read, I was not poor. That realisation made me less afraid.

One of my favourite Vietnamese proverbs says: 'Trong cái rủi có cái may' — 'Good luck hides inside bad luck'. The bad luck was that the creditors took away our belongings, but the good luck was that they weren't readers and didn't know about the value of the books we had on our shelf. Looking back, I know now that the most precious possession in our home at that time was our bookshelf, which my father had built from bamboo he'd harvested himself, and which my parents had filled with books they had bought with their savings. My parents were avid readers, and they had chosen translated literature as well as tales written by Vietnamese writers.

We didn't have access to a library at that time, and the only bookshop in our town was a government bookshop, which sold mainly textbooks or books produced to advance the government's policies. Literary works were rare and expensive for my parents, so I held on to our books as if they were the most precious jewels. I read them again and again, so often that the covers fell off and my father had to replace them with cut pieces of cardboard as well as sewing the pages together.

Every day after school, after many hours working in our rice field or selling things on the street or in the market, I looked forward to escaping into a book. Sitting with a book in my hand, my feet were still dusty or muddy, but I felt uplifted, transformed, hopeful. Thirty years later, this experience was fictionalised in my second novel, *Dust Child*, in which Trang, a bar girl who had to serve American soldiers during the war, found strength and consolation in books.

Each evening, after coming home from work, Trang would scrub herself with a scented soap bar to remove all the filth. Then she would curl up on the floor, next to her sister Quỳnh, with a book. She re-read the ones she'd brought from home and devoured new titles that she'd purchased. The stories transported her into another world, purified her. As she travelled into women's tales from ancient times until now, into the lives of the Trưng warrior sisters, the Empress Nam Phương, and the poet Hồ Xuân Hương, she absorbed their strength.

Back in the '80s, in Bạc Liêu, we had no television or movie theatre, no phone or internet, so books were my only way to escape. And what a magical escape it was. I remember how wonderful it felt sitting in the shade of a tree in our garden, next to our fishpond, with the wind roaming free above my head. The books that I read soothed my soul, consoled me, let my imagination soar.

Looking back, I don't know how I could have coped at that time without books. And yet our troubles were not over. Our belongings weren't worth much and soon the creditors were suing my parents in court. The court decided that my parents had to pay a punishing interest rate, as high as 20 per cent per month, backdated from the time that my parents had first borrowed the money. As each month passed, our debts increased.

So my parents immediately tried to sell our house. Many people visited, but no one wanted to buy. Because the house was located right next to a large cemetery, filled with plenty of uncared-for graves, they thought it would bring bad luck. The house's location, hence its cheap price, had been the very reason my parents could afford it in the first place.

During the many months as we waited for a buyer — someone who would take away our home but would at the same time rescue us — I tried to stay calm by focusing on the work I had to do, and reading as many books as I could. I re-read the books we owned, and I borrowed from everyone I knew. When I ran out of books, I made up stories inside my head. I wrote in my diary. In those early entries, I recorded what I was witnessing around me: the economic crisis, the impact of the American War in Việt Nam, which had ended thirteen years earlier, the many people who were still waiting for their loved ones to return from the war, the many people who were fleeing Việt Nam illegally by boat due to the harsh political and economic conditions. By writing down what I was seeing, I became more curious. I paid close attention to the many turmoils that were happening around me. Unbeknown to me, I was researching the books that I would write one day.

When we finally managed to sell our house (to the unsuperstitious son of a monk who lived in a nearby pagoda), my parents used most of the money to pay their debts. With the rest, they bought a small patch of rice field behind the cemetery. My brothers and I helped them dig up the earth from half of the rice field and pile it on to the second half, to make the foundations of our new home. We used bamboo poles and coconut leaves to erect a structure with two rooms and a cooking area. Although our new house was just a hut, it became our home as soon as we put inside it a bookshelf filled with our books.

Even though we still owed people a large amount of money, I could begin to dream again. And what I dreamed was that I would become a published writer. I dreamed that one day, my words would have the power to make someone feel less lonely, less scared, as books had done for me. I dreamed that the characters in my books would inspire, give strength and hope, just like the characters in the books I had read.

These characters in my favourite books remained my friends. They travelled with me to Hồ Chí Minh City in 1991 when I passed the entrance exam to the Foreign Trade University. They cheered me on when in 1992 I became the top first-year student then won a scholarship to study in Australia.

When I arrived in Melbourne in February 1993, my parents still owed people money. My mother had to sell ice cream on the street, and my father was still working in our rice field. Being in Australia gave me a great opportunity to help: I worked in supermarkets, cleaned people's homes, saved from my generous scholarship, and sent all my savings home. I was relieved when my parents were at long last able to pay off all of their debts.

My parents have given me many precious gifts throughout my life: their unconditional love, their resilience, their fighting spirit, and their love for storytelling. My mother sang me many lullabies when I was small, and my father told me fairytales and legends. The books they gave me to read broadened my horizon, inspired me to become a writer, and enriched my life.

At thirty-three years of age, after having worked at many different jobs, I returned to my dream of becoming a writer, a beautiful dream that has now been realised with the publication of twelve books of fiction, poetry, and nonfiction. In these books, my characters continue to reflect about the importance of books and reading. In my debut novel, *The Mountains Sing*, Grandma Diệu Lan tells her granddaughter Hương, 'If our stories survive, we will not die, even when our bodies are no longer here on this earth.' Hương was twelve when she experienced American bombings. She hated America for tearing her parents away from her and sending them to war. But later, she fell in love with American people through reading American literature. She thought to herself: 'I had resented America, too. But by reading their books, I saw the other side of them — their humanity. Somehow, I was sure that if people were willing to read each other, and see the light of other cultures, there would be no war on earth.'

In my second novel, *Dust Child*, the importance of literature continues to be highlighted. In this book, not just Vietnamese people find strength in books, but Americans, too. Books help Dan, an American veteran, understand and manage his trauma. 'Over the years, he'd read books by American veterans, to try to understand his experiences, to know he wasn't alone. Still,

Vietnamese literature opened his eyes. The book that had affected him the most was *The Sorrow of War* by Bảo Ninh, his former enemy. Reading it was like looking into a distorted mirror. He could easily have been Kiên, the Northern Vietnamese veteran in the novel. The title said it all. When he told his vet friends, they were surprised he chose books written by people who had once tried to kill them. Whom they had once tried to kill. But he needed to understand the people he'd dehumanised during the war. In searching for their humanity, he was trying to regain his own.' Dan also loves his book club. 'For him, a conversation about books represented the most intimate discourse. It revealed a person's values, beliefs, fears, and hopes. Experiencing the same books enabled people to travel on similar journeys and brought them closer together.

One of the best things about being a writer is that I can consider reading a part of my job. I read every day, in Vietnamese and in English. I love discovering new writers and revisiting my favourite titles. I try to diversify my bookshelf by reading stories from marginalised groups and minority cultures. In the past, reading saved me, and now reading sustains me, gives me joy, and infuses me with new knowledge. I enjoy recommending my favourite titles to my readers. I take pride in spreading the love for reading. And I know the best gifts I can give myself and those I love are books.

My parents are in their eighties now and living in Hồ Chí Minh City. They remain avid readers. Due to my husband's job, I am a global nomad, having lived in Bangladesh, the Philippines, Belgium, Indonesia, and now Kyrgyzstan. One of the best ways for me to stay connected with my parents is via books. Our best conversations are often about books: the books we read together, the books we have read independently, the books I have written, and the books I am going to write. And every few months, I gift my parents a stack of books, ordered from an indie bookseller who helps me select titles that we both think my parents would love.

In February 2024, I returned to Việt Nam and took my parents on holiday. I will never forget those mornings and afternoons when we sat side by side on the beach in Hồ Tràm, the vast blue ocean in front of us, the soft white sand under our feet, and the tall, lush green coconut trees shielding us from the brilliant sun. We sat there, in silence, each of us reading a book. All that could be heard was the wind in the trees around us and the ocean lapping against the shore. Occasionally, we took a break, drank our coconut water, talked about the books we were reading, laughed, and read some more.

In my memory, the sky is a speechless blue above us — so immense, as immense as my parents' love and hopes for me. That sky will stay blue and brilliant in my mind, even when the sun is gone.

Author's note: I finished writing this essay on 23 March 2024. Sadly, shortly after, at the beginning of April, when I was in the US for my book tour, I received the news that my father had just been diagnosed with a serious illness. I cancelled my tour and flew home to Việt Nam to be with him. We spent the last three months of his life together. He passed away on 24 June, aged eighty-six.

My father, Nguyễn Thanh Cẩm — my teacher, my personal hero, my inspiration — lives on in my writing. This essay is dedicated to him.

MATT OTTLEY

I have remained passionate about picture books …
because I have always embraced the notion of active
participation: they are as essential to my diet as
vegetables. They make up much of the fibre of
my thinking.

Matt Ottley is an artist, composer, and author, best known for the forty or so books for children and young adults he has illustrated, written, or both. Matt's works have won many awards including the Children's Book Council of Australia's Picture Book of the Year Award and the Prime Minister's Award for Children's Literature. One of his most recent works, *The Tree of Ecstasy and Unbearable Sadness*, was inspired by his lived experiences of bipolar disorder and comprises a lavish picture book and a symphony, also a film. This has attracted international attention, including a Special Mention at the BolognaRagazzi CrossMedia Awards. As a composer, and an endorsed Yamaha musician, Matt has written scores for many of his picture books as part of an initiative known as 'The Sound of Picture Books™'. He has performed these works with musicians and orchestras across Australia and internationally.

A lineage of gifts

I have two images in my mind of the very first schoolhouse I attended as a four-year-old in the tiny township of Mount Hagen in the Western Highlands of Papua New Guinea. The year was 1966 and my family was part of the small but growing contingent of Australian expats who lived in PNG as part of a drive during the late '50s and '60s to push development in that country. In the early years of the 20th century, Australia had been granted PNG as a mandated territory and tasked by the United Nations to introduce it, with all its myriad cultures and languages, to a Westminster-style government, with the aim of leading it eventually to become a self-governing, independent nation.

Although PNG was never technically a colony of Australia, there was something of a colonial attitude in the way the Australians governed the highlands. All white people were referred to and addressed as 'Masta' by the Indigenous people, and most of the Australian families I knew had 'houseboys'. For the Australians, it was a frontier of sorts: when I was a child, the patrol officers were still making first contact with some of the very remote peoples. For the highland Melanesians, it was also a frontier, but of a wholly different kind. It was only much later, as an adult, that I came to realise how monumentally disturbing it must have been for the peoples of an ancient civilisation, one that had existed in isolation for well over 10,000 years, to have had, in a relatively short time, everything they understood about existence — their belief systems, their local politics, their perceptions of what the world was — completely upended.

My family left PNG when I was twelve, just prior to the country achieving independence in 1975. Although I could not have known it at the time, I had borne witness, in those first years of my life, to a narrative of clashing cultures, of violence and worlds in upheaval, but also of love and friendship across language barriers — a microcosm of the entire arc of human history.

My mother, Jacqueline Johnston, was one of the very few professional Australian artists to have painted the landscape and the Melanesian villages of those years in the highlands. When I was four, she did something that encapsulated that extraordinary, complex narrative as it was distilled into my childhood experience: she painted the schoolhouse.

My memories of the interior of the building are scratchy and blurred around the edges, but the exterior remains clearly in my mind because of my mother's painting. It was a small, single room of about six by eight metres with thatched walls and a thatched roof, a typical Melanesian dwelling.

My mother's painting was a gift to the community in that it is part of the record of Australian life in PNG at that time. Years later, she shared with me a photograph of the painting. Ironically, it isn't the painting that is imprinted in my mind — I've never actually seen the original work itself (it probably hangs in a home somewhere in PNG or Australia) — it's the photograph. If she had never shared this, my recollections of the schoolhouse and some of the activities there may have remained completely buried in my subconscious.

As we were looking at the photograph, a decade after we'd moved to Australia, my mother told me that there was a blackboard in the schoolhouse that had hinges on its bottom edge and a fastener at the top. When school finished for the day, the blackboard would be folded out to become a bar where the men in the community would drink at night. There was a morning roster among the women: whoever was teaching that day would latch the blackboard back to its wall setting, then mop up the spilled beer and sweep up any broken glass before the small gaggle of children in the community arrived for their lessons.

Although I have only a vague memory of the blackboard, I recall much more clearly some of my experiences inside the schoolhouse. One of these, in particular, may have been part of the mix of life experiences that determined that I would become a writer and illustrator. One day, the teacher read a picture book to the children, not an unusual happening in a kindergarten or preschool, but for some reason one of the images in that book has remained in my mind with extraordinary clarity. I can't remember what the book was about, or who authored and illustrated it, but there was a double-page image of a cow in a meadow that was one of the most magical things I'd ever seen in my short life. Although my love of painting was embedded in my relationship with my mother, seeing that particular artwork in that picture book was a wholly memorable, passion-inspiring moment.

When I was four, my mother had a small easel made for me and I would stand beside her as she painted the landscape. Gently she taught me to paint in oils, a priceless gift of love and patience. During our field trips, I'd seen many spectacular things: gatherings of 200 highland warriors, their athletic bodies glistening with pig grease, their extraordinary bird-of-paradise headdresses waving up and down in unison as they danced to the thunder of their kundu drums. I'd seen the beautiful, rare, and huge flightless Victoria crowned pigeons in the rainforest, and enormous bird-winged butterflies — but for some reason, the image of the cow has trumped them all. I'd been gifted a glimpse of a world that was so much larger than the one I knew, and more importantly, although I couldn't have conceptualised it at the time, a world that I, too, could somehow be part of because I loved drawing. A fascination for books was burgeoning in me.

At home, my father had a study at one end of our small bungalow. There was a bookcase in that room, and I was fascinated by the spines of the novels packed neatly into it. In my sixth and seventh years, I began drawing science fiction novel covers (because that was predominantly the genre my father read). I didn't bother thinking up the stories these covers would enfold. (The novels seemed to contain an unnecessarily large number of words — how could any manageable story be that long!) However, I did give them elaborate and painstakingly written titles (probably direct copies of the titles on my father's books).

Then, when I was eight, my mother gave me another priceless gift: she began sewing sheets of butcher's paper together into booklets and pasting cardboard covers onto them so that I could start creating my own stories. My love of books, and particularly of illustrated books, began in this very hands-on way. More importantly, it was an organic part of the nurture my mother gave me.

My grandmother set up a bookshop in Mount Hagen. Given that the expat population was so small, and that very few of the Indigenous people had learned to read English at that time, her little store was a labour of love more than an economic enterprise. There were no telephone links to Port Moresby (the capital of PNG, on the coast), let alone Australia, so I can only imagine the slow and convoluted process it must have been ordering books from Australia. The turnaround for mail took weeks, so it would have been months before stock arrived via the flights from Sydney to Brisbane to Cairns to Port Moresby and then by truck over the perilous unsealed mountain passes into the central highlands.

One of the books that made that arduous journey was a copy of *Digit Dick on the Great Barrier Reef* by Leslie Reese. I had only seen the ocean once, during a trip to Australia to see my other grandparents, but I'd been too young to take much of it in. I remembered the salty smell of the sea, so different to the rivers I was used to, but I was so taken with Leslie Reese's book, I wrote and drew my own version of it, called *Ottley Octopus on the Great Barrier Reef*. I recently found a copy of *Digit Dick* in a second-hand bookstore in Sydney and was pleasantly surprised to discover that my story was very different from its inspiration — in fact, it was utterly different, the only similarity being that my octopus has an encounter with a whale, just like Digit Dick. But given that being swallowed by either a fish or a whale is a fairly common meme in children's stories (although Digit Dick isn't swallowed but actually rides on the back of the whale), I think I can be forgiven for borrowing it.

My mother's willingness to sit and discuss my drawings and paintings in great detail also helped me to develop my sense of narrative and primed me for storytelling through my art. Most of my drawings up to that point had had some kind of narrative attached to them — the bird is building a nest but a storm is coming, or the cuscus (possum-sized arboreal marsupial) has climbed out of the cage and is escaping into the forest.

Picture books are, for young children, so much more than printed words and pictures: they are a part of the world of play, and as such can become a part of their physical being. Recently I read of a mother's response to Maurice Sendak about a drawing he'd made for her child. She wrote, 'Jim loved your card so much he ate it.' As adults we become consumers of literature in a different way. We engage, but we don't participate in quite the same visceral way as children do. In my case, perhaps I have remained passionate about picture books and made them a large part of my career because I have always embraced the notion of active participation. Like Jim, I have loved to 'eat' them: they are as essential to my diet as vegetables. They make up much of the fibre of my thinking.

My career as an author and illustrator began relatively late: I was thirty-one before I decided to take the leap and make picture books the mainstay of my working life. I'd had a few illustrations published in my early twenties, and my first picture book, *Albert's Rainy Day*, was released when I was twenty-two. That book was moderately successful, but only, I think, because of the diet of visual art and narrative I had received from a very early age. I really had no idea about what I was doing: at that stage, I was operating entirely from intuition. Through my twenties I did a variety of jobs to sustain myself while I studied both visual arts and music. Then, at thirty-one, I experienced — for the first time in my life — Maurice Sendak's *Where the Wild Things Are* and a door in my mind opened — just a chink — to let in a shaft of light.

As I read *Wild Things*, something wonderful was being revealed to me, but I couldn't quite understand exactly what it was. I realised that the work was a metaphorical romp through a child's temper tantrum, that much was obvious, but something else was speaking to me that was just out of my grasp — it was to do with particular details in the images. Max is naughty, so is confined to his room, in which a jungle grows and an ocean appears. He travels across the ocean in a boat to meet the Wild Things on a small island. It seemed to me that a jungle growing and an ocean appearing were not unusual metaphors for a child's imagination, but the moon in the images was the detail that really made an impact. In some spreads we see a quarter moon and in others it's full. There is a time-warping element in this work that is a subtle but powerful insight into the seemingly never-ending feeling of disquiet a child senses when they believe themselves to be unheard by their parents. They don't yet have the maturity to know that this will eventually evaporate. What happens in a few minutes *feels* like it's lasting a full lunar cycle. I only understood that, however, after looking through a book on Golden Age Dutch art one evening and coming across a reproduction of Johannes Vermeer's painting *A Girl Asleep*. That door in my mind was suddenly flung fully open and an idea came streaming in on the light that had everything — and nothing — to do with Golden Age Dutch painting.

In *A Girl Asleep*, a young woman sits at a table, head bowed as if she has just nodded off. She could also be bowing her head in prayer. Vermeer encourages us, enables us, to look closely by engaging our sense of good manners. If she were awake, perhaps looking in the viewer's direction (not even necessarily directly *at* us), we would feel obliged not to scrutinise her too intensely. I believe that even though we are looking at a painting, those deeply inground social niceties operate at a subconscious level, so Vermeer has conveniently closed her eyes, allowing us to really *look* at the young woman ... And perhaps that's because this painting is about an exploration of the deeper self, what goes on just under the level of consciousness. Just to the right of the girl there is a door, ajar, leading our eyes across a corridor into a far room in which we can see the edge of a mirror. There are reflections in that mirror that we can't quite define, reflections of the self that are in those deep rooms within us that sometimes only dreams reveal. There is much else in this painting that is enticing, invites discussion: the half-revealed slightly larger-than-life-sized egg that sits directly in the girl's line of sight should she open her eyes; the tilted bowl of fruit and drinking vessel; the foreground chair that is at an odd angle to the table. It's as if this is a house being unpacked.

It occurred to me that picture books could be an art form as powerful for adult audiences as Vermeer's image was to me in that moment. And I realised that Sendak had done exactly that — he had created artworks in *Wild Things* every bit as compelling as Vermeer's painting. It was the narrative nature of *A Girl Asleep* that triggered this idea. And weirdly, it made me think of opera. It seemed that picture books were potentially a form more akin to opera than to their closer cousins in the literary world because they are a combination of words and images: they are multimodal. Vermeer's painting has nothing to do with books (other than that it is often reproduced in them) and is not part of a sequence of paintings intended to tell a story, but it contains its own discreet narrative that can be read at a deeply metaphorical level in many different ways. There has been much debate about what Vermeer intended his painting to say, and it occurred to me that, in fact, it says them all. This to me was the as-yet unleashed power of the picture book, a literary form that can explore themes and ideas in a way unlike any other narrative-driven art form because of the metaphorical, even allegorical potential of images. Visual art is not prescriptive, so the bandwidth of meaning for individual readers is enormous. I still believe picture books are a largely untapped art form for adults that the publishing industry has not yet recognised.

The first time I experimented with a similar depth of layering to my artworks was for a book called *Luke's Way of Looking*, written by Nadia Wheatley, first published in 1999.

The corporeal relationship I have with visual arts is

something most people can relate to with music. People often talk about feeling music at a gut level. I have worked at various times in the past decades as a performing classical and flamenco guitarist. Music has also become an intrinsic and inseparable part of my career as an author and illustrator. Although I trained originally as a guitarist, my real passion was always for composing, and what began as a thwarted university degree in my early twenties has, over many decades, become a journey of self-education in music composition. I now write scores for all of my picture books, creating a series that has become known as 'The Sound of Picture Books™'. Coupling music with literature is not a new idea, but there has been little bespoke music written for picture books. We all know Prokofiev's *Peter and the Wolf*, but that was conceived as a musical work and only much later recreated by various authors and artists in book form. There's a handful of similar works, but really not many.

Along with musicians from various ensembles, I have been performing 'The Sound of Picture Books™' since 2014, and what I've discovered is just how powerfully stories can move people when their hearts are opened by music. Perhaps I've witnessed storytelling more akin to how it was before the invention of the printing press and the widespread ability to read. Once upon a time, storytelling would have *always* been performed, whether by a single individual or a group. The printing press and the spread of literacy have allowed the art of storytelling to flower in a different way, just as written music has influenced the direction of music composition: taking these forms beyond the limitations of human memory.

There is arguably one element of this original form of storytelling that has been lost in post-industrial societies: the immediacy of community. The printing press may have been the greatest gift for humanity, but like many valuable gifts, it has come at a cost.

Some years ago, at the end of a performance of a book collaboration with author John Marsden, called *Home and Away*, one of the teenagers in the audience sat sobbing. *Home and Away* begins in Australia and ends in an imagined country called Hollania after war has come to Australia and a young family is forced to leave their suburban, middle-class home in Sydney and flee on an unseaworthy boat. The story ends in a detention prison in Hollania, with the fifteen-year-old protagonist and his two siblings having lost both their parents.

When I approached the weeping girl, she said she was devastated because she had 'hated these people' (asylum seekers) and she now felt utterly ashamed of herself and her family's attitude. What I think was most powerful for that young woman was that she couldn't contain herself, that her grief was shared. There would be no turning back for her, no hiding her newfound sense of empathy and compassion. Her peers had all seen how moved she was, and I could see by the expressions on some of her friends' faces that they were shaken by her honesty. Such is the power of storytelling and the potential of picture books for young adults and adults, especially when shared in community.

When I think of my mother's painting of the schoolhouse, or Vermeer's *A Girl Asleep*, what is miraculous is that I experienced both in books — the Vermeer in a hardcover volume and my mother's painting in a photo album. Like Mum's work, I've never actually seen Vermeer's original, it hangs in the Metropolitan Museum of Art in New York, but in both cases these are works that have, in extraordinary ways, illuminated a path before me and changed the direction of my life. When I think of that young woman in the *Home and Away* workshop and the small gift I gave to her — opening a window onto other ways of thinking

— I can see the lineage of gift-giving: from my mother's gentle teaching to the extraordinary knowledge and wisdom contained in the books I have cherished, all precipitating what I delivered in that workshop. And miraculously, it didn't stop there. That young woman's grief emerged from her deep involvement in the stories that were shared that day.

We not only share stories but how we feel about them, and this becomes the connective tissue of empathy and compassion that humanises us all.

ALICE PUNG

Auntie Stella and Uncle Martin gave me a beacon of light, the gift of reading. There was no library near our house when I was growing up … But I got to go places because of these books — places that were safe and warm and suffused with love and reason.

Alice Pung is an award-winning writer, editor, teacher, and lawyer born in Australia to ethnically Chinese refugees from Pol Pot's Cambodia. She is the bestselling author of two highly acclaimed memoirs, *Unpolished Gem* and *Her Father's Daughter*, an essay collection, *Close to Home*, and the editor of the anthologies *Growing Up Asian in Australia* and *My First Lesson*. She has also written two novels, *Laurinda* and *One Hundred Days*, as well as a number of books for children. Her work has been published internationally, including in the US, UK, Italy, Germany, and Indonesia.

Alice is a qualified lawyer and works part-time as a legal researcher in the area of minimum wages and pay equity. She is also an Adjunct Professor in the School of Media and Communication at RMIT University. She lives with her husband, Nick, and three children at Janet Clarke Hall, the University of Melbourne, where she is Writer-in-Residence.

In 2022, Alice was awarded the Order of Australia Medal for her services to literature.

The gift of hope

Every year on our birthdays, Uncle Martin and Auntie Stella would drive to our concrete house behind the carpet factory and gift me and my brother a book. They brought us *Haffertee Hamster*, *Haffertee's First Easter*, and other titles from this series. They brought *Betsy Glowworm Shines Her Light* and *Friska, My Friend*. There was a biography of the African American surgeon Ben Carson. My first *Children's Illustrated Dictionary*. Even when our parents forgot our birthdays, this elderly couple always remembered. These gifts continued throughout all of my childhood and teens, until I was well into my twenties.

When my parents first arrived in Australia, they thought the government had put them in a five-star hotel. The Midway Migrant Hostel was just a group of sturdy brick buildings that looked like brown slab cakes — but compared to the cardboard and plastic tents in the camp at the Thai–Cambodian border where they'd been staying until only a month before, these buildings were evidence of a life after death: the death of half of our family in the Killing Fields. In this glorious afterlife, the residents of the Midway Migrant Hostel even had visitors, souls so pure and kind that they could only be sent from God.

And indeed they were. Uncle Martin and Auntie Stella visited the Hostel to befriend and help the new arrivals: they delivered food, gave toys to the children, and brought second-hand furniture for the families who'd moved into their own houses. They invited us to their church, but their love was not conditional on conversion. They called themselves our godparents, and neither they nor my family thought anything unusual about this arrangement.

Uncle Martin and Auntie Stella were in their seventies and had four grown-up children. When I was born less than a month after my parents arrived in Australia, they came to visit us at the hospital and marvel at the first Chinese baby they'd ever seen, with a mop of black hair. My father proudly told them that he'd named me Alice because he thought Australia was a wonderland and he was happy that I'd grow up in such a paradise. Auntie Stella wrote my birthday in her little floral pocket notebook, and every single year of my life until I became an adult, she delivered me a present without fail. They visited us at home and never judged the mess in our house or commented on my grandmother's Buddhist shrine.

We secretly wanted to believe that we were their special favoured family, but we guessed that Uncle Martin and Auntie Stella were doing this for other refugee families as well. I knew that other children's names and dates of birth would be in Auntie Stella's little book and that every year she and Uncle Martin would bring them all a gift on their birthdays, too. We did not mind this. The magnitude of their love was extraordinary, and in such abundance that there could be no cause for envy.

The books were simple, earnest, and good. Haffertee was a toy hamster Ma Diamond made for her daughter Yolanda when Yolanda's real hamster died. It was named Haffertee because Yolanda thought her hamster was a girl and wanted to bring her home to 'have her tea'. Haffertee, an inanimate toy that comes to life through sheer love, showed us the power of imaginative empathy. The families in those books also had imaginative empathy as the adults had reasoned discussions and talked to children as if their thoughts mattered.

In our world, adults were often angry giants. They loved us but they also yelled at us and controlled everything, from when and what we ate, to what we were allowed to have and wear, and who we were allowed to see at any given time. Those who have the least often have the most inadequate physical buffers against the world: the chemicals of the factories were closer to our lungs, the vehicles we drove were made of thinner metal, the clothes we wore were made of poor-quality fibres and textures.

Our parents loved us, but their love was imbued with anxiety, the real fear that bad things had happened and could happen again, things beyond mortal control. They talked a lot about who was 'smashed', who was starved, who was lost. They'd talk this way at any time — over dinner, crossing the road, looking at tins of food in the supermarket, even when they were content and shelling peanuts on the front verandah of our first house.

Uncle Martin and Auntie Stella were different. They talked to us as children, even when we failed to maintain eye contact, even when we hid behind sofas and doors, too shy and ashamed and guilty over our inability to express true gratitude. But my brother and I read the books over and over again until we could memorise lines and copy the illustrations. I even tried to sew myself a Haffertee hamster.

My parents forgot birthdays, school interviews, and concerts, not from indifference, but from the foggy-mindedness induced by the sort of invisible and exploitative work that delivered comforts to wealthier households. So, as children, we didn't know how to be likeable, no one had ever taught us. We'd only been taught how to make ourselves useful.

The books Auntie Stella and Uncle Martin gave us were all about being useful, but they also contained things that had never crossed our minds before: that work was to be appreciated, not just expected, and that it was possible to find contentment in life through living it with great care, consideration, and purpose, not just as a short 'happily-ever-after' paragraph at the end.

These were simple books, not the perennial literary childhood classics, and many of them are now out of print. Most of them — aside from the *Children's Illustrated Dictionary* — had some kind of lesson at the end. Betsy Glowworm, for instance, lit up the cave so Billy Badger could see his food, while the naughtier Beryl Glowworm kept them all stumbling in the dark.

Auntie Stella and Uncle Martin gave me a beacon of light, the gift of reading. There was no library near our house when I was growing up. Our suburb had a tool library for men with anger issues yet no book library for children with nowhere to go after school. Besides the free government guides on *Dangerous Snakes and Spiders* and the hospital's *Bringing Home Your Baby* book, for a while these gifts were the only other English books we owned. I got to go places in my childhood because of these books — places that were safe and warm and suffused with love and reason.

Over the years, there were of course presents that weren't books: a set of two beautiful knitted, stuffed dolls, an embroidery set, chocolates and Easter eggs. But these things are long gone, or passed on to younger cousins. What remain are the books.

This was the gift of reading that was given to me, and over the years I made little books for Uncle Martin and Auntie Stella for Christmas. Uncle Martin always told me in great earnestness, 'You learned English so well, we are amazed by how well you speak and read, and how wonderfully you write.' To more sophisticated minds, these words might be misconstrued as patronising. To us, they were anything but.

When Uncle Martin passed away many years after his

beloved Stella, their daughter Ruth sent me a message. She'd found her late mother's diary when cleaning the house. In an entry from 4 January 2000, Auntie Stella had written: 'We went to buy birthday presents specially book for Alice Pung.'

*

When I go to children's bookstores with my own children, I see they are filled with big bright titles like *Kindness*, *In My Heart: a book of feelings*, and *I Am Peace*. But I believe children are born with the full spectrum of human feelings. They don't need to be told how to love or be kind or generous. They also don't need to be taught how to feel the pettier emotions: annoyance, resentment, jealousy, misery.

What they probably need now, more than ever, is the power of a good story, larger than their egos or even capacity for feeling. I still have all of Auntie Stella and Uncle Martin's book gifts. This is the legacy they left us, and I will pass these books on to my children. In *Betsy Glowworm*, they may learn that just because you are having a bad day, you don't dim your light. You do not block out the light of others.

Sometimes, you just have to do what has to be done, even when you don't feel like it. I learned this lesson from watching the adults around me. They did not want to work in low-skilled jobs when they might have been nurses or engineers back home, but they did. They did not want to be polite to the racist store assistant who would never address them directly, just speak to their children, but they were. And they did not want to take anything or anyone for granted.

Every year at Christmas, we'd visit Uncle Martin and Auntie Stella. We children would sit on the floor and bask in the light of our Australian godparents — and we could see, even in the faces of the adults, that they felt truly *seen* — not for who they were, but for what they still might become.

In that diary entry of Auntie Stella's, she'd written at the very top a passage from her favourite book: 'Let everything I do reflect my love for you.'

We were blessed by this love, but through the books they gave us, the gifts of reading, we were also given the gift of hope.

DIANA REID

*... if we can lay our finger on what novels do for us,
if we can distil the gift of reading at its best, we might
be more thoughtful about how we share it with the
next generation.*

Diana Reid is an Australian novelist, currently based in London. Her debut novel, *Love & Virtue*, described by *The Guardian* as 'a formidable debut novel', was an Australian bestseller and winner of the Australian Book Industry Book of the Year Award (also the Literary Fiction Book of the Year), the Australian Booksellers Association Fiction Book of the Year Award, and the MUD Literary Prize, as well as being shortlisted for numerous other awards. In 2022, Diana was named as one of *The Sydney Morning Herald*'s Best Young Novelists. Her second novel, *Seeing Other People*, released in 2022, was also highly acclaimed. Her third novel, *Signs of Damage*, was released in 2025.

The gift of forgetting: reading
to escape our reflection

While the author wrote, he forgot his name; while we
read him, we forget both his name and our own.
— *E.M. Forster,* Aspects of the Novel

The question of which books to gift the young people in our lives is one that I am ill-equipped to answer. I had the fortune of growing up in a household that was gloriously unselective when it came to books. Books lined the walls, they were dissected over dinner, they were the most common shape beneath the Christmas tree. This atmosphere of profligate bookishness was established, of course, by my parents.

Of an evening, my father could most often be found reading in the little courtyard that adjoined our living room. He sat outside, whatever the weather: so unchanging was this habit that an awning was erected to accommodate it. (I'd always assumed his aversion to indoor reading was because he wasn't allowed to smoke inside, but even when he kicked the habit, he still ventured out beneath the awning. It turned out that his most abiding addiction — more than smoking, more than literature, even — was fresh air.) As to *what* he read, his tastes tended towards espionage. But to his immense credit, more often than not he selected a book for the sole reason that my brother or I had enjoyed it. So there he sat: in the rain, cigarette in one hand, a Star Wars spin-off, or the latest Harry Potter in the other.

And my mother was, to *her* immense credit, more generous with books than anyone I have ever met. Friends were forever leaving our house with a book in hand (less often dropping by to return them — as any reader will know, 'lending' is invariably gifting). She was the enthusiastic organiser of a monthly book group which, twenty-five years later, is still running. Popping up to the local shop to buy every member a copy of the latest month's selection, she would invariably spy something that I might like. The booksellers must have seen dollar signs whenever they saw her coming. As well as generous, my mother was totally uncensorious. Whatever she read, I could read. Anything lying around the house was fair game. If I learned about some of the worst horrors of history, or humanity's darkest impulses at a younger age than the school curriculum would have dictated, then at least I was reading.

It was, therefore, an unquestioned tenet of my upbringing that books — novels, in particular — were one of the greatest gifts in life: you could never have too many or read too much. But now that I contemplate *which* novels I might gift a young person, I am forced to ask: *what is it about books?* What — exactly — are we gifting? A good time? An education? A friend? A community?

Because if we can lay our finger on what novels *do* for us, if we can distil the gift of reading at its best, we might be more thoughtful about how we share it with the next generation.

*

I decided to start my inquiry by the usual method of approaching books: beginning with the cover. For covers contain not only a title and an author's name, but also a promise — from another author, from a marketing department — about what the book will *do*. I tried this in my own local bookshop, focusing on the 'new releases' table. One promise shouted louder than the others, repeated on every second cover:

'Charming and relatable'

'Wildly funny, almost alarmingly relatable'

'Relatable, profound, and beautifully heartfelt'

Although it's only a small sample, I suspect that these claims would be echoed in bookshops all over the world. It often seems in contemporary culture that the most we can ask from a book, from art in general, is that it be relatable. Which would suggest that the best gift for the next generation would be a book tailored to the individual recipient: one populated with characters who are, in some way, *like* their reader.

But in what does this likeness consist?

The most obvious likeness — and, I think, what is most commonly meant by the term *relatable* — is factual: a congruence of circumstance. You relate to characters who share features of your identity. You might relate, for example, along vectors of age, race, nationality, gender, or sexual orientation. When I was a young reader, I related, like many nerdy young women, to Hermione Granger, a character of my age and gender who shared my values: books, hard work, academic success. Let's call this 'factual identification' — the recognition of demographic parallels between character and reader.

It is no wonder that this mode of relatability is so widely praised. There is power in factual identification: the power, first, of self-knowledge, an enhanced ability to understand and articulate your own experiences. And then there is the self-confidence to be gained from knowing that you are not alone in those experiences. And perhaps most powerful of all is the fact that relating to fictional characters — recognising ourselves in them — not only validates who we are, but expands the possibilities of who we might become.

No doubt other authors (perhaps even some of those writing for this collection) will better articulate the power of relatability: what it means, especially for marginalised peoples, to be represented in literature. What I would like to explore is a second, subtler, perhaps occasionally overlooked mode of relating to fictional characters.

When I look back at my own reading life, I related most intensely to characters who were strikingly *unlike* me. I, an abundantly privileged, white, Australian girl, read Khaled Hosseini's *A Thousand Splendid Suns* and felt the pain, the harrowing injustice of life as a woman under Taliban rule, as if Mariam's suffering were my own. I read *The Remains of the Day* and felt the pressures of a repressed, middle-aged English butler as keenly as I did the anxiety of my own homework. And then I read Tolstoy in my twenties and found that I related to everybody all at once.

Is it inaccurate to say that I found these characters relatable? I don't think so. I was able, despite our differences, to find parallels between their experiences and mine. In *Anna Karenina*, yes, I related to the young heroine's frustrations, but I also related to her husband for his pettiness, his love of the moral high ground. And I related to the hero Levin for his existential dread, his anxiety about finding fulfilment in work. These latter two experiences of relatability were certainly not based on circumstantial *facts* about my life — needless to say, I have never been a respected official with an adulterous wife, or a land-owning master of serfs. And yet I found in these characters a semblance of my own struggles.

We relate, in this mode, not as members of particular identity groups, but as humans. No closer parallel is necessary. It is the inner life not the outer circumstance that resonates. Because we can look at totally foreign experiences and say — not *that's happened to me* — but *if that were to happen to me, I would react the same way.* Thus, we can relate to a character, to their values or particular foibles, even if we can't relate to their experiences. Indeed, we can relate so intensely that we almost forget the gulf of circumstance that divides us.

This mode of relating — let's call it '*imaginative* identification' — has many of the same benefits as factual identification. It expands your emotional vocabulary, even equips you to understand experiences you haven't yet had. And it has the effect of legitimising your struggles, of making you feel less alone. Not because we are members of the same community, but because we sense that perhaps communities might be transcended — that our membership in one or the other doesn't preclude connection with outsiders.

So we have two modes of 'relatability': one factual, the other imaginative. Both are valuable, although the former is perhaps more fashionable. So fashionable, in fact, that I worry we are losing sight of the second one, that our culture is so focused on validating identities, we forget that there is value, too, in transcending identity altogether and relating to something as banal as 'common humanity'. Indeed, I will argue that what books are *uniquely* equipped to provide, and what young people need now, is imaginative identification.

*

In order to identify with a fictional character, either factually or imaginatively, we need to have an understanding of that character's circumstances. That is, we must have a sense of who this fictional person is and where they have come from. We must look, then, to narrative arts: novels, films, television, plays.

Among these art forms, novels are uniquely positioned to engender *imaginative* identification for the simple and obvious reason that novels grant their readers access to the characters' thoughts. The sorts of similarities that engender *factual* identification are visible on a screen. A character who looks like you, who lives near you, who is the same age as you, is likely to be relatable. But to imagine yourself sharing their inner life, you need the psychological detail that only novels can afford.

And there is another less academic, more depressing reason why novels are uniquely suited to engender imaginative identification — depressing because it requires talking about books not as works of art but as cultural products for sale. That reason is: books remain charmingly, anachronistically, algorithm-resistant.

So much of contemporary cultural consumption, from streaming films and TV shows to streaming music, is conducted online. At every turn, 'recommended for you' pages tell us what we might like, based on demographic factors (are we the age, gender, sexual orientation, nationality for which this particular piece of 'content' was designed?) as well as more personal considerations. What have we watched before? Did we stop after two episodes or did we binge-watch to the end? So our tastes are gradually identified and consolidated, until we find a corner of the internet populated entirely by people who are demographically 'like' us, who like the same content as us.

Of course, books are not immune from this market manipulation. There's the annual glut of 'most anticipated' new releases, and the inevitable 'book of the summer'. There's also TikTok's ever-expanding book platform: BookTok. (In 2022, seven of the top ten books on the *New York Times* bestseller list gained their popularity through TikTok. In 2023, TikTok was credited with turbo-charging the popularity of a whole new fantasy genre, 'romantasy'.)

But! It is still possible — as old-fashioned as it sounds, it *is still possible* — to have an experience with a book, from purchase right through to consumption, wholly offline. Firstly, because bookshops and libraries, unlike that 20th-century relic the video store, still flourish. And once we have made a purchase, perhaps guided by a recommendation from a friendly staff member in a bookshop, or something we saw online, or even motivated by nothing more than a pretty cover and our own whims, then the act of reading — the actual experience of immersing ourselves in a novel — occurs offline. Yes, there are Kindles and ereaders, but there seems to be no risk that these will replace physical, printed books. And the physicality of the reading experience, its distance from surveillance capitalism's data-gathering forces, is transformative. As Zadie Smith, novelist and essayist, explains:

> A book does not watch us reading it; it cannot morph itself, page by page, to suit our tastes, or deliver to us only depictions of people we already know and among whom we feel comfortable. It cannot note our reactions and then skew its stories to confirm our world view or reinforce our prejudices. A book does not know when we pick it up and put it down; it cannot nudge us into the belief that we must look at it first thing upon waking and last thing at night, and though it may prove addictive, it will never know exactly how or why. Only the algorithms can do all this — and so much more.

Books, then, more so than other narrative art forms, are resistant to the smoothing distortions of algorithms. The author's focus, when they write fiction, is to render the fictional world to the best of their ability. They are concerned with artistic truth, not with servicing an imagined audience. So it is no surprise that their creation, when you finally pick it up off the 'new releases' table, is more like a window into another world than a mirror.

If we read always to see ourselves, looking always for *factual* relatability, then we are depriving ourselves of one of novel reading's unique gifts: the opportunity to relate to somebody who is entirely unlike us. And it is critical that we keep turning to books to seek out these opportunities, because they have much to teach us.

*

The current enthusiasm for 'relatability' in its most conventional sense surely stems in part from our culture's wariness of imagination. From the popularity of memoirs, to the push for writers — even of fiction — to limit their work to their own lived experience, we are all alert to the idea that the only way to truly understand something is to live through it. So it is important to acknowledge, before defending imaginative identification, what it *can't* do. Imagining that a fictional character's struggles and triumphs are your own, relating to them *as if* you have lived through things you haven't, is not a way to acquire knowledge. Books cannot teach us what it is to be someone else. But they *can* teach us how to care about other people. Though that might seem a modest offering, I would argue that it is an urgent gift for the next generation.

Henry James stated that the task of the writer was to become 'the kind of person on whom nothing is lost'. In order to create a fictional world, the novelist must be a finely tuned instrument, alert to the subtlest changes in emotional weather, capable of recognising the complex pulls of obligation and love and resentment that make up the fabric of society. Like dew on a cobweb, it is for the novelist to cling to these interconnecting relations and render their patterns visible.

The philosopher (and avid reader) Martha Nussbaum has argued that this perspective is not only aesthetically useful — in that it makes for interesting, complex, beautiful books — but it is also *morally* useful. When the author succeeds, the reader is able to adopt this same perspective, coolly observing the web of the novel's interrelating characters. It is from this vantage that we are in the ideal position to make moral judgements, for the simple and obvious reason that we are not *in* the novel, we have nothing to gain or lose by what occurs on the next page. As Nussbaum puts it, our relationship to the characters is the 'only human relation characterised by genuine altruism'. We are capable of seeing and judging without the distortions of self-interest.

This egoless perspective that Nussbaum describes is undermined if we are reading for the first kind of relatability. If we read looking for our likeness, then suddenly we have a stake: we want to see ourselves, or the group to which we belong, represented in a flattering light — or, at least, in a way that accords with our own view. Which is not to say that this mode of reading has no value (indeed, I defended its value above), it is only to observe that factual identification cannot promise us the same egoless perspective as imaginative identification.

To illustrate how such a perspective might be useful, let's look at a passage from one of the great novels. In George Eliot's *Middlemarch*, the heroine, Dorothea, has recently come to believe that the man she loves has given his heart to another woman. She is devastated and, over one long, lonely night, wonders how to proceed:

She began now to live through that yesterday morning
deliberately again, forcing herself to dwell on every detail
and its possible meaning. Was she alone in that scene?
Was it her event only? …

It had taken long for her to come to that question,
and there was light piercing into the room. She opened
her curtains, and looked out towards the bit of road that
lay in view, with fields beyond, outside the entrance-
gates. On the road there was a man with a bundle on his
back and a woman carrying her baby; in the field she
could see figures moving — perhaps the shepherd with
his dog. Far off in the bending sky was the pearly light;
and she felt the largeness of the world and the manifold
wakings of men to labour and endurance. She was a part
of that involuntary, palpitating life, and could neither
look out on it from her luxurious shelter as a mere
spectator, nor hide her eyes in selfish complaining.

See how our heroine gradually works towards an egoless
perspective? When Dorothea asks, 'Was she alone in that scene?',
she challenges the assumption that she is the main character.
Then, her perspective widens even further as she looks out of the
window and sees the villager with the baby — she looks to stories
about *other* people, stories in which she does not feature at all.
And then she goes wider still, thinking of 'the manifold wakings
of men to labour and endurance', to all the stories that she will
never know: the ones where she has *no* role, not even that of
spectator. Slowly, she backs away from her own ego. And with
each step, her perspective comes closer to that of a reader. For
we are not a character in this drama, either. And, over the course
of 800 or so pages, we have watched Dorothea's story weave in
and out of the stories of several other citizens of Middlemarch.

As she grows alert to 'the largeness of the world', she sees herself as we have seen her this whole time: a delicate thread in a wider, richer tapestry.

Eliot is careful, however, to distinguish Dorothea from the reader. Her perspective is not *exactly* ours, for hers is not that of a 'luxurious spectator'. She cannot just close the book, sigh, and resume her own life. It remains for Dorothea to *do* something.

Reading, then, can only show us what an egoless perspective might look like; it can provide us with an ideal to work towards. And the model is certainly useful. Because, whatever our best intentions, we can only do the right thing if we can first *see* the obligations before us: if we are the kinds of people 'on whom nothing is lost'. Whether we have the moral fibre, the energy, or the opportunity and resources to go on and fulfil those obligations, is another matter entirely.

It is certainly not the case that people who read are more virtuous or that they behave better than people who aren't familiar with a reader's egoless perspective. I am only saying that we can learn something about morality from caring about characters in novels. And, perhaps most usefully of all, we can learn what it feels like to love.

When we love someone, we care about them, not as minor characters in *our* story, but as characters in their own right. We adopt something like Dorothea's perspective. Just as Dorothea takes an interest in the villager out the window and all the men she cannot even see — our interest in our loved ones is not dictated by our proximity to them. It is an egoless passion: we do not care about what our loved ones may *do* for us, we care about them on their own terms.

Think of my father, sitting under the awning on a rainy night reading teen fiction that no doubt left him cold, just because *I* liked it. What is that if not a portrait of love? A love we practise every time we pick up a book and find ourselves caring about the characters, not because they are like us, or because they validate us, or even empower us, but because they ring true.

That, to my mind, is a great gift: to familiarise young people with the experience of loving without ego. And it seems a timely gift for the next generation, especially when so much art is dominated by Big Tech, and each industry — from music to TV and film, even publishing — is invested in turning every surface into a mirror.

*

So, after all that, which book would I choose to gift to the next generation? Well, for better or for worse, the category is now rather broad: any book that might inspire imaginative identification. In other words, any book in which the main characters are not obviously *like* the recipient. Perhaps my mother modelled the perfect approach, after all: whatever happens to be lying around the house.

But I can extract, from my exhortation to read for imaginative as opposed to factual identification, a few guidelines.

Do not worry about whether the young person is represented in the novel. Worry instead about whether it's any good.

To that end, a classic is probably a safe bet. Of course, lots of excellent books are omitted from the canon, but anything that has survived the sieve of time is more likely to appeal.

Do not worry about it being too hard. A book is like a friendship: it must be voluntary, not coerced. There is nothing wrong with gifting a young person a book that they can rise to meet when they're old enough.

When in doubt, George Eliot's *Middlemarch* might be a good place to start.

NILANJANA S. ROY

The reader's creed is simple — there is a rhythm to giving and receiving, a flow to the reading life where your pleasure is doubled by sharing all that has warmed you, changed you, helped you become more yourself.

Nilanjana S. Roy is an Indian author, editor, journalist, literary critic, reader, and book-lover. She has written two award-winning fantasy novels, *The Wildings* (2012) and *The Hundred Names of Darkness* (2013). Her third novel, *Black River* (2022), is Delhi noir fiction and in 2024 was named one of *The New York Times'* 100 Most Notable Books of the Year and an Amazon Best Book of the Year. She has also written an essay collection, *The Girl Who Ate Books*, about the lifelong love of reading, and is the editor of two anthologies: *A Matter of Taste: the Penguin book of Indian writing on food* and *Our Freedoms*.

Over a more-than-twenty-year career as a columnist and literary critic, Nilanjana has written for *The New York Times*, *The Guardian*, the BBC, *The Business Standard*, and many more. She currently writes about books for the *Financial Times*.

Nilanjana lives in Delhi with her husband and four irrepressible cats.

To Adventurers:
the world in your hands

Being enchanted, its floor was not like the floor of the
Forest, gorse and bracken and heather, but close-set grass,
quiet and smooth and green. It was the only place in the
Forest where you could sit down carelessly, without getting
up again almost at once and looking for somewhere else.
Sitting there they could see the whole world spread out
until it reached the sky, and whatever there was all the
world over was with them in Galleons Lap.
— *A.A. Milne,* The House at Pooh Corner

I found an old diary recently, a bit of childhood flotsam, with entries in turquoise, cerise, and black ink:

A True Account of the Earthly and Galactic Voyages of
An Accomplished Adventurer,
N.S.R, aged 12 and ½.
*** SORRY ADULTS NOT ALLOWED INSIDE EXCUSE PLEASE ***

The cover illustration, in vivid purples, reds, and golds, shows a rocket escaping an exploding volcano, steered by a cheerful dragon and a messy-haired girl.

The Accomplished Adventurer had voyaged to an impressive list of places: Calcutta, Murshidabad, the Hundred Acre Wood, the Emerald City, Darjeeling, Gangtok, Bombay, the Kingdom of Shundi, Narnia, Jaipur, Alwar, Bikaner, Meerut, Bag End in Hobbiton, Bayport, St Mary Mead, Wonderland, Agra, Hyderabad, Bhubaneswar, Koschei's castle and forest, Lilliput, the Sahara Desert, Alma-Ata, the Faraway Tree, Red Rock Lakes in Montana, Zuckerman's Farm in Maine, and assorted parts of outer space among them.

I guess you might argue that only some of these places are real, but to that twelve-year-old Adventurer, there was no difference between the Indian cities and towns I'd really been to and the places that I found in stories. Winnie-the-Pooh, Dorothy from *The Wizard of Oz*, Satyajit Ray's travelling singers Goopy and Bagha, J.R.R. Tolkien's Hobbits and Orcs, the Hardy Boys and Miss Marple, Alice in Wonderland, the Firebird from Russian folktales, Gulliver, the Little Prince, and a thousand other characters were my friends and fellow explorers, as much and perhaps more than my classmates from school.

Books took me everywhere, just as surely as trains and cars, and it was through the gift of books and reading that imaginary worlds and foreign countries became real to a child growing up in Calcutta and Delhi.

*

Few Indians travelled outside the country in the 1970s and 1980s unless they were students; the world was a lot more closed back then. Only millionaires, maharajahs, politicians, and criminals vacationed abroad. But I grew up with two gifts in that pre-globalisation childhood, though I took both for granted until I arrived at middle age — the broad and calm part of the river where you look back at the streams that fed and nurtured you.

I'd had the luck to be born into a large, noisy, cheerful, squabbling family of readers; books were an everyday part of our lives. Calcutta was a city of readers, in general, and introduced me to democracy in action in two forms. Bengali books were cheap, but beautifully calligraphed and illustrated, and I met readers everywhere, in the maidans and in the mansions, crossing at least some boundaries of class. And through my family's diverse bookshelves, which I was allowed to raid for the most part, I discovered that reading was a democracy in itself.

Mashis and didimaas, beloved aunts and grandmothers, who never stepped out of their allotted roles, wearing their printed silk saris just so, handling a thousand domestic and office duties without complaint or let-up, had the freedom to be themselves as readers. As a young democracy, we had already been introduced to harsh censorship in the 1970s, and would be introduced to brute majoritarianism a few decades later. But families and countries can have different Constitutions for themselves, and the unspoken rule across our family's many branches was that reading was a censor-free zone.

One aunt could smile demurely at exacting relatives, be the perfect Bengali wife — and collect shelves of the bloodiest, most chilling crime novels, dismembered bodies and grimy city streets housed right above the haldi-stained cookbooks. One of my grandmothers wore only the simplest of white cotton saris, but loved the annual Durga Puja anthologies brimming with racy fiction, along with soulful, sensuous poetry; the other, whose wardrobe was briskly bright and modern, read the Vedas and Upanishads in the original Sanskrit, but had three book cupboards packed with Mills & Boon, Silhouette, and Harlequin romances, the pulpier the better.

A great-grandfather I'd never known — he died years before I was born — came to life through his love of languages. His books, housed on the highest shelves of the family library, encompassed Persian, Arabic, Sanskrit, Urdu, Hindi, High Bengali, and everyday Bengali as well as English. They gave me a deeper sense of literature and language as another kind of clan gathering, where you could be plural, multilingual, mixed-up, and still at home. Thanks to his collection, I stumbled across Sappho:

Love shook my heart,
Like the wind on the mountain
Troubling the oak-trees.

And then the Persian poet Hafez:

The subject tonight is Love
And for tomorrow night as well,
As a matter of fact
I know of no better topic
For us to discuss
Until we all
Die!

I knew nothing about love and its thousand torments back then, but I understood that the poet from the Greek island of Lesbos (born around 610 BCE) and the poet from Shiraz, Iran (born around 1325 CE), hailed from the same family. That kinship leaps across the gap of centuries, rendering time insignificant.

*

If the first gift was the belief that literature and reading are inherently democratic, the other became apparent many years later, long after childhood. I was one of the last generation of readers to grow up before the internet, without much television.

You take the decades you live in for granted, but these useful absences pushed many of my generation of writers outside, to play in gardens and scramble around mountainsides, to invent imaginative games, to climb trees and roofs like errant stray cats. Back at home, we'd find corners where we could quietly read a book and disappear into a thousand Elsewheres.

It's harder for today's 'anxious generation' to find time to read among the many pulls and pressures of their lives, even though it's Gen Z and the Millennials who have driven a TikTok-led reading revival. For many of them, books are just one pathway in a map bristling with highways and avenues, one option in a glut of plenty, a constantly beckoning supermarket of choices. It was far simpler for us to divide the day into school, playtime, and reading hours; my schedule was never as stressful as my nieces' and nephews' lives seem to be.

I became an eclectic reader by default, but the way books come to you is rarely straightforward. Even for bookworms who know the insides of their city's libraries and bookshops by heart, much of our reading is guided by chance. So much of what shaped me comes down to the generosity of other readers, and accidents of fate and history. My father brought home Soviet books, their rich colours both startling and beguiling, from Olga Perovskaya's *Kids and Cubs* to Yuri Olesha's *Three Fat Men*. The Russian imagination sang with folklore, like our Bengali fairytales, and was backlit by a sense of faint menace, reflecting the turbulence of Indian politics. My parents' more glamorous, globe-trotting friends gave us gifts from the Free World: Archie comics, set in a cartoon-colour Riverdale brimming with burgers and drive-ins, where nothing bad could ever really happen.

My mother had briefly spent time in the US as a foreign exchange student and she made friends with the Litts, a wonderfully warm-hearted Jewish American family in New York. Even though thirty years passed before she visited America again, those bonds have endured for three generations, sparking visits back and forth across the Atlantic, invitations to one another's family weddings and christenings. We have shared a lifetime of joys and sorrows.

The oldest of their family, Gert Landau, was in her seventies then, and for the next fifteen years sent us regular packages — magical book parcels that we opened with hushed reverence, to reveal sumptuously designed editions of A.A. Milne's *Winnie-the-Pooh* and *The House at Pooh Corner* or L. Frank Baum's *The Wizard of Oz*. She sent a steady stream of *National Geographic*s, too, and one year, a boxed set of E.B. White's books.

Sometimes the books that leave the greatest mark on you aren't the ones you love as much as the ones that strike strange, new chords. *The Trumpet of the Swan* was the first book I'd read that gave words to what eventually revealed itself as a love of wild places, and wild things, not an easy emotion for a city-child to express or even guess at.

Part of my affinity with *The Trumpet of the Swan* was based on cross-cultural misunderstanding. E.B. White's protagonist, Sam Beaver, was eleven years old, strong for his age, and 'had black hair and dark eyes like an Indian'. In the pleasure of discovering a book from the Western world that featured an Indian(ish) main character, I forgot that America had its own Indians and decided that Sam and I were going to be fast friends forever.

Sam befriends a Trumpeter Swan, Louis, who can't trumpet but can spell a lot of words, including 'catastrophe'. I could spell catastrophe, too, I thought, and settled down to read, and re-

read, the adventures of Louis and his travels. And Louis stole my heart with his declaration: 'Safety is all well and good: I prefer *freedom*.' We had something in common, even if I was not a glorious swan and lacked stunning white feathers — we both loved freedom, and we were good spellers.

Sam Beaver was my first writing teacher. He journalled long before Instagram made journalling fashionable:

> Every night, before he turned in, he would write in the
> book. He wrote about things he had done, things he had
> seen, and thoughts he had had. Sometimes he drew a
> picture. He always ended by asking himself a question
> so he would have something to think about while falling
> asleep.

I cadged a notebook off my father, who was as generous with his stationery as with his bookshelves. Following Sam's lead, I began to scribble every day, not quite daring to want to be a writer, but getting there crabwise in the end.

*

Many of my closest friends are writers, and while we bring each other gifts of food and art, tales of our travels, and warm writing advice, what we most often carry from one continent to another, swearing and repacking because hardbacks take up weight and precious space, is books. So much of Indian and Asian writing is unavailable or unpublished in the West, especially when it comes to translation.

On trips abroad, I used to carry as gifts the late Eunice de Souza's *Nine Indian Women Poets*, Agha Shahid Ali's Kashmir poems, Girish Karnad's plays, Mahasweta Devi's short stories,

Arvind Krishna Mehrotra's translations of the saint-poet Kabir, and Ranjit Hoskote's translations of the mystic Lal Ded. Over time, I added books by Geetanjali Shree, Sheela Tomy, Devika Rege, Hansda Sowvendra Shekhar, Vivek Shanbhag, and many others. Poetry, plays, and novellas are wins for the modern traveller: you can fit six slim volumes into the space taken up by one Big Fat Booker Winner!

The reader's creed is simple — there is a rhythm to giving and receiving, a flow to the reading life where your pleasure is doubled by sharing all that has warmed you, changed you, helped you become more yourself. I married a reader, and every six months my husband and I sort through the flood of books that come into the house for reviews and blurbs, yielding to the temptation to keep just a few of the ones we love, but passing the rest on to local libraries. It's not hard to part with books, truly; so much harder to leave a book unloved and unread for years at the back of your own bookshelves.

*

The streets taught me what reading can be, and also what books can mean for readers who grow up without the luxury and privilege of having books in their own homes and access to libraries. India has a wealth of literary festivals, but a dearth of good public libraries, and for many, regular visits to bookshops remain unaffordable.

Over the last ten years, a wave of protest movements rolled across the country, as citizens from all walks of life — farmers, students, women, Muslims, all beleaguered in a time of growing political warfare and communalisation — took to the streets, risking their liberty and lives in their attempts to preserve democracy.

And time after time, in North Delhi and in Lucknow, in small towns in Bihar and on highways near the border of the state of Haryana, on pavements in the freezing winter, or under the makeshift shade of tarpaulins or broad banyans in the scorching North Indian summer, little libraries became places of rest, learning, and community. If you took the time to linger and talk to protestors, you were met with a kindness and hospitality that bordered on overwhelming — from cups of chai and massive steel tumblers of lassi and lunch thalis, to tips from the women on how to combat tear gas by soaking your dupatta in a solution of vinegar and salt water. I brought books in sturdy jute bags as a way of saying thank you.

'What kind of books do you want?' I asked one pavement librarian. I thought he might say more of Arundhati Roy's essays and writings, or the writings of the towering founding father, jurist, Dalit leader, and reformer Dr Bhimrao Ambedkar, or Mahatma Gandhi's perennially popular *My Experiments with Truth*.

'Everything,' he said. 'Children's books. Cookbooks. Histories. Japanese crime novels. Hell, bring me refrigerator manuals if you have them. In the lulls when the police leave the protestors in peace, they finally have the time, away from their household and farming duties, to read — and they want to read everything, absolutely everything.' Books in Hindi and Punjabi drew the most readers, but at the back of one of the libraries at the Delhi–Haryana border, I saw rows of adults poring over Dr Seuss and old copies of Richard Scarry's alphabet books — protests were a great place to step up their English-language learning. If a protest lasted for months, the libraries morphed again, becoming unofficial secular prayer rooms. Every morning, protestors would join together, reading out prayers from three of India's major faiths, for the Hindus, Sikhs, and Muslims in the audience, and closing with a prayer from the most plural of all texts, the Constitution of India.

They recited each line in English or Hindi first, then translated it further into local languages, including Punjabi or sometimes Bengali or Tamil for migrants.

> WE, THE PEOPLE OF INDIA, having solemnly resolved to constitute India into a SOVEREIGN SOCIALIST SECULAR DEMOCRATIC REPUBLIC and to secure to all its citizens:
>   JUSTICE, social, economic and political;
>   LIBERTY of thought, expression, belief, faith and worship;
>   EQUALITY of status and of opportunity;
>   and to promote among them all
>   FRATERNITY assuring the dignity of the individual and the unity and integrity of the Nation.

The promises, so familiar, shone with fresh light as their voices soared above the sounds of traffic, the loudspeaker announcements, and the frequent threats from the police.

One day at the protests, I thought I could recognise a speech in Hindi — it sounded familiar, but I couldn't immediately place the author. Rabindranath Tagore? The poet and freedom fighter Sarojini Naidu? And then it came to me: the speaker was translating the words of James Baldwin on the fly. His friend, a young woman with a serene face and a command (I discovered later) of six Indian languages, read out two sentences in English; he listened and translated them into Hindi; another young scholar, standing by his side, then translated his translation into Punjabi.

> One discovers the light in darkness, that is what darkness is for; but everything in our lives depends on how we

bear the light. It is necessary, while in darkness, to know that there is a light somewhere, to know that in oneself, waiting to be found, there is a light.

When the three had finished, the crowd of farmers, who had sat and listened in silence, rose to their feet, roaring and applauding their approval. 'More! More!' they called, summoning Baldwin's spirit back from France and America, hailing him as a fellow comrade, a friend who understood their struggles, their weariness, and their wounds, but also their aspirations and battles.

Jimmy, I thought as I hitched a ride on the back of a tractor, returning to my city with empty book bags that would be filled again and again with the books of Baldwin and other adventurers, how far your words have travelled. How far your books have come, across time and continents, to be read and passed from hand to hand, from voice to voice. Books and ideas and dreams: they were meant to travel, to cross borders and barriers, to be received and gifted and shared, over and over again.

NIKESH SHUKLA

*'Basically, the tl;dr of what's about to happen is read
what you want, build your own personal canon,
and always trust in James Baldwin.'*

Nikesh Shukla is an award-winning author and screenwriter.
Nikesh wrote the recent Spider-Man India graphic novel *Seva*
for Marvel Comics. He has published a number of novels for
adults and young adults and a memoir, *Brown Baby: a memoir of
race, family and home.* He has also written a book about writing
(*Your Story Matters*), a children's book (*The Council of Good
Friends*), and edited the bestselling essay collection *The Good
Immigrant* (as well as co-editing *The Good Immigrant USA*).

Nikesh is the co-founder of *The Good Journal* and The Good
Literary Agency, a fellow of the Royal Society of Literature,
and a member of the Folio Academy. He has been awarded
honorary doctorates from the University of Roehampton and
the University of Bath. Nikesh has been named one of *Time*
magazine's cultural leaders, *Foreign Policy* magazine's 100 Global
Thinkers, and *The Bookseller's* 100 most influential people in
publishing.

[There are no] rules for reading

No, darling child, you don't want me to tell you what to read. The shit I like won't be the shit you like. I have very specific tastes. I grew up reading Marvel comics, Archie comics, sci-fi books, books set in contemporary New York, and sports dramas. A strange combo. Hard to pin down.

You also don't want me to promise you that books will teach you to be empathetic. God, no. We both know this is absolute nonsense. Some of the most villainous people in the world are the best read. Some of the most racist, transphobic, and misogynistic people have reams of books lining their homes. It seems these books taught them nothing good.

I don't even think you want me to promise you that a book will take you around the world, teach you a thing or two, because I read a lot of books about science and I still don't really know how light refracts through an eye. I don't even think light does refract through an eye. Basically, the tl;dr of what's about to happen is read what you want, build your own personal canon, and always trust in James Baldwin.

1) Find a book that's important to you for reasons that only you truly understand. A book that changes you isn't a book from a

list of books other people think you should read 'cos it's going to inspire you, or from the great canon of the 100 best, most indispensable, and most important whatevers or whatever. It's a book that arrives in your life at the right time, in the right frame of mind, with the right amount of time to be present in it. How many times have I given a book that moved me to someone else and they thought, yeah, that was fine? How many times has someone passed something on to me saying it changed their life, and I read it, and it didn't change my life? The variables were different. The time and space were different. The arrival point was different. I guess what I'm trying to tell you is, the books that will change your life won't arrive when promised. They will creep up on you. They will find you when you least expect it. Get under your skin when you're at your most vulnerable. When you're feeling most robust. When your defences are up. When you're in a slump. When you've decided books are for losers. When you've dismissed the book. When you've picked it up because of a cover or a review or a quote from a solid writer or a first line. The sneak attack. That's what you want. I can't pass you that book. You can't even seek to earn that book. You just have to not fight it when it arrives.

2) Find a book that makes you fall in love, just a little, with one or two or more or all of the characters. The type of love where you fan-cast an actor you fancy as one of the protagonists, and then you fan-cast yourself as the love interest in your daydreams, and you stare at the wall and think, ooooh, David-Duchovny-as-Protagonist, you are a very attractive and dry man, how naughty. Oh my, Gillian-Anderson-as-protagonist, I hang on your every word, your every smirk, your every shimmy. It's totally normal to fall in love with characters in a good book. In the same way it's totally normal to run your index finger along the seams of

the empty crisp packet when no one is looking and lick the tip like it's a baby's dummy. The best books are the ones filled with characters you want to spend time with. They could be sitting in a cafe shooting the shit about how modern life is rubbish, or they could be rushing to stop the lab from exploding, releasing the zombie juice into the earth's atmosphere, or they could be falling in and out of love over quiet tender fragments of moments where everything's unsaid over three years at a prestigious Dublin college. All we want to do is spend time with them. That's love. The plot is irrelevant. It's the story we care about, the emotional journey our characters take us on. It's easier when we're in love.

3) Find a book that makes you laugh. For god's sake. There are many levels of literary elitist out there. They'll give all manner of reasons why this book is incredible and this book is a piece of shit. And these are all rules these boring bastards made up! The literary elitist I particularly hate (with the close second being the gatekeeper who drones on about how 'smart' the author is) is the elitist who thinks funny books are unworthy. How effing dull, eh? Laugh! Laugh like everyone is watching. I remember, years ago, when podcasts weren't the thing they are now, walking along listening to Adam and Joe on BBC 6, and I would find myself laughing in the unlikeliest places to someone bellowing 'maybe you shouldn't be living heeeeeere' or 'Steven!' And people would look at me like I was a strange person. What on earth was I listening to? Anyway, I seem to have crowbarred this whole narrative of being into podcasts before it was cool to be into podcasts into a list item about finding stuff that makes you laugh. Okay, yes, back to the scheduled programming.

Look, the world is on fire, and there is so much to worry about, and our phones are in our faces, we've got our noses glued to social media timelines that give you war, war, war, war, war, a nice jumper, infographic on what you're complicitly silent about, infographic on what you're complicitly silent about, infographic on what you're complicitly silent about, infographic on what you're complicitly silent about, a slimline wallet to streamline efficiency (30 per cent off). Everywhere is bad and our heads are filled with information on what's wrong with the world, what we're not doing enough of to stop the world being bad (hey corporations and governments, really? Us? Our sole responsibility?) and stuff we could buy to make ourselves feel better. The fact that I've picked up a book instead of the addiction-device, my goodness, wouldn't it be nice to be transported into a lighter realm where I can laugh. Either escapistly (not a word, I know, but I don't care, it made me laaaaaugh) or the world's fucked but here's an absurd thing we can laugh at-ly or other. With so many funny books out there, find the one that hurts your stomach as you convulse with guffaws.

4) Find all the books that James Baldwin wrote and read them. And always trust in James Baldwin. Always. I think of this quote often: 'You think your pain and your heartbreak are unprecedented in the history of the world, but then you read … It was books that taught me that the things that tormented me most were the very things that connected me with all the people who were alive, who had ever been alive.' It's from his *Life* magazine essay in 1963, 'The Doom and Glory of Knowing Who You Are'. Baldwin wasn't writing for me. And yet, on my twenty-first birthday, when two people important in my life gifted me a copy of *The Fire Next Time*, it changed everything. The effect that book had on me was beyond profound. Perhaps it was because Baldwin was writing to his nephew in the first instance, but the passion and the grace got me. Hooked me. Pulled me under its spell. There is a clarity, a moral fury in the text. It sent

me in search of everything he wrote that I could lay my hands on, eventually finding this, in an essay in *Notes from a Native Son*: 'I imagine one of the reasons people cling to their hates so stubbornly is because they sense, once hate is gone, they will be forced to deal with the pain.' The laden fatigue that comes with experience of 'I imagine ...', the double meaning of 'sense', the choice of verbs, from 'cling' to 'sense' to 'forced to deal' ... it is a masterclass in explaining the inexplicable to a child. That cliché, hurt people hurt people, it feels like it started here.

I'm asked constantly whether writing can change the world. And I think that perhaps it cannot. To speak in such a macro way, to not acknowledge that the world is filled with people and it is people who dictate its ebbs and flows, then perhaps changing the world in itself feels like an impossible task. But to move one person, to change the way they see the world, to show them the possibilities and boundlessness of their imagination. To move another, to hold up a mirror and say, I see you, to make them feel less alone, to make them feel like what they experience can make sense. That is all we can do.

But then, as Baldwin said: 'You write in order to change the world, knowing perfectly well that you probably can't, but also knowing that literature is indispensable to the world ... The world changes according to the way people see it, and if you alter, even by a millimetre, the way a person looks or people look at reality, then you can change it.' That's why we always trust in James.

5) Find books that stimulate your curiosity in the world, in people, in things, in magic and wonder and brilliance, and find them on your own terms. Books can't teach you how to care about other people. That bit's up to you. You can do it. It's the way you're raised and where you're raised and by whom and who you

look up to and how you move through the world and it's a series of choices and decisions, some made by you and some made by others, that make you think about others. Besides, do we want didactic books? Books to teach us moral lessons and tell us what to think? I hate the idea of that, to be honest. I want to see the world reflected through complicated and messy characters and maybe they can open up the way we see the world or the perspectives that guide how the world might be the way it is, but how we feel, that's up to us.

That's why I'm perpetually irritated by writers who aren't curious. Surely, kindness and curiosity are the way to navigate the world. To treat people with a basic level of kindness that isn't self-serving, and to want to know more. Writers who want to know something head out on a journey of discovery, talk to people to learn more, look up at the sky to learn more, put things under a microscope to learn more, those are the writers who will give me something. Maybe they can open the world up for me, and maybe they won't come to an easy conclusion, and maybe they won't come to any conclusion, maybe it really is the journey itself that matters and not the destination. Maybe the answer to the question is less important than the meandering we did to get to that answer. Either way, a curious writer can open things up for you.

As I said before, I have met some well-read racists, and I have met some extremely 'highly educated' dickheads, and they've all read a bunch of books, and it taught them nothing, it would seem, about the human condition. So, I'm not always convinced books can teach us empathy. It's a nice thought. But also, it's one that makes for nice memes rather than practice where it matters.

There you have it … instead of a bunch of books to read, as gifts, I've given you some rules for reading. But here's the thing: do what you want. These rules aren't for following, nor are they didactic. More, just a general feeling of why I read in the first place. You know how I said I hate writers who tell you stuff they know rather than take you on a voyage of discovery through what they don't, well I skirted close to the line of being guilty of that myself. But hey … I love being a bit mischievous. Good luck. The world is yours. It always was. I don't know if it's being handed to you in the best state. But hopefully you can make sense of what comes next by reading about what came before. I love you. Keep going. Above all else, keep going.

Here are some books for you:

A book that changed me: *The Buddha of Suburbia* by Hanif Kureishi

A book that made me fall in love with the characters: *Normal People* by Sally Rooney

A book that made me laugh: *Sag Harbor* by Colson Whitehead

A book that made me trust Baldwin: *The Fire Next Time* by James Baldwin

A book that stimulated my curiosity in the world: *When We Cease to Understand the World* by Benjamín Labatut

NARDI SIMPSON

... in the space between lines and stanza and paragraph and page, amid the foundations of word ... we, the daughters of non-written worlds, exist. It is here we take breath. Expand. Grow and play.

Nardi Simpson is a Yuwaalaraay storyteller from the north-west freshwater plains of New South Wales in Australia. Nardi's debut novel, *Song of the Crocodile*, won the 2017 Black&Write! Fellowship and the Association for the Study of Australian Literature's Gold Medal, and was longlisted for the 2021 Stella Prize and Miles Franklin Literary Award.

As a member of Indigenous duo Stiff Gins, Nardi has travelled nationally and internationally for the past twenty-six years. She is also a founding member of Freshwater, an all-female vocal ensemble formed to revive the language and singing traditions of NSW river communities.

Nardi is a graduate of Ngarra-Burria: First Peoples Composers and is currently undertaking a PhD in Composition. She is the current musical director of Barayagal, a cross-cultural choir based at the Sydney Conservatorium of Music.

Nardi currently lives in Sydney and continues to be heavily involved in the teaching and sharing of culture in both her Sydney and Yuwaalaraay communities. Her second novel, *The Belburd*, was released in October 2024.

Yilaalu

Yaama. I am speaking to you from an office in downtown Sydney. I can feel and see the bustle of George Street from my desk, the Sydney Town Hall rising at its back as trams and pedestrians fill the concrete and bitumen pathways. Here is Gadigal Land. Offices and shops now rise from the place named for the Xanthorrhoea. 'Gadi' is the local First Nations word for this plant, commonly called Grass Tree. The suffix '-gal' denotes belonging, literally translating to 'the people or place of'. This language instantly allows us to picture not only a landscape but a people within and shaped by it. Gadigal — the place of the Grass Tree. Gadigal — the people belonging to Grass Tree country.

Soak through paper and ink to this place with me now. Ask your eyes to read while your mind floats with me across this ageless yet changing place. Grass Trees rise from undulating ground. Around them, rugged Banksias push their golden cones and serrated leaves into pulsating blue skies. Bottlebrush and Paperbark and Mat Rush sway in the soft, salt breeze. Nectar-laden shafts of the slow-growing Gadi stretch high. Native bees and butterflies drink and flap at their sweetness. Green arching fronds and sturdy black trunks dominate the scrub floor. Gadi is everywhere, sprouting from rich soil smattered white — a combination of the dark ground that promote Warrigal and Yam and other edible roots and the light sand of the beaches and crumbling coast nearby. Sandstone and dirt also encourage Turpentine and Red Gum. They tower, building-like, to cast shade upon their delicate, ground-covering cousins. Golds and reds and greens and purples wink from the various flowers and grasses and shrubs of the lush undergrowth. The image made all the more resonant by the hint of salt that loiters on the breeze. It has come to our lips, through time and the page. Greet it. Roll Gadigal onto your palate if you are able. She welcomes you and wishes you joy.

Here, I wish us to peer closer, absorb ourselves into the landscape, become part of it. This is sometimes a tricky skill to pull off. Getting closer in a deeper way is not done by looking more intently. Or by concentrating harder on the thing before you. In fact, it can only be attained by the opposite. To move inside, we must let words and thoughts go. Give your head a rest. Stop looking. Forgo reading. Let your mind wander. We are forced to navigate with a source other than our eyes. When going deep, words become a distraction, a decoy to the true richness happening before us. So, invite your eyes to be torch only so that your heartwood can take over. Once you have connected with it so that it may steer you, we can go.

Although the ground is dense and sprawling, faint pathways snake through Gadigal's undergrowth. These passageways are nothing but a delicate unfolding of foliage. A Bracken Fern corrected in the slightest of turns, an exposed root smoothed. Blue Flax stems fanning to a single side rather than in a full, glorious expanse. These trails are almost invisible to the eye. Lucky we are using our heartwood, or centres, to see! Once they appear, we notice the shy trails mark much of the bush. They bring energy into the landscape. Suggest bustle. And business. How apt. The pathways are evidence of thousands of feet on innumerable journeys. Reading people in place is incredibly important. How else are we to understand the enormity of a landscape, its power and effect on us? Whenever we see country, we must also read movement of people within it. In our way, people and country are indivisible. The Gadigal pathways illustrate the beautiful way a single landscape holds slow-growing ancientness alongside vigorous progression. The tracks enter Gadigal from the west via Wangal country, the north via Birrabirragal, the south through Kaymaygal, and the south-west through Bediagal clan lands. Further afield, sections of trail wind through Dharug, Gandangara, and Dharawal nations. The lines trace wondrous possibility. They point to different environs, unique knowledge systems, particular social structures, exceptional custom, and crucial practice. Each of these are home to communities. Families. Kinship networks. Despite their understated appearance, the footpaths herald an overflowing network of ecosystems, landscapes, places, *and* peoples. Oh, how precious these pathways! They hold the imprint of peoples magnificent and complex and full.

One final dive will take us as far as perhaps we can travel together. But this journey should be easy for us now. Most of the hard work absorbing and going deeper than words allow has already been done. Through the beat of your heartwood, wherever in your body that may reside, dissolve all that you know. Don't worry, you won't be lost to yourself. Bodies know what they need and are great at taking care of themselves. Your absence will be refilled, perhaps with something greater. Clearing a space in yourself invites sacredness to enter. Now, remembering the page was once a tree — robust trunk, ranging branches, fresh, exhaling leaves — find the remnants of the tree's breath in the fibres that float around us. Then enter, nose first into its fabric.

You have found us. Welcome, my friend. Sit so that our knees may touch. Lean against my shoulder and rest if you can. It is here, in the space between lines and stanza and paragraph and page, amid the foundations of word, that we, the daughters of non-written worlds exist. It is here we take breath. Expand. Grow and play. I love this space because it is soft and generous and intimate. Here I am surrounded by creation. In this space between reading and writing and speaking and feeling, relationship is key. The filaments of paper that swirl among us were once forests. The ink that marks it once dyes extracted from the earth. They lend themselves to us in a different form so that we may dissolve between them, for they know this is rich territory for daughters of the unwritten and unread.

In the un-transcribed parts of pages, I co-create. All I am connected to join me here, in the margins, to enrich the ideas and words I will eventually make. Here, in the unwritten, I commune with Great Creators, environments and ancestral lines, am soaked in the swirling, circling time of dreaming. I am infused with the language of totem, land, sea, and cosmos. I drink from already made story, taste never-ending song, and move in time to the unstoppable dance of lore. My arrival is a request these elements effect and they grow my making. It is beautiful, serendipitous even, that I converse with the greatness beyond written language from within the structure of a typed page. From deep beneath that which is written, space bars become community and tabs the land. Full stops are hearths at which my ancestors gather to ensure the words I sculpt belong to more than just myself. It is a warm, full place to inhabit. It is also the perfect place from which to create stories that connect and share. I wanted to show you this place so that you can know that intense beauty and feeling can exist outside or under words on a page. It has been the way of many people since the first sunrise threw pink and orange and lilac into the sky.

Moving away from each other and back into ourselves — me, a Yuwaalaraay writer and maker held and loved by many over long stretches of time, and you, a stranger yet loved and held in similar ways — we can now speak freely, with certainty. Hopefully now you understand it when I say reading extends much further than words. Our starting point showed us that. Reading country is a skill, a speciality that can take us to innumerable, exciting, unexpected places. A Gadi tree can ignite chapters. Connection, story, culture, language, obligation, and country flowing from its page. Relationship follows. These are also read. My wish in our time together was to make a connection with you. I wanted this so you would understand me when I told you not all things worthy of being known are written. It is possible to orient away from words and read other things. Important things. I wanted you to feel the truth of the idea that it is good for eyes to give way to mind and heartwood sometimes. That stories can exist in blank spaces, too. That we need to believe in more than what we can read.

A preoccupation with reading does not honour the expertise of aural communities who have refined ways of embodied storytelling over generations. For us, people and places, emotions, thoughts are important archives also. This is why I shrug when authors or teachers state, 'to be a good writer you have to read.' I know there is another way. Other material that can inform and colour my world. I read country. In languages as old as speech itself but that have never, ever been captured in text. I also read relationship. I do this by using landscape as the great thesaurus of connection. My reading is a defiance, a sovereign assertion. I do it in the face of a systemic dismantling of my own native tongue. Our peoples continue to read in these ways despite the silencing of First Nations languages during the process of colonisation. It is unthinking and unfair to insist to an

Indigenous child the reading of language, writing, and words in a coloniser's tongue is the key to their success. We are the longest continuing storytellers in the world. Perhaps our techniques of aurality and aural knowledge, transmission, and teaching are something worthy of notice, too.

I formulate words between us now in this space, on this page to assert that daughters (and sons) of the unwritten must continue to read in our ways as well as the ways of others. We must pore over the textbook that is country. The volumes of relationship. Serials of connection. Anthologies of obligation. Articles of exchange. All these great texts are unwritten. And reside in people communing with place. We do not seek to have our great volumes only rest upon a shelf. We wish them to lean against family, upon a homeland, animated and buzzing within the relationships that shape it. And have it pass on to our next generation of cultural readership, so that they may add their chapters and pass on again. Yilaalu, for all time.

MADELEINE THIEN

*...what I find so unnameable is how this piece of writing
sounds a bell in me, how it will sound this bell in another,
and how I am joined to this person and to this other, no
matter the time, no matter the space.*

Madeleine Thien is the author of five books: the story collection *Simple Recipes* (2001); and four novels, *Certainty* (2006), *Dogs at the Perimeter* (2011), *Do Not Say We Have Nothing* (2016), and *The Book of Records* (2025). *Do Not Say We Have Nothing* was shortlisted for the Booker Prize, the Women's Prize for Fiction, and the Folio Prize, and it won the 2016 Giller Prize, the Governor-General's Literary Award for Fiction, and an Edward Stanford Award. Madeleine's novels and stories have been translated into twenty-five languages, and her essays have appeared in *The New Yorker*, *Granta*, the *Times Literary Supplement*, *The New York Review of Books*, and elsewhere. She lives in Montreal and teaches part-time at the City University of New York.

On Walter Benjamin's
Berlin Childhood

Now let me call back those who introduced me
to the city.

A few weeks after my fiftieth birthday, I sat down to read 'A
Berlin Chronicle' and was bewildered to find entire passages
marked and underlined. My handwriting filled the margins
before vanishing two-thirds of the way through and re-emerging
at the end. Paging through the essay, I felt unmoored: I had no
recollection of reading the work. The scribblings in the margins
offered irrefutable proof that 'A Berlin Chronicle' — described
by scholar Carl Skoggard as 'a run-on fragment' — had spoken
to me forcefully at some distant point. I saw that the reader
within me was housing another reader, a thousand other readers,
each dimly or not at all aware of the others. Early in the essay,
Benjamin asks *whether forty is not too young an age at which to*
evoke the most important memories of one's life. Is fifty, I wonder,
too late an age to wonder to whom my memories belong? They
seem to visit me from some other place. The present, this vast
sea, carries what was distant into proximity, and its waters crash
over me.

Near the opening of *Berliner Chronik*, 'A Berlin Chronicle', Benjamin writes that a person searching through their own buried past must conduct themselves with the *tone and bearing of a man digging*. I glimpse the bent form of this searcher. Hearing the clang and bite of their spade, I listen for that unknown quality: the *tone* of a person digging. Benjamin describes the places in which his childhood and youth were lived: one memory evokes the next, like notes and noticings that fragment and transform, vanish yet circle. He describes how past, present, and future coexist in a single image, as if, for instance, a ship is the past, the ocean is the present, and the hazy outline of the mountains is the future.

Benjamin wrote 'A Berlin Chronicle' in the spring of 1932. At first, he believed he was composing the preface to another piece, but this prelude quickly became the work itself. The following year, fascist laws made it illegal for Jewish writers to publish in Germany; in March 1933, Benjamin fled Berlin and took refuge in Paris. For a time, and despite the danger, he continued to publish under different pseudonyms, but eventually that, too, became impossible. 'A Berlin Chronicle' did not appear during his lifetime; today the work is included in a volume of his collected writings, *Reflections*, edited by Peter Demetz. A second — connected though very different — work, *Berlin Childhood circa 1900*, was also completed in the 1930s. Despite Benjamin's strenuous efforts to find a home for it, this piece, too, was not published until 1950, nearly a decade after his passing.

Language, Benjamin writes in 'A Berlin Chronicle', isn't the spade, the implement, or the tool, but is itself the site of memory. Interred within this site are images of the past. He warns the reader that it will not be enough to keep an inventory of the remembrances unearthed here. The richest prize is to preserve *the dark joy of the place of the finding itself*.

*

Benjamin — not a poet, novelist, journalist, or academic, not precisely a philosopher, theologian, mystic, or Marxist — was one of the 20th century's great writers. He fashioned language in ways that turned essays and reflections into edifices and passageways, rooms and galleries created by constellations of images; this, too, was storytelling. He says, quite matter-of-factly, that if he is more skilled in the German language than most of his peers, this is because he assiduously followed a single rule: never to use the word 'I' except in letters. Perhaps, without that pronoun's centrifugal force, language revealed other ways of knowing. Perhaps his restless syntax, straying from paths ordained by the word 'I', nurtured, as Marcel Proust writes in *Time Regained*, an ear and a longing for 'the only true voyage of discovery … to behold the universe through the eyes of another, of a hundred others, to behold the hundred universes that each of them beholds, that each of them is'.

Benjamin tells us that he was invited to write a series of glosses on noteworthy places in Berlin, and to articulate what the city had become for him. In prefacing these pieces, he found himself, to his surprise, relying on the pronoun 'I', which appeared useful, perhaps, as a kind of spade. Returning in memory to vanished establishments or to rooms no longer accessible, he needed the guidance of his younger self in order to find what still remained. Or perhaps, pushing open a door of memory, he found not only former lovers, barmen, shopkeepers, his parents, and lost friends, but also the same recurring yet opaque figure — the self he had been, or still remained, or had once understood himself to be.

'A Berlin Chronicle' consists of twenty-three passages that connect multiple points of space in Berlin's West End district;

the fragments are united by a quality of deep concentration and a feeling of descent — the tone, perhaps, of a man dislodging the ground on which he stands. Benjamin wrote the Chronicle in the spring of 1932, a few months before his fortieth birthday. That summer, he made detailed plans to die by suicide. He did not carry out these intentions; when fall arrived, he returned to the Chronicle and decided to recast it as a series of titled notes — 'Loggias', 'The Telephone', 'Tiergarten', 'The Reading Box', 'Misfortunes and Crimes', etc. — which together might form a unity. By the end of 1932, he had gathered forty-something notes into a manuscript he named *Berlin Childhood circa 1900*; recently, in 2015, an exceptional translation and commentary was published by Carl Skoggard. *Berlin Childhood circa 1900* is like a singular tree whose roots can be found in its shadow: the much looser, more ragged, run-on fragment, 'A Berlin Chronicle'.

In March 1933, seven weeks after Hitler came to power, Benjamin fled Germany. While searching for a publisher for *Berlin Childhood circa 1900*, he continued to revise its pieces, adding and removing passages. Six years later, with the book still without a home, he composed a foreword. 'In the year 1932,' he begins, 'while I was abroad, it began to become clear to me that soon I would have to take leave of my native city for a lengthy period, and perhaps forever ... I attempted to keep my yearning in bounds through insight into the necessary and irretrievable loss of the societal past, and not that of my own, with its accidents of biography. A special destiny, it may be, is reserved for such images.'

Both texts, which sought to call forth images of a collective past — of streets and passageways he had once traversed alongside innumerable Berliners — were published years after Benjamin's death, and both remain in print in many languages. 'A Berlin Chronicle' and *Berlin Childhood circa 1900* also outlived his family home, 4 Magdeburger Platz in Berlin's West End, which was destroyed by bombs during World War II.

*

'A Berlin Chronicle' could be read, without haste, in two hours.

It opens with a dedication to his fourteen-year-old son, Stefan, and begins with Benjamin's first memories of being led into the city by nursemaids: *Now let me call back those who introduced me to the city.* As I read, I lose the firmness of the ground; I hear the burrowing of the spade and the clank of metal against stone. Describing the removal of an ice skate, Benjamin writes, *If you then slowly rested one calf on the other knee and unscrewed the skate, it was as if in its place you had suddenly grown wings, and you went out with steps that nodded to the frozen ground.* My own feet tingle: they remember a leather skate loosened and pulled away; unburdened, my feet seemed made of clouds. Benjamin describes the facade of a building he once knew intimately in childhood; passing it years later, the facade means nothing to him. But entering its heavy doors and coming face to face with a staircase, he discovers that this particular place — at the foot of the staircase, beneath so many colliding angles — recognises him. This shock of being recognised by a site — in which he is not the seeker but the one discovered, as if he is a fragment of time recognised by a fragment of space — binds the 'I' not only to this location but, also, in unforeseen ways, to himself.

Images sharpen and constellate: he recalls school corridors, an aunt at her window like a goldfinch in its cage, a local flood in which he arrived home and took hold of the rings of the doorknocker as if they *were now lifebelts*, a telegram from a friend who had died by suicide, the affluence in which he came of age and which he took for granted, the great purveyors and procuresses of fruits and fish and birds, guarding their market stalls.

Benjamin reflects that the 'I' permits the *capacity for endless interpolations into what has been*; he also warns himself that everything that the 'I' represents — the subject-hood of oneself — *deserves more than to be sold cheap.*

For a long time, I sit thinking about the 'I' interleaved into that which was; and about the sacred trust of the 'I' that is not a vehicle, a commodity, an object to be displayed. What will each of us do with our subject-hood, this sacred trust that is our handful of time in this world? As I continue to read, Benjamin's pages open up a staircase around me. I am grateful to leave myself, to look up to where they lead, to exist beside him, listening. *You did not read books through; you dwelt, abided between the lines, and, reopening them after an interval, surprised yourself at the spot where you had halted.*

*

The man sending his spade into the soil is not looking to unbury a treasure, to disinter a body, to bury himself, or to plant a seed. We might say that this seeker is not even looking, but rather moving his spade through the ground and, by this action, making himself aware of the soil. That soil, Benjamin tells us, is the present, and the one engaged in the struggle to remember is trying to hold the present as much as the past. And maybe that is why, as I follow 'A Berlin Chronicle' with my mind, I seem to float down a hallway — as do all the objects in my vision: the little cup beside me, the candle, the phone, the thimble with flowers, and the placemat that shows various ways of cooking potatoes. The present becomes a sea in which I am suspended. Time is transcribed onto space; and in this way, I feel the transcription of space onto memory. My feet, which just a moment ago felt as if they had wings, are now confused, as if their solidity is dissolving. The present, growing larger and more viscous, blurs my edges. Outside, crickets are chirping, an all-encompassing, silvering sound.

*

The run-on fragment of the Chronicle is imagined by Benjamin as a topographical memoir and a map in which personal notes show the way to a collective life, a shared city, a lived Berlin. *I have long, indeed for years, played with the idea of setting out the sphere of life — bios — graphically on a map.* He could, he thinks, colour-code locations that have marked his childhood and youth: the homes of friends, the rooms of lovers, park benches, meeting houses, the graves he saw filled; so many sites of wonder, trepidation, lust, satiation, grief. He wonders *what kind of regimen cities keep over imagination*, and how the city — with its demands and hassles, in which the incessant struggle to survive permits the individual *not a single moment of contemplation* — compensates us, shores us up, by flowering in our memories. The city, he realises, covertly weaves a veil out of our lives.

Several fragments later, he is seized by the idea of drawing a diagram of his life, and he understands, with almost blinding clarity, how to draw such a diagram. Certain relationships, he decides, are primordial; arising from family relationships, neighbourhood, school friendships, companionship on travels, and even mistaken identity, these relationships mark separate entryways into the labyrinth of one's life. Moreover, these webs of human relation are inscribed in certain streets, roads, districts, and meeting points: urban geographies pre-trace our routes and furnish the paths along which we live. Aren't these primordial relationships, he asks, ultimately governed by hidden laws?

> 'If a man has character,' says Nietzsche, 'he will have
> the same experience over and over again.' Whether or
> not this is true on a large scale, on a small one there are
> perhaps paths that lead us again and again to people who
> have one and the same function for us: passageways that
> always, in the most diverse periods of life, guide us to the
> friend, the betrayer, the beloved, the pupil, or the master.
> This is what the sketch of my life revealed to me as it took
> shape before me ... the people who had surrounded me
> closed together to form a figure.

Perhaps this figure reveals the 'I' not as a centre but as a vessel of companionship, a needle pulling thread, a linkage whose meaning is not its stability or solidity but the way it joins and thereby creates. In ways we can and cannot perceive, we have been woven into this singular world.

My question returns: do my memories belong to me? Or have they remained in rooms and streets, and in the minds of others, inside forgotten pages, where I, too, unexpectedly encounter them? Benjamin reminds us, also, that there are places we have frequented, people we have encountered countless times, on whom we have left no imprint and no trace at all. What governs the pressure of our existence on this world, and the speed or slowness in which these traces dissolve from view?

Benjamin confesses that he wants the emotional power of personal memories, over time, to numb him to their feeling; he is meticulously planning to inoculate himself against the pain of loss. He knows he is leaving Berlin, either by his death or by exile. The exercise of the Chronicle, as well as its antecedents, is the exercise of seizing hold of memory in order to release it. I can't help but hear, again and again, the foreword to *Berlin Childhood circa 1900*, in which Benjamin writes that he is seeking *insight into the necessary and irretrievable loss of the societal past, and not that of my own, with its accidents of biography.* He communicates that all of us, not just himself or those he knew and loved, are about to lose something monumental. There is an abyss approaching, as near in time and space as the Landwehr Canal stood to his childhood home. Berlin, he says, even more than other sites, has more of *those places and moments when it bears witness to the dead, shows itself full of dead.* He taps his spade against the locations of his past, hoping that images, cut free from that era, will retain, and thus safeguard, vantage points peculiar to childhood. *For childhood, knowing no preconceived opinions, has none about life. It is as dearly attached ... to the realm of the dead, where it juts into that of the living, as to life itself.*

Throughout the Chronicle, the word *threshold* recurs, transforming, extending, and encircling its meanings. Benjamin writes of the threshold of childhood, the threshold of one's class position, standing at the threshold of a house, approaching the threshold of memory. He says that ghosts *sniff at thresholds like a genius loci* — the protective spirits of a place. A threshold might be as innocuous and eternal as a line of treetops seen against building walls; it could be a railway crossing; it could be the frontier region between the language of children and that of adults; it waits in the unmarked boundaries *that mysteriously divide the districts of a town.* At the point where two things are nearest — where opposing fields are on the verge — life pauses. Such locations, he believes, are prophesying places.

*

Each time Benjamin catches hold of a memory, I find myself submerging into a memory of my own, as if I were a net he has cast out.

I am thinking of a particular fruit and vegetable stand near to where we attended church each Sunday in Vancouver. The ground here was always slick, and the faces of the shoppers desperate and closed. This was, and still is, an impoverished neighbourhood, full of vibrancy but also human anguish; it was our neighbourhood.

Searching for what was good and affordable, my mother never showed a moment's uneasiness. Everything was precious. Everyone moved through our world, and we moved through the worlds of others. I remember looking into my mother's face in order to be reassured: was she frightened, wary, relaxed? Were we safe and could I let my guard down? In my memory, I am searching for her guidance — the silent navigation a mother embodies for her daughter; a way of being that soundlessly teaches me how to exist in the world. She has been gone for almost twenty-five years, and I have not thought of this place, this search, in decades. She flickers vividly, momentarily, into life once more.

I am a half-step behind my mother, who continues her task while I, distracted by the wind in the trees, the rumble of idling engines, a pungency in the air, lose myself in time.

*

The Anhalt Station, or Anhalter Bahnhof, was a gateway and terminus railway station during Benjamin's lifetime, one from which he frequently departed and to which he returned. The station instilled an emotional tremor in him, a *stricken violence*. He sometimes saw, above the yellow, sandy-coloured train station, the dunes of the Baltic Sea appearing *like a fata morgana.* Generated by bands of heat in the air that create a refracting lens, a fata morgana is a visual illusion: an object in the distance will appear to have iterations of itself, sometimes upside down or distorted or stacked up over and against itself — and even all of these permutations at once. It is a mirage. *But the vista would indeed be delusive if it did not make visible the medium in which alone such images take form, assuming a transparency in which, however mistily, the contours of what is to come are delineated like mountain peaks.*

In the 1930s, the platforms of Anhalt Station carried 16 million people each year, and was the largest train station in Europe. Benjamin died by suicide in the summer of 1940; displaced from Paris, he was attempting to flee occupied France. Beginning in 1941, nearly 10,000 Berlin Jews were sent from Anhalt Station to Theresienstadt, from where more than 90,000 Jews were transported to death camps. The train station was bombed and rendered unusable in 1943 and 1945, and demolished in 1960. A part of the facade of Anhalt Station remains. This ruin, which for an older generation evoked historical memory, devastation, and a warning, is, like all images, subject to time. Now it is a visual stand-in for past horror, and a disturbingly beautiful wreck. A new meaning is erasing the old one; the ruin leads nowhere, not even to memory.

Benjamin, who in 1932 glimpsed the exterior of Anhalt Station as a mirage delineating the future, observed that one's legs *become entangled in the ribbons of the streets.* The diagram of our relations, and the topography of our routes through the city, give us the possibility of glimpsing, however fleetingly, what the city has made of us. Do not let the 'I' be sold cheap, he reminds us; let go of the accidents of biography and seek out an *insight into the necessary and irretrievable loss of the societal past.* Pay attention to what the world has woven of our lives. Keep sight of the sacred, which flickers into view only through and within our entangled existences. He made a home for himself in language, and this endeavour led him to build a text made from the words of others. This unfinished creation, *The Arcades Project*, is perhaps his most recognisable work; he was a collector intent on gathering bits of text dishevelled in the air of his time.

When I read 'A Berlin Chronicle', I think of how others call me into being in my many forms, and I hope I do the same for them. How to see the present? How to face the loss of an entire city, or cities upon cities? Their buildings, their collective memories, their threshold places, their dead jutting into the world of the living, their millions of childhoods, their shadows of tree lines against walls, their fields of life where time has stilled? What are we to do? What are words against this catastrophe?

*

The Chronicle, upon so many readings and re-readings, fell into my hands again as I stood waist deep in middle age. I do not know why I reached across the shelf, hesitated, and picked it up once more. So much is forgotten, so much lies in wait. There are moments, Benjamin writes, when we are beside ourselves, and our deeper self is touched by a shock and lit like *a little heap of magnesium powder by the flame of the match*. We are granted a sudden illumination, the possession of a moment, which itself receives *the gift of never again being wholly lost to me — even if decades have passed between the seconds in which I think of it*.

These findings touch the questions — on existence, meaning, mortality — to which our lives can provide no certain answer. How do we prepare ourselves to receive a finding so valuable? There must be some activity, some internal alteration, like a clearing of the heart. *Gift* comes from the root *ghabh*, to give or receive, and is connected to the words *hand* and *hold*. In some languages, *gift* also means *poison*, deriving this meaning from *dose, a portion prescribed, a giving.* I think about the portion of life we are given, how the moment we begin to taste its wonder we are also tasting mortality. Perhaps this is why the Chronicle seems to make space for my own very personal, and quite different, memories — Benjamin's fragments concentrate their energies on calling things to life. Transported by them, I, too, am visited by the city of my childhood, my deceased parents, my family, my happiness, by rooms inside rooms, and childhoods within childhoods. We don't live forever, but we have this capacity to call out — to call things towards life.

Benjamin, contemplating insurmountable loss, facing exile from his home, entrusted these memories — no more than a series of images — to the substance of language, and thus to strangers who might one day enter the labyrinth of their pages. *But to lose oneself in a city — as one loses oneself in a forest — that calls for quite a different schooling. Then, sign boards and street names, passers-by, roofs, kiosks, or bars must speak to the wanderer like a cracking twig under his feet in the forest, like the startling call of a bittern in the distance, like the sudden stillness of a clearing with a lily standing erect at its centre.*

Today, what I find so unnameable is how this piece of writing sounds a bell in me, how it will sound this bell in another, and how I am joined to this person and to this other, no matter the time, no matter the space.

All these images, Benjamin writes, *I have preserved.*

JOHN WOOD

*Think about the next generation, the thousands
of future doctors, entrepreneurs, teachers, scientists, and
perhaps even Nobel Prize winners who will have their
chance at a better life because of the work we
are collectively doing to make their university
dreams come true.*

Talent is universal. Opportunity is not.

John Wood is the founder of two of the fastest growing social
enterprises in world history, first Room to Read (established in
2000) and more recently U-GO (2022). At Room to Read, he
was the founding CEO and later board chair, leading the teams
that raised over $750 million in philanthropic capital and have
thus far brought their award-winning education programs to
over 45 million children in twenty-eight low-income countries.
He views U-GO as his 'logical next step' — 'As the students
get older, and they ask for help going to university, how can I
possibly say no?'

John has published five books, including *Leaving Microsoft
to Change the World* and the children's classic *Zak the Yak with
Books on His Back*. *Leaving Microsoft* was named a Top Ten
book of the year by both Amazon and Hudson's Books and has
been translated into twenty languages.

John has been named by Goldman Sachs as one of the world's 100 Most Intriguing Entrepreneurs and an 'Asian Hero' by *Time* magazine. He was the inaugural winner of the Microsoft Alumni of the Year award, presented by Bill and Melinda Gates. He served three terms on the Advisory Board of the Clinton Global Initiative. In 2014, Queen Silvia of Sweden awarded him the World's Children's Prize, also called the Children's Nobel Prize. John is currently a Henry Crown Fellow at the Aspen Institute and makes regular media appearances.

From library card holder
to library builder

Wanderlust has been an omnipresent part of my adult life. I blame it on the Happy Hollisters.

Who were the Hollisters, and why were they happy? Well, you'd have to be a pretty sad sack of a kid to be a Hollister and *not* to be downright giddy with perpetual excitement, as this children's book family was constantly heading off on all kinds of adventures. They were a classic 1960s nuclear family — mother, father, five kids, a dog, a cat, and a donkey. The kids, who ranged in age from three-year-old Sue to twelve-year-old Pete, had a super-fun hobby — solving mysteries that seemed to drop out of the sky and into their lives.

The family sleuthing often involved journeys to the most fantastic destinations — Alaska, Hawaii, ancient Mayan temples, and the Swiss Alps. It seemed as if they had no raison d'être other than travelling to the most amazing places. This family was kinetic energy personified. They hiked steep mountain passes looking for a Belgian diamond thief on the run from the Swiss Guard. Headed off to Cape Cod to search for buried pirate treasure. Took overnight train journeys to Quebec. They rode horses across million-acre dude ranches in the Rockies. And best yet, absolutely everything went their way — just as the Alpine pass was closed by an avalanche, a chopper pilot would show up and offer them a ride.

What I love most as an adult who now reads to our four-year-old son, Orion, is how reality never has to get in the way of a good story. Despite Mr Hollister being the owner of a humble hardware store, and even though his wife did not have paid work, the family was somehow able to afford nonstop travel. They could get anywhere in the world on very short notice. No Hollister was ever made grumpy by jetlag, there were no lost bags, middle seats near the toilet, or flight delays. Even the above-mentioned helicopter was big enough and had enough fuel to accommodate seven additional passengers with no prior notice. And who was taking care of that donkey the whole time?

The eight-year-old version of me was lucky — my local library in small-town Athens, Pennsylvania, had the entire thirty-three-book set of Hollister mysteries. There is no way my parents could have afforded all of these books. Each promised a new mystery to be solved, a new adventure to embark on, a new part of the world to be discovered. Long before I became a backpacking world traveller, my brain was eagerly taking journeys. I'd often make 'repeat trips' — I went to Alaska three times before the age of ten. And even today, I can remember how little Ricky, upon arriving (by chartered plane, naturally) at the remote Alaskan outpost of Ketchican, yelled 'Catch me if you Ketch-i-can' as he stepped off the plane. Without being aware of it, I was learning both wordplay and geography.

*

I was also soon immersed in lessons about entrepreneurship. One day as I perused the book stacks, my eye was drawn to *One Hundred Pounds of Popcorn*. From my earliest years, I had been a *popcorn-i-vore*, as our family tradition was to spend Sunday nights viewing *The Wonderful World of Disney*, snacking on my mother's stove-popped corn. I naturally wasted no time adding this book to my reading pile. The premise was that a family out for a drive noticed that a large bag of popcorn had fallen off the back of a truck. Pulling over to investigate, they discovered the biggest bag of unpopped kernels they could ever have imagined. The parents called the company's switchboard, only to be told that as a gesture of thanks for doing the right thing, they were welcome to keep it. What does one do with 100 pounds of popcorn? Naturally, you pop it, and you sell it. The kids set up a production line — half the family was in the kitchen, while the other half was out making sure that their product sold — *mixed-metaphor alert* — like hotcakes!

Now here's the part of this essay where I reveal that I'm kind of a capitalist at heart. My parents would teach their five-year-old to count by giving me a huge pile of coins. But I decided I did not want to *count* coins. I wanted to *earn* them and *spend* them on life's most important things — candy and Matchbox cars. So, I put on my best salesman's smile and began selling my paintings door to door. Five cents a painting, and unlike Henry Ford who only had one product (the Model T — you could have any colour you liked as long as it was black), I had two — barns and sailboats. When my mother noticed me counting out a huge pile of coins and asked where I had got the money, I told her about my new endeavour. 'Tomorrow, when I go out again, I am only going to sell sailboats. Everyone likes them and I sold out. But nobody likes those dumb barns.' My mother of course tersely informed me that I would not be doing any more door-to-door selling. My little enterprise was strangled at birth.

So, five years later, how could I not have been jealous of this family of popcorn hustlers? Their parents *encouraged* them to embrace door-to-door sales in a way that would make a modern-day multi-level marketing scheme look tame in comparison. And they reaped rewards on par with modern skincare startups. I tried to imagine how many new cars *those* boys must be buying.

Every time our family drove anywhere, I would look for random stuff to fall off trucks. Never happened. But the seeds of entrepreneurship had begun to pop.

*

As I entered first grade, my parents shared the shocking news that we'd be moving from Connecticut to Pennsylvania. I don't remember how I reacted to this surprise revelation. But I do remember the bribe. As my father was overseeing the construction of a new home, he promised my older brother and me that we'd each get our own bedroom. And they'd finally acquiesce to our constant demands for a family dog.

On the day we adopted an adorable little beagle from the Stray Haven animal rescue centre, there was a family debate about what to name her. Even though I am the youngest of three, I have never been afraid to argue. And I fight to win.

'Let's call her Pretzel,' I suggested.

'Why Pretzel? That's a stupid name for a dog,' opined my older brother.

'Well, I just read a book about a dachshund. All the other dogs made fun of him for being so long and thin. But then he showed them all the cool tricks he could do, like tying himself up in knots and even looking like a pretzel.'

'This is not a dachshund. This is a beagle,' my older sister, Lisa, pointed out.

'I don't care,' I cried. 'Pretzel is a great name, and we should call her Pretzel.'

I won. Pretzel came into our lives and became my best friend. Because my siblings were five and seven years older than me, I would get Pretzel to lie on the floor while I read aloud my favourite stories.

*

The Happy Hollisters were not the only ones solving mysteries — so was my hero Encyclopedia Brown (E.B.). Or, to quote the titles of his books — *Encyclopedia Brown: boy detective*. Brown, whose real name was Leroy, was the son of a police chief in the seaside town of Idaville. The chief would often bring to the family's dinner table the cases on which he was most flummoxed. His brilliant son would close his eyes, breathe deeply, and try to find some inconsistency in the story.

But E.B. did not just help his father — he also ran an independent detective agency out of the family garage, with the aim of helping the kids in his neighbourhood to solve their own mystery cases. His fee: '25 cents per day, plus expenses'. His motto: 'No case too small.' Every detective story needs an antagonist, and in E.B.'s case it was the local ruffian and bully, the delightfully named Bugs Meany.

E.B. did not work alone — he also had a 'bodyguard' named Sally Kimball, on whom he had an obvious crush. *But hey, there's no time for romance, we've got serious cases to solve.*

It's fun to look back after a full life to contemplate the wonder of children's books, and how innocent and naive (as the father of a precocious four-year-old boy, I use that latter word in a positive way) I was as I joined those journeys. What possible expenses could a twelve-year-old detective incur? How could Bugs Meany be so vile that E.B. and Sally's cases could run to a vast pantheon of twenty-nine books? And did I really check out a library book titled *Encyclopedia Brown and the Case of the Disgusting Sneakers*?

*

It turns out I did not just read mysteries; I wrote them. And became a published author at the age of eleven. As I spent dozens of hours reading and re-reading the boy detective's adventures, I was inspired to create another crime-solving hero. It is here that I have the pleasure of introducing you to Secret Agent 117.

117 was of course modelled on E.B. He also had his own sidekick — not a girl on whom he had a crush, but a beagle with the unlikely name of Potato Chip. I spent hours trying to come up with sleuthing scenarios in our crime-free town of Athens for this brave young boy and his loyal canine companion.

And now — confession time. As a mystery writer, I had a lot to learn. First of all, a secret agent needs to be at least a tad bit clandestine. I did not have an editor, or else they might have told me that since I lived at 117 Hillcrest Drive, I should have invented a more *secretive* name. Also, my dog in real life was named after another salty snack.

These groan-inducing errors did not stop this young author from once again going door-to-door. I believed that my fiction was good enough that any housewife would gladly pay ten cents for a welcome distraction from her otherwise-humdrum days. I was not shy about ringing every bell, knocking on every door. The adult version of me thinks of the scene in David Mamet's *Glengarry Glen Ross* — 'ABC. Always. Be. Closing.'

My poor mother was embarrassed and appalled. She once again slammed on the brakes, this time on my nascent publishing empire. My only consolation — I had experience in self-publishing before it was even a thing.

*

Children's books did not just affect my childhood in a big way. They had an even bigger influence on my life as an adult than I could ever have imagined.

Partly as a result of being a lifelong autodidact, I was fortunate to get through what was then one of the most gruelling interview processes in the business world — that of a then little-known but hugely ambitious software company called Microsoft. Despite knowing almost nothing about software, I figured I could make up for what I lacked by reading voraciously. And good news, dear reader — it worked!

By 1998, I was seven years into a globetrotting career. The company was growing so quickly that they threw a lot of responsibility my way, even though I was not trained or ready for it. Because the international markets were exploding and I was one of the only team members who was not married with children, I often heard these happy words from my superiors: 'Go home and pack your bags, Wood. You're heading to Taipei in the morning.'

I found myself in the enviable position of being sent — in comfy business-class seats, no less — to far-flung and fascinating destinations — Auckland, Sydney, Hong Kong, Singapore, Dubai, Johannesburg, Seville, Paris, and London. On one long flight, after a weekend doing an add-on trip to track wildlife in South Africa's Kruger National Park, I had a revelation: 'This is an even better gig than the adventures of the Happy Hollisters.' After all, they were volunteers, whereas I was being paid a generous salary and had a nice swathe of stock options in a company whose market capitalisation seemed to go nowhere but up and to the right. 'Take that, Ricky, you little imp!'

I loved the travels, but I never really bought into the *rah*

rah rah that it was going to be technology that would change the world. I had seen so many places where people were living in abject poverty, not even able to afford food, the most basic shelter, or clothing for their children. Being in Cambodia in 1994, shortly after the end of the Khmer Rouge genocide, opened my eyes to a different need. A young man in his early twenties offered to rent me a motorbike for the day in order to explore the ancient temples of Angkor Wat. I agreed, and then he also sold me a driver — himself. 'It's very dangerous out there. The Khmer Rouge are still in the jungle and there are landmines everywhere. For an extra two dollars, I will be your driver.'

Several times during our afternoon tour, he pointed out schools that had been burned to the ground by the Khmer Rouge. It was not just the schools, the guide explained. They also threw all of the books onto the fire, and murdered the teachers for being so-called enemies of their revolution. 'How will we ever recover and join the modern world if our children do not have schools and books and teachers?'

As the hot sun beat down upon us, I tried to imagine a childhood with no Happy Hollisters, no popcorn entrepreneurs or crime-fighting child detectives. Nothing to offer a different version of the world to children whose lives had been robbed of hope. This generation of children in Cambodia would be trying to build a new world on foundations of ash.

*

A different version of this story hit me four years later while trekking in the Nepalese Himalayas in 1998. After seven years of twelve-hour days, I needed a break from the relentless pace of Microsoft. So I grabbed my hiking shoes, my backpack, and a large stack of books to embark on an eighteen-day circumnavigation of the Annapurna range, a jagged set of 8,000-metre peaks that helped to define the border between Nepal and Tibet.

At the end of a hot and gruelling first day's trek, I grabbed a shaded seat at a bhatti (local teahouse) and imagined the cold beer that would soon be in my hands. My waiter was the eleven-year-old son of the teahouse owners; he explained that they were out in the fields planting the spring crop. I had no idea whether it was legal to order a beer from such a youngster, but rolled the dice. He soon returned with a dusty bottle of Tuborg that felt as hot as my tired feet. 'This is *tato*,' I said in my best *Lonely Planet* Nepalese. 'Do you have *chiso* beer?' 'No *chiso*, only *tato*,' he replied. Then suddenly he said, 'Sir, please wait five minutes,' at which point he began running down a steep hill to the nearby river. Plunging the bottle into the icy glacier melt, he looked back up with a wide smile. 'Sir, your beer will soon be cold,' he yelled as he gave me a thumbs-up.

I heard a laugh and turned to see a Nepalese gentleman drinking his duit cha (milk tea) at the neighbouring table. 'Are all children in Nepal this clever?' I asked. He chuckled and said that many of them were smart, but that the local community lacked a strong school.

It turned out that my new friend Pasupathi worked for the education department of the local province. There were seventeen schools, but as he explained to me: 'I am the District Resource Officer. For a region that has no resources.' No longer young himself, he'd walk hours on end along donkey paths from village to village, listening politely to the requests of the teachers, but unable to offer them much more than empathy.

Then his face lit up. 'Sir, would you like to visit the local school at Bahundanda tomorrow? It's only a three-hour walk.' *Only*, I thought? But this guy was two decades my senior, wearing beat-up tennis shoes, so if he could do it … As he went to roll up in his sleeping bag, we shook hands and I agreed to accompany him, musing about how awesomely different this was from being in a crowded conference room talking about Microsoft Windows.

Morning broke early on the day that would change my life forever. Pasupathi took the liberty of showing himself into my tiny nook of a room, rousing me at 6.30 am with a hearty namaste. I have never been a morning person, and things were about to get worse as Pasupathi took a seat at the foot of my single bed, lit a cigarette, and told me how excited he was to show me the school in Bahundanda. I debated lobbying him to find me a cup of coffee, but instead rolled out of my sleeping bag and loaded up the backpack. 'If we hurry,' he assured me as he pointed upwards at an alarmingly steep angle, 'we can get to the school at the same time as the children.'

*

No day that starts with a mountain trek in the morning sunlight can be a bad day. We walked along the boulder-strewn river, a surprisingly large volume of water rushing downstream beside us. Green terraced rice fields were carved into impossibly high steep hillsides. As the sun burned off the morning chill, the only sound was our footsteps, making good time along the dirt trail. All seemed right with the world.

After two hours of flat terrain, we came upon a steep series of switchbacks — the approach to Bahundanda. This was the first of dozens of difficult switchbacks I would experience with burning pain in my legs over the next few weeks. The village clung to a lofty perch on the side of the hill, looking down into the river valley.

Pasupathi, twenty years my senior and on his third cigarette of the morning, was still in front of me. He crested the hill and without waiting marched towards the school. Children clad in uniforms of dark blue pants and powder blue shirts ran past us as a clanking school bell signalled the start of the school day. They smiled and greeted the foreign backpacker. 'Namaste. Hello, sir. Good morning, sir.'

Pasupathi introduced the headmaster, who quickly offered a tour. The first-grade classroom spilled over with students. There were seventy in a room that looked as though its capacity was half that number. The floor was packed earth, and the sheet-metal roof intensified the late morning springtime sun, baking the room. There was no natural ventilation. The children sat on rows of long benches, crammed closely together. Lacking desks, they balanced their notebooks on bony little knees.

We visited each of the eight classrooms; all were equally packed. As we entered, every student stood without prompting and yelled, 'Good morning, sirs!' The headmaster next took us to a dark room where a sign proudly announced SCHOOL LIBRARY. As a lifelong library nerd, I was excited for this part of the tour. But as we walked in, it hit me that the room was completely empty. The only thing covering the wall was an old, dog-eared world map showing — ten years after the fall of the Iron Curtain — the Soviet Union, East Germany, Yugoslavia, and other countries that had ceased to exist. The books were noticeable only in their absence.

I phrased my question in the politest way possible.

'This is a beautiful library. Thank you for showing it to me. I have only one question. Where, exactly, are the books?'

The headmaster stepped out of the room and began yelling in Nepalese. A teacher soon appeared with a key to the rusty padlock on the cabinet where the books were locked up. The headmaster explained — books were considered precious. The school had so few that the teachers did not want to risk the children *damaging* them. I wondered how a book could impart knowledge if it was locked up, but kept that thought to myself.

My heart sank as the school's tiny treasure trove was revealed. A Danielle Steel romance novel with a couple locked in a passionate, semi-clothed embrace on the front cover. A thick Umberto Eco novel, in Italian. *The Lonely Planet Guide to Mongolia.* And what children's library would be complete without *Finnegans Wake*? The books appeared to be backpacker cast-offs that would be inaccessible (both physically and intellectually) to the young students.

The headmaster had earlier told me that the school had 450 students, so all I could think about was 450 kids without children's books. It boggled my mind. How could this be happening in a world with such an abundance of material goods?

Without prompting, the headmaster then said: 'Yes, I can see that you also realise that this is a very big problem. We wish to inculcate in our students the habit of reading. But this is impossible when this is all we have.'

I thought that any educator who used the word *inculcate* with a straight face deserved better teaching materials. I wanted to help, but would it be considered condescending if I offered? The headmaster saved me the trouble of thinking this through. His next sentence would change the course of my life.

'Perhaps, sir, you will someday come back with books.'

*

A year later, I returned to Nepal with 3,000 books collected from friends from around the world who had responded to my online 'Books for Bahundanda' campaign. I had not expected to return with my seventy-three-year-old father, Woody, as my right-hand man. The trip was his reward for having done so much to help me get the book drive off the ground, and to serve as the receiving point using his garage in Colorado. He was so dedicated to the project that he had moved his two antique cars out into the harsh Colorado sunlight to make room for all the books.

And now here we were — on 'Woody and John's Excellent Adventure'. With the help of a few local volunteers, we loaded those books onto the back of six rented donkeys. The group's leader, Dinesh, suggested we 'share the wealth' so that more than just one school could benefit. This led to five times the fun. At each school, the young students eagerly greeted our donkey train. When the books were unloaded, it became a bit of a mosh pit as the kids dove upon the stack — for many, it was the first time they'd seen brightly coloured children's books similar to the ones I'd grown up with. Their eyes were as big as pizzas. Small groups would form a circle under a tree and share their reading adventures. Woody high-fived me and told me how proud he was that I'd taken on this project. And yes, I get teary-eyed twenty or so years later as I think that I have lost him, but will always have these memories.

We were interrupted by a gentleman wearing a down jacket, blue dress pants, and hiking shoes. 'You have brought so much joy to these children,' he exclaimed as he shook our hands. 'I am wondering if you can also help my students? I have walked three hours this morning from my village.' He pointed to the other side of an impossibly steep-looking mountain. He pulled an airmail envelope out of his jacket pocket, handed it to me, then held my hand in his own while looking me in the eye. 'This letter is important. I wish to petition you to bring books to my school. I know these books have already found homes. But perhaps the next time you come back to Nepal, you can visit my school.

When our students see you coming with books, they will jump so high that their heads will hit the ceiling.'

He then shook my father's hand as if to close the deal. I looked at Woody — his face was lit up with a warm smile. 'What do you think?' I asked. 'Same time, next year?'

*

From little things, big things grow. Those first five libraries soon became ten, ten became 100, 100 became 1,000, and 1,000 became 10,000. That headmaster who had undertaken a round trip of six hours on foot had convinced me that I had to — using the words of Microsoft's CEO Steve Ballmer — 'Go big or go home'. The world had over 750 million illiterate people, the vast majority living in the low-income countries where I'd travelled, like Cambodia, Nepal, India, Tanzania, and so many others. As Pasupathi had told me at our first meeting, 'We are too poor to afford education. But until we have education, we will always remain poor.' I knew that I had to quit Microsoft, because if my library project was no more than a part-time hobby, well … hobbies don't scale.

By late 1999, I had jumped out of the Microsoft airplane while praying that my parachute would deploy successfully. Room to Read would soon be born, with the goal of opening as many libraries in low-income countries as Andrew Carnegie had endowed in his lifetime (approximately 2,500). I did not have Carnegie's riches, but I had a lot of energy, was not shy about asking for favours, and at age thirty-five I had a long runway in front of me. Once I escaped from Microsoft's strong gravity field, there was nothing to distract me from the ultimate mission — to bring the gifts of reading to millions of young people who would otherwise, due to the random circumstances of their birth, never experience the same joy that had been such an integral part of my childhood.

*

By 2003, we had begun working in Cambodia and Vietnam and had both India and Sri Lanka on the drawing board. With the help of a huge global army of volunteers, Room to Read had opened our 1,000th library. And we were on track to beat old Andy Carnegie by 2005. There was just one issue. It was not enough to open libraries. We also had to become a book publisher.

My career in business had taught me that *What gets measured, gets done.* It's not enough to simply *assume* that the work you are doing is impactful and valued by the community. Our founding team decided to test our assumptions by asking the students and teachers what were we doing well and what could we do better?

Perhaps unsurprisingly, the number one response was for more books in the mother tongue. Most of the books we were providing were in English, the second language taught in the schools. But for a child to gain literacy, it's important that the books they read in school are in the language they speak at home. Every year we had a budget line for local-language books; the issue was that we could not find very many of them. Why? Because the for-profit publishers did not have the economic incentive to publish books in languages spoken predominantly by poor people. When a family lives on one or two dollars a day, children's books are an undreamed-of luxury item. So while you could find thousands of titles in English, German, French, Italian, and Japanese, good luck if you wanted them in Khmer, Vietnamese, Tamil, Sinhalese, or Nepalese.

And so the next evolution began. I was both giddy with excitement and wracked by serious trepidation over making this leap. But we knew it had to be done, and fortunately Dinesh quickly volunteered to pilot the program in Nepal. Some experts told us the quickest path would be to overlay Nepalese or Khmer script onto existing books, but we could not imagine a child in rural Cambodia reading *Heidi* or *Pippi Longstocking* and being able to relate. We made a vow — we would only publish original children's literature written by local authors and illustrated by local artists. Not only would our students have books that were culturally relevant, but we'd also be creating economic incentives out of which a publishing industry might begin to emerge. In my words: 'We will find the J.K. Rowling of Nepal, the Dr Seuss of Cambodia, the Tintin of Tanzania.' Perhaps there would even be child detectives in Cambodia solving *The Mystery of the Missing Motorbike*, or chapatti entrepreneurs in Nepal.

And it worked! The range of creativity that was unleashed was not only inspiring, it also brought me back to the childhood wonder of seeing a new book for the first time. Only now I was not the reader, but the publisher. In Nepal, Tommy Tempo (the local word for a tuktuk) was a mischievous character who kept running away from his human driver in order to splash pedestrians who were standing too close to mud puddles and steal the caps off unsuspecting policemen. In Laos, children could learn simple arithmetic by following the adventures of a dog running his own coconut cart. *The dog has ten coconuts, but one of them is stolen by a monkey. Now how many does he have?* In Cambodia, a little parrot is thrilled to be given a new pair of shoes, but he continues to misplace them, so he enlists the reader in helping him to track them down.

Again, from little things, big things grow. In just two decades, what started with ten original titles in Nepal has grown beyond our wildest dreams. Room to Read's book publishing program has created nearly 5000 original and adapted children's books. They've been published in over fifty-five languages in twenty-eight countries.

There's an adage that if any founder knew how difficult his or her journey would be, they would never have embarked upon it. To achieve the above, I was in constant recruitment mode and led this crazy peripatetic life that made my years at Microsoft seems sleepy in comparison. My road trips were often measured not in days, but weeks. During one particularly busy stretch, I did not see my home for twenty-eight days. We estimate that over twenty years, I flew 15 million miles as we launched operations in twenty low-income countries while simultaneously raising money in wealthy cities from Aspen and Amsterdam to Sydney, Tokyo, and Zurich. And yes, I gave up a lot of money by refusing to consider lucrative post-Microsoft private-sector roles. And yet … there is one True North Star that makes it all worthwhile — over 43 million copies of these books have been distributed to over 45 million eager young readers.

Fun fact: to distribute this many books, you'd need 84,000 donkeys. That would be a donkey train 150 miles long.

*

What started in Bahundanda changed my life forever. I'd have it no other way. Secret Agent 117 may never have been a bestseller in the mode of John le Carré. But for the first time in their lives, thousands of authors and artists were given a paid opportunity to show off their talents while helping their nations to develop a generation of literate young book-lovers. Instead of selling popcorn, my entrepreneurial skills were devoted to solving social issues. I did not have a Bugs Meany in my life, but I did have a consistent adversary — the lack of opportunity that prevents so many millions from reaching their full potential. And I have experienced the joy of travel to dozens of countries the Happy Hollisters had never heard of.

THELMA YOUNG LUTUNATABUA

Poetry reminds us that climate change is not just charts and numbers but also the stories our grandparents tell us, the shoreline walks we cherish, the babies we squeeze.

Thelma Young Lutunatabua is a digital storyteller and activist. She is the co-founder, with Rebecca Solnit, of Not Too Late, a project inviting newcomers to the climate movement as well as providing climate facts and encouragement for people who are already engaged but weary. Thelma and Rebecca have also co-edited *Not Too Late: changing the climate story from despair to possibility*, a collection of essays and interviews bringing strong climate voices from around the world to address the political, scientific, social, and emotional dimensions of the most urgent issue human beings have ever faced.

Thelma currently works at The Solutions Project. Before that, she worked in various roles supporting the global climate movement, as well as other human rights endeavours around the world. She calls Fiji and Texas home.

Making more magic

The first climate-change book I ever read was *Heat*, by the British journalist George Monbiot. I had just started working for a climate-specific organisation and was transitioning to the phase of my life where I was thinking constantly about CO_2 emissions and their impacts. I remember reading the book on a flight and realising that I should probably stop flying. Even before the plane landed, I was feeling the heaviness of the boulder, the perilous reality of our existence and our future. How were we ever going to get on the right track?

I have found that I often don't read as many climate books as I should. My rationale is that I work on the issue day in and day out, poring over countless news articles, reports, and social media posts such that when there is time to sit and read for pleasure, my brain seeks a release from the pressure. For so many years, all I could see when I looked at the broader reality of our climate crisis was pain, uncertainty, and enormous weight.

There's a line from the classic teen fairytale film *Ever After* where the wayward prince says, 'I used to think that if I cared about anything, I would have to care about everything and I would go stark raving mad.' Though this was said back in 1998 and in a very unserious film, the sentiment still resonates for many of us. We scroll through Instagram and there's footage of dead bodies in conflicts, then a split second later we scroll up and there's a delightful recipe for a refreshing beverage. Our brains are constantly being fractured into thousands of daily pieces of content that undermine the stability of our emotions as well as our morality. We are so afraid of opening up the faucet of caring about injustice, just in case it becomes an overwhelming flood. And so we become stunted in our work towards a better world.

There's also a new form of 'whataboutism' that is going around. If you say you care about the climate crisis, you might then get a barrage of responses: 'Well why don't you post about Congo ... or Sudan ... or reproductive justice?' This concept dates back to the late 1970s during the Cold War and has developed as a convenient way of deflecting the focus in an argument, as a tactic in political maneuverings, not with the purpose of *actually* producing concrete solutions to crises that are not getting attention or improving social justice conditions but merely as rhetorical arguments to gain the upper hand. There's a nervousness now about the possibility of being 'called out'. And so it can be easier not to care than to persevere along the path of our activist journey. The mental load of being a concerned human being feels like it's becoming so layered, so complex, that sometimes it seems impossible.

Books are critical tools in helping people figure out what they think about the world, how they want to use their skill sets for the common good. Social media and the internet can help inform — but books slow us down, take us deeper, create an atmosphere of mindfulness. We can take our time to reflect, learn, and not get distracted. Even if the subject matter engenders a sense of heaviness or grief, we can set the book down, take some breaths, and explore these emotions, not just race onwards. To make sure our minds and hearts stay intact while doing social justice work, we have to build a bookshelf of guides who can help us find our way. Even now, if I'm having a hard week, if I sit down and read a bit of Leo Tolstoy, Eduardo Galeano, or Rebecca Solnit, I'm immediately restored and better able to process what's happening.

After five years of working at the climate group 350.org, staff are offered a sabbatical, a much-needed opportunity for rejuvenation. For the first two weeks, I had daily to-do lists, which meant that my brain was still in a constant state of hectic rustling. However, one day at the beach, I sat and watched the coconut trees sway and sway and sway — and I realised that I needed to embrace stillness. I deleted my social media apps and for the rest of my sabbatical immersed myself in the glorious pages of books.

I was hungry to learn more about the world we could build. So many climate organisations are great at speaking to what we must fight against — the fossil fuel industry, injustice, political corruption — but not always so effective at articulating what we are fighting for and the world we can create. I sat outside as often as possible and read through the wisdom of Grace Lee Boggs and especially her book *The Next American Revolution*. She writes: 'The physical threat posed by climate change represents a crisis that is not only material but also profoundly spiritual at its core because it challenges us to think seriously about the future of the human race and what it means to be a human being.' I searched for examples of a non-dystopian future (which are shockingly hard to find). Thankfully, adrienne maree brown and Walidah Imarisha put together a collection of stories from various writers, called *Octavia's Brood*. Referencing the visionary work of Octavia Butler, they write in the introduction: 'Whenever we try to envision a world without war, without violence, without prisons, without capitalism, we are engaging in speculative fiction. All organising is science fiction.' I continued to let my imagination explore and tantalisingly experiment with what life could look like if we got things right. The beautiful reality is that once you start looking for solutions and possibilities, you see them more and more.

During my sabbatical, I also let myself read poetry again. And it's odd to say 'let myself' — because even that is a testimony to the twisted pressures of productivity imposed by our society. Poetry is an essential part of our fight for a livable future, not least because it can embrace the complexities of death, destruction, hope, and courage in ways that prose can't. When I was at the COP21 Paris climate talks I saw a swarm of journalists surrounding the poet Kathy Jetñil-Kijiner. Coming from the Marshall Islands, a low-lying atoll nation highly at risk from rising sea levels, Kathy's poetry is abundant with an urgency to act, as well as an urgency to nourish culture and community. Kathy's devotion to her family and her islands was a percussive wave of emotion that struck every activist, journalist, and delegate on that day. One of her most well-known poems, 'Dear Matafele Peinem', was written for her daughter and performed at the opening ceremony of the UN Secretary-General's Climate Summit in 2014:

Here's a short extract:

no one's drowning, baby
no one's moving
no one's losing
their homeland
no one's gonna become
a climate change refugee

or should i say
no one else.

Poetry reminds us that climate change is not just charts and numbers but also the stories our grandparents tell us, the shoreline walks we cherish, the babies we squeeze. It teaches us how to hold grief, uncertainty, possibility, and love, all at the same time.

Poetry also enforces a change in pace, prompts us to breathe — and breath is an essential part of revolution, quietening, centring, helping us not to go stark raving mad. Many years ago, I was learning how to meditate from the Burmese activist monk Ashin Issariya. Living in exile after propelling the 2007 revolution, he never gave up on his efforts for a better world. We would meditate together and then discuss and reflect, inevitably ending up in a discussion about politics. So one day I asked him — how can you be present in the world as a meditative practice dictates, while also planning future social justice campaigns? He reminded me that you can never plan for the future unless you are grounded in the present. If we lurch forward in a constant state of panic and fear, we will inevitably accept solutions that carry the potential for more harm. Poetry is the pause we need to reconnect, touch the earth, reflect, and reconsider our ways.

These days, when I read books, it's mostly at the end of the day, when I sit with my young son. We go through his bookshelf and pull out many of his favourites, taking time to cuddle and laugh. My husband and I met while doing climate campaigning and so we often discuss not just what the future will look like for our son, but how we will raise him. One of the books that is helping with that discussion is *The World Is Ours to Cherish: a letter to a child* by Mary Annaïse Heglar. She begins the book by saying, 'There is magic all around you,' then journeys with the reader through the imagery of our magically beautiful world, how it's changing, and then how we'll protect it: 'We'll build a world where we take the magic we have and use it to make more.'

So much of the climate crisis is an imagination crisis. We are trained by disaster films, nightmarish headlines, and endless streams of doom that a bleak future is inevitable. We need books, we need poetry to help us see the magic all around us, as well as the magic that could be. I would also encourage people to read not just nonfiction books about politics, economics, and the environment, but also works of fiction.

Right now we need tales of heroes. We need reminders that people can band together to defeat evil. In our climate work, hope is a valuable emotion — but so is courage. There's a reason we still reference David versus Goliath in social justice campaigns. The story continues to be a reminder that even if you are small, a well-targeted shot can destroy even the most powerful.

The future is not certain, but in that space there is so much possibility. We need people with imagination who can see new ways of being, and we need people ready to rally their courage and take on this enormous quest.

Afterword

JULIA ECCLESHARE

The simple and unbridled delight in the stories absorbed in childhood, and the extraordinary influence they have on a lifetime, are celebrated in each of the moving and meaningful essays in this collection. Steeped in nostalgia of the best kind, each contribution draws on the details of the writer's childhood experiences of reading, sometimes as a very young child, sometimes later on in life. For many, their thoughtful consideration of their early encounters with reading and the profound and lasting effects of those stories, leads them to conclude that childhood reading may be the most important reading experience of a lifetime.

Why those stories reverberate, and why they burn such a lasting impression that they urgently need to be shared with the next generation, has no precise answer. The joy of this collection is that the universality of these reading experiences is threaded through these essays as each contributor conjures up the intensity of their own memories.

Having listened to many people talk about how they became a writer, I know that behind every writer there is a child who was enchanted by story. But becoming a reader, a child for whom books really matter, requires a meaningful introduction to books and stories as well as access. In these essays, the precise alchemy that shapes each reading path depends on cultural and individual circumstances — but being given books or borrowing them from the local library underpins many of the childhood memories recalled, many of them strongly associated with a person or a place.

For Shankari Chandran it was her Appamma who soothed her to sleep with stories from the *Mahabharata*, while for Horatio Clare, the last thing he heard at the end of every day was his father reading aloud in his beautiful voice, 'soft, rich, and clever'. For both of these writers, the source of the story is associated with love and the intimacy of sharing something special. It is not the book alone that holds the power, it is also the web of emotions that matters. In the absence of a person who could provide that in her early years, Alice Pung, a child refugee from Cambodia at the time of Pol Pot, was given what she describes as 'a beacon of light, the gift of reading' by her adoptive godparents in Australia. 'I got to go places because of these books — places that were safe and warm and suffused with love and reason.'

That gift of travelling through time and space, bolstered by human understanding and empathy, is described by many contributors as the greatest of all the things that reading can do. For Imtiaz Dharker it is poetry that fills the role most perfectly. She makes her claim profoundly when she writes, 'Poetry travels without a passport. It is able to eavesdrop on the world. It says things the heart knows before the world catches up.' Ursula Dubosarsky's reflections on herself as a reading child are similarly expressed with passion: 'As I read and re-read the stories, I knew that more than anything that I wanted to enter this world, this realm of ideas, of beauty, of the imagination, of the impossible. This is what reading is for.'

For others, the gift of reading in childhood was the mind-blowing expansion in otherwise unobtainable knowledge. Tristan Bancks remembers going to the public library 'partly to disappear into other worlds'. The other world he best remembers finding came from a sex education book. 'Surely this wasn't how babies were made. Couldn't be. Reading it was a communal, educational and subversive pursuit. It blew our little minds. A gift, indeed.' Nicola Davies was also impressed by the other worlds entered through information books and especially their illustrations. Reflecting on the impact of the illustrations in the encyclopedias her father bought from a door-to-door salesman, she extols the importance of picture books in sharing the gifts of reading. 'The books I most often give to both children and adults are picture books. They cut to the chase. They deal with big things in a way that delivers clear understanding at an emotional level.'

From the oldest fairy stories, myths, and legends to the newest social and political commentary, stories for children have presented everyday guidance and moral choices in the least didactic way. From their earliest exposure, readers learn about fear and friendship, honesty and trickery, inclusion and discrimination. Absorbed young, these experiences simply become part of how a reading child views the world. Pico Iyer's essay is an introduction to the children's books that have guided him through life, including Michael Bond's stories of Paddington Bear and the fantasies of Ursula Le Guin. He stresses how much these books matter. And he goes further in expressing his heartfelt belief that books and literature exercise power 'in the use of the law and debate to determine what society sees as the ever changing "limits" to freedom of speech'.

Other ideas abound throughout this collection, showing the power and beauty of stories, reading across time and place and in different forms. In the hands of these brilliant writers of today who remember their reading experiences from the past, this is a wonderfully diverse collection of essays that is as full of surprises as it is of heartwarming moments of recognition.

Truly, these are gifts of reading to be shared with the next generation.

The gifts of reading for
the next generation

Robert Macfarlane

Maurice Sendak, *Where the Wild Things Are*

Reader's Digest *Field Guide to the Birds of Britain*

Susan Cooper, *The Dark is Rising*

Ursula K. Le Guin, *A Wizard of Earthsea*

Victor Kelleher, *Forbidden Paths of Thual*

Jennie Orchard

Vera Brittain, *Testament of Youth*

Kahlil Gibran, *The Prophet*

Steve McCurry, *On Reading*

Meg McKinlay and Matt Ottley (illustrator and composer), *How to Make a Bird* (from Matt Ottley's 'Sound of Picture Books™')

John Marsden, *Prayer for the Twenty-First Century*

Dina Nayeri, *The Ungrateful Refugee*

Maria Popova and Claudia Zoe Bedrick (editors), *A Velocity of Being: letters to a young reader*

Tristan Bancks

Gus Gordon, *Herman and Rosie*

Jean Craighead George, *My Side of the Mountain*

Gary Paulsen, *Hatchet*

Louis Sachar, *Holes*

Morris Gleitzman, *Once*

Katrina Nannestad, *We Are Wolves*

Claire Zorn, *The Sky So Heavy*

William Boyd

Rudyard Kipling, *The Jungle Book*

H. Rider Haggard, *King Solomon's Mines*

H. Rider Haggard, *Allan Quatermain*

H. Rider Haggard, *She: a history of adventure*

H. Rider Haggard, *Nada the Lily*

Shankari Chandran

Veda Vyasa, *Mahabharata*

Kamila Shamsie, *Home Fire*

Arundhati Roy, *The God of Small Things*

Louisa May Alcott, *Little Women*

Christine Shamista, *Soft Side of Red*

Horatio Clare

Bill Peet, *The Gnats of Knotty Pine*

Russell Hoban, *The Mouse and His Child*

Philip Hoare, *Leviathan*

Robert Westall, *The Machine Gunners*

Astrid Lindgren, *The Brothers Lionheart*

Nicola Davies

Shaun Tan, *The Red Tree*

Maria Gulemetova, *Beyond the Fence*

Barroux, *Where's the Elephant?*

Mariajo Illustrajo, *Flooded*

Robert Macfarlane and Jackie Morris (illustrator), *The Lost Words*

Nicola Davies and Jackie Morris (illustrator), *Skrimsli*

W. Keble Martin, *The Concise British Flora in Colour*

Imtiaz Dharker

Pascale Petit, *Mama Amazonica*

Carol Ann Duffy, *The World's Wife*

Neil Astley (editor), *Staying Human*

Jean Rhys, *Wide Sargasso Sea*

Audre Lorde, *Sister Outsider*

Ursula Dubosarsky

Junko Nakamura, *Chez Bergamote*

Madeleine Winch, *Come by Chance*

Arnold Lobel, *Fables*

Ulf Nilsson and Anna-Clara Tidholm (illustrator), *Goodbye Mr Muffin*

Marcia Williams, *Greek Myths*

Maisie Fieschi

Geoffrey McSkimming, *Cairo Jim in Search of Martenarten: a tale of archaeology, adventure, and astonishment*

William Makepeace Thackeray, *The Rose and the Ring*

Ursula Dubosarsky and Tohby Riddle (illustrator), *The March of the Ants*

May Gibbs, *Snugglepot and Cuddlepie*

Joan Lindsay, *Picnic at Hanging Rock*

Ethel Turner, *Seven Little Australians*

Pico Iyer

Michael Bond, *A Bear Called Paddington*

Ursula K. Le Guin, *A Wizard of Earthsea*

Hergé, *Tintin in Tibet*

Peter S. Beagle, *The Last Unicorn*

Alan Garner, *Red Shift*

Wayne Karlin

Leo Tolstoy, *Anna Karenina*

Isaac Babel, *Red Cavalry and Other Stories*

Barbara Kingsolver, *Demon Copperhead*

Charles Frazier, *Cold Mountain*

Nguyễn Phan Quế Mai, *Dust Child*

Colum McCann

Mary Lavin and Edward Ardizzone (illustrator), *The Second-Best Children in the World*

Jim Harrison, *Letters to Yesenin*

Michael Ondaatje, *Coming Through Slaughter*

Louise Erdrich, *Tracks*

James Joyce, *Ulysses*

JohnMichael McCann

Gabriel García Márquez, *One Hundred Years of Solitude*

Toni Morrison, *Jazz*

Vladimir Nabokov, *Pale Fire*

Herman Melville, *Moby Dick*

Italo Calvino, *Invisible Cities*

Allen Ginsburg, *Howl and Other Poems*

Walt Whitman, *Leaves of Grass*

Ann Morgan

FOR YOUNGER READERS

Reda Gaudiamo and Cecillia Hidayat (illustrator), *The Adventures of Na Willa*, translated from Indonesian by Ikhda Ayuning Maharsi Degoul and Kate Wakeling

Marguerite Abouet and Mathieu Sapin (illustrator), *Akissi: tales of mischief*, translated from French by Judith Taboy and Marie Bédrune

Karen Hottois and Delphine Renon (illustrator), *Emmett and Caleb*, translated from French by Sarah Ardizzone

Cao Wenxuan and Meilo So (illustrator), *Bronze and Sunflower*, translated from Chinese by Helen Wang

Jörg Mühle, *When Dad's Hair Took Off*, translated from German by Melody Shaw

FOR YOUNG ADULTS

Tété-Michel Kpomassie, *An African in Greenland*, translated from French by James Kirkup

Faïza Guène, *Just Like Tomorrow*, translated from French by Sarah Ardizzone

Sonia Nimr, *Wondrous Journeys in Strange Lands*, translated from Arabic by M. Lynx Qualey

M.T. Vasudevan Nair, *Kaalam*, translated from Malayalam by Gita Krishnankutty

Trifonia Melibea Obono, *La Bastarda*, translated from Spanish by Lawrence Schimel

Galsan Tschinag, *The Blue Sky*, translated from German by Katharina Rout

Ismail Kadare, *Broken April*, translated from Albanian by New Amsterdam Books and Saqi Books

Michael Morpurgo

Robert Louis Stevenson, *Treasure Island*

Jean Giono, *The Man Who Planted Trees*

Rudyard Kipling, *The Elephant's Child*

Antoine de Saint-Exupéry, *The Little Prince*

Michael Morpurgo, *Magical Myths and Legends*

Michael and Clare Morpurgo, and Olivia Lomenech Gill
    (illustrator), *Where My Wellies Take Me*

Dina Nayeri

Rainer Maria Rilke, *Letters to a Young Poet* and *The Dark Interval:
    letters for the grieving heart*

Roland Barthes, *A Lover's Discourse: fragments*

Bertrand Russell, *The Conquest of Happiness*

Albert Camus, *The Stranger*

Edward Said, *Out of Place: a memoir* and *Orientalism*

George Orwell, *Facing Unpleasant Facts: narrative essays*

Simone de Beauvoir, *The Woman Destroyed*

Sylvia Plath, *The Bell Jar*

Nguyễn Phan Quế Mai

Markus Zusak, *The Book Thief*

Elif Shafak, *There Are Rivers in the Sky*

Gabrielle Zevin, *The Storied Life of A.J. Fikry*

Ann Morgan *Reading the World: how I read a book from every
    country*

Jennie Orchard (editor), *The Gifts of Reading*

Matt Ottley

Guus Kuijer, *The Book of Everything*

Laura Cumming, *Thunderclap: a memoir of art and life and sudden death*

Maurice Sendak, *Where the Wild Things Are*

Margaret Wild and Ron Brooks (illustrator), *Fox*

Anthony Doerr, *All the Light We Cannot See*

Tamlyn Teow, *SoXiety*

Alice Pung

Beverly Cleary, the Ramona series

John Marsden, *Letters from the Inside*

Ruth Park, *Playing Beatie Bow*

Janet and John Perkins, and Gillian Gaze (illustrator), *Haffertee Hamster*

Shaun Tan, *The Red Tree*

Markus Zusak, *The Book Thief*

Diana Reid

George Eliot, *Middlemarch*

Kazuo Ishiguro, *The Remains of the Day*

Virginia Woolf, *A Room of One's Own*

Zadie Smith, *On Beauty*

Richard Flanagan, *The Narrow Road to the Deep North*

Nilanjana S. Roy

A.A. Milne, *The House at Pooh Corner*

L. Frank Baum, *The Wizard of Oz*

E.B. White, *The Trumpet of the Swan*

Arundhati Roy, *The God of Small Things*

Arvind Krishna Mehrotra (translator), *Songs of Kabir*

James Baldwin, *Go Tell It on the Mountain* (or *If Beale Street Could Talk*)

Nikesh Shukla

Hanif Kureishi, *The Buddha of Suburbia*

Sally Rooney, *Normal People*

Colson Whitehead, *Sag Harbor*

James Baldwin, *The Fire Next Time*

Benjamín Labatut, *When We Cease to Understand the World*

Nardi Simpson

Daniel Browning, *Close to the Subject: selected works*

Anne-Marie Te Whiu (editor), *Woven: First Nations poetic conversations from the Fair Trade Project*

Ngarukuruwala Women's Group with Genevieve Campbell, *Murli la: songs and stories of the Tiwi Islands*

Linda Martin and Elfie Shiosaki (editors), *maar bidi: next generation black writing*

Tracey-Anne Cameron and Dr Benjamin Nickl (hosts), *Deep Listening: stories of country* (podcast)

Madeleine Thien

Alexis Wright, *Carpentaria*

Adania Shibli, *Touch*

Wong May (translator), *In the Same Light: 200 Tang poems for our century*

Y-Dang Troeung, *Landbridge: life in fragments*

John Berger, *Portraits*

John Wood

Kate DiCamillo, *The Miraculous Journey of Edward Tulane*

Kate DiCamillo, The Mercy Watson Series

Roald Dahl, *Fantastic Mr Fox*

Joe Todd-Stanton, *Arthur and the Golden Rope*

Calef Brown, *Polkabats and Octopus Slacks*

Thelma Young Lutunatabua

Kathy Jetñil-Kijiner, *Iep Jāltok: poems from a Marshallese daughter*

George Monbiot, *Heat*

Rebecca Solnit and Thelma Young Lutunatabua, *Not Too Late: changing the climate story from despair to possibility*

Mary Annaïse Heglar and Vivian Mineker (illustrator), *The World Is Ours to Cherish: a letter to a child*

Grace Lee Boggs, *The Next American Revolution*

adrienne maree brown and Walidah Imarisha (editors), *Octavia's Brood*

Acknowledgements

First and foremost, I would like to express my deep thanks to Robert Macfarlane whose support for *The Gifts of Reading* and *The Gifts of Reading for the Next Generation* has been critical to the development and success of these two collections.

I am also truly indebted to all of the authors who have contributed essays for these two collections. There are so many demands imposed upon writers today — events, festivals and endorsements, to name but a few — and it is extraordinarily generous to agree to write something without receiving payment. Special gratitude to Pico Iyer and Nguyễn Phan Quế Mai who made many suggestions about others who might become involved.

John Wood, founder of the two organisations benefiting from these publications — Room to Read and U-GO — has provided unwavering support. Many thanks, also, to his wife, Amy Powell, to Noelene Palmer, and to the 'A' team of volunteers become lifelong friends: Pam Cook, Sarah Farmer, Jodi Mullen, Mihiri Udabage (who even commissioned a 'Gifts of Reading' cake!), and Margaret Wilcox. Author Tristan Bancks has been indefatigable in his promotional efforts. Other committed advocates include Deborah Abela, Shankari Chandran, Susanne Gervay, Melina Marchetta, Nguyễn Phan Quế Mai, and Markus Zusak.

My friend Julia Eccleshare, doyenne of the children's publishing world in the UK, has joined the 'team' and provided generous advice in relation to *The Gifts of Reading for the Next Generation* as well as writing the Afterword.

Special colleagues in publishing and the media have also helped ensure the longevity of *The Gifts of Reading*. Susan Wyndham, Drusilla Modjeska, and Nicole Abadee in Sydney, Bron Sibree in Perth (Western Australia), and Ginny Dougary in London have all made a difference.

Even though this second anthology has been released by Scribe, I remain grateful to my first publisher Lettice Franklin at W&N, for her continuing support. Alan Samson has also been a fount of encouragement.

Sadly Jenny Dereham, friend and mentor, who gave me my first job in publishing — at Michael Joseph, many moons ago — died in 2022, but this is an opportunity to express my enormous gratitude for all that she taught me. After *The Gifts of Reading* was released, she wrote to say how much she had loved the book but also: 'I was/am a bit unhappy about there being 23 authors — because I hate odd numbers! Not "odd" as in the opposite of "even", but "odd" as in unsettled. I don't mind a book ending with chapter 21 because 21 is a "real figure" but not 17, or 19 or 23! … But it is of course brilliant … a really inspirational book.' How I wish she were alive to see that I had taken her advice and found 24 individuals prepared to write essays for this second anthology.

I am absolutely thrilled that this new collection is released by Scribe, who publish 'books that matter'. I have so much enjoyed working with Marika Webb-Pullman, who is enthusiastic, responsive, and light of touch. Alice Richardson has borne the onerous responsibility of managing the many agreements with great patience and grace. I would also like to mention Molly Slight (previously) in Scribe's UK office because it was Molly who first expressed interest in this anthology and encouraged me to contact her colleagues in Australia. Many thanks also to the book designer, Laura Thomas, and the jacket designer, Guy Ivison, for their beautiful work, and my enthusiastic and supportive publicists in Melbourne and London, Sophia Benjamin and Nicola Garrison.

There are so many more people who have joined me on this journey, and I am sure to neglect someone who has been important. Many thanks for many different reasons to Bassam Aflak, Anna Baillie-Karas, George Dovas, Eirlys Hunter, Lee Keylock, Amber Melody, Arti and Shonee Mirchandani, Phil Perry, Louise Pfanner, Elizabeth Phillips, Catherine Platt, Stephanie Poletti, and Rachel Robson.

I am enormously thankful for ALL of the friends around the world who have bought and gifted the first anthology, hosted gatherings, and shared feedback. Their wonderful efforts and support are so much appreciated.

And finally, thanks to my family, all of whom have become increasingly involved in my 'gifts of reading' world: Rupert, Angelina, and Alice; Gareth and Belle; Duncan; and of course Ivor, tireless supporter of all the literary and non-profit endeavours I have been involved with over the past few decades.

Permissions

EPIGRAPH
Ben Okri, 'Ten and a half inclinations', 2022
Copyright © Ben Okri 2022. Reproduced by permission
of Ben Okri c/o Georgina Capel Associates
Ltd., 29 Wardour Street, London, W1D 6PS.

JENNIE ORCHARD / INTRODUCTION
Thanks to Markus Zusak for permission to quote from his
memoir, *Three Wild Dogs and the Truth* (Pan Macmillan,
2024).

IMTIAZ DHARKER / THREE POEMS FROM *SHADOW
READER*
Thanks to Dr Suzanne Fairless-Aitken, Rights Manager at
Bloodaxe Books, for permission to include three poems from
Imtiaz Dharker's latest collection, *Shadow Reader* (Bloodaxe
Books, 2024).

DIANA REID / THE GIFT OF FORGETTING
The passage from Zadie Smith's essay, 'Fascinated to Presume:
in defense of fiction', was published in *The New York Review of
Books*. Permission to reproduce this has been granted by her
agent, RCW Literary Agency.

NILANJANA S. ROY / TO ADVENTURERS
The extract from Sappho's poem, 'Love Shook My Heart', is translated by A.S. Kline. The extract from Hafez's poem, 'The Subject Tonight is Love', is translated by Daniel Ladinsky.

MADELEINE THIEN / ON WALTER BENJAMIN'S
BERLIN CHILDHOOD
The quotations in italics are from 'A Berlin Chronicle' in *Reflections: essays, aphorisms, autobiographical writings*, edited by Peter Demetz, translated by Edmund Jephcott (Mariner Books, 2019), and from *Berlin Childhood circa 1900*, translated by Carl Skoggard (Pilot Editions, 2019).

THELMA YOUNG LUTUNATABUA / MAKING MORE MAGIC
The extract from Kathy Jetñil-Kijiner's poem, 'Dear Matafele Peinem', is reproduced by kind permission of the poet.

Room to Read and U-GO

The contributors to *The Gifts of Reading for the Next Generation* have generously agreed to donate their royalties to the two organisations founded by John Wood: Room to Read and U-GO.

Room to Read

Founded in 2000 on the belief that World Change Starts with Educated Children®, Room to Read develops children's foundational literacy skills, as well as life skills that promote gender equality. Room to Read nurtures these essential skills in children by training and coaching educators, creating quality learning materials and spaces, strengthening education systems, and delivering programs directly and with partners — all while honouring the dignity of every child. Committed to accelerating learning outcomes for more children, more quickly, Room to Read has benefited more than 50 million children across 28 countries. Room to Read envisions a world free from illiteracy and gender inequality, where all children have room to read, learn, and grow.

www.roomtoread.org

U-GO

After being asked by numerous parents in multiple countries to help their daughters to find a path to university, in 2022 John Wood founded U-GO as the 'logical next step' in his life. The team works not just with Room to Read, but also twelve other stellar partners to fund long-term university scholarships for female students in low-income countries. By the end of 2024, well over 4,300 ambitious and promising young women in Bangladesh, Cambodia, India, Indonesia, Nepal, Pakistan, Philippines, Tanzania, and Vietnam had been invited to join the U-GO family. John's medium-term goal is to have 20,000 U-GO scholars by 2030 and 100,000 graduates by 2040.

The U-GO model has been publicly endorsed by Nobel Economics Prize–winning Dr Richard Thaler, who has spoken of the incredibly high ROI that U-GO provides on the philanthropic dollar.

'Talent is universal. Opportunity is not.'
www.ugouniversity.org